THE MANAGER'S GUIDE TO
FINANCIAL STATEMENT ANALYSIS

The Manager's Guide to Financial Statement Analysis

Stephen F. Jablonsky
Noah P. Barsky

JOHN WILEY & SONS, INC.

New York • Chichester • Weinheim • Brisbane • Singapore • Toronto

This publication is designed to provide accurate and authoritative information in regard to the subject matter covered. It is sold with the understanding that the publisher is not engaged in rendering legal, accounting, or other professional services. If legal advice or other expert assistance is required, the services of a competent professional person should be sought.

Library of Congress Cataloging-in-Publication Data:

Jablonsky, Stephen F.
   The manager's guide to financial statement analysis / Stephen F.
Jablonsky, Noah P. Barsky.
     p.   cm.
   Includes bibliographical references and index.
   ISBN 0-471-24727-8 (alk. paper)
   1. Financial statements — United States.   2. Managerial
accounting.   3. Business enterprises — United States — Valuation.
4. Corporations — United States — Valuation.   5. Business enterprises —
United States — Finance.   6. Corporations — United States — Finance.
7. Wal-Mart (Firm)   I. Barsky, Noah P.   II. Title.
HF5681.B2J23   1998
658.15'12 — dc21
                                                                97-32010
                                                                  CIP

Printed in the United States of America.

10 9 8 7 6 5 4 3

Contents

CONTENTS

Contents

Preface

In today's global business environment, managers need to know how to read financial statements and use that information in the formulation and implementation of their firm's overall business strategy. Managers also need to know how the expectations of creditors and shareholders influence the development of the firm's business strategy. Once managers understand how to make sense out of the financial statements and market information about their firm, they will be able to function more effectively as members of their management teams.

In writing this book, we have emphasized the need for managers to be able to communicate with one another in order to accomplish their shared objectives. It is one thing to be able to develop a personal understanding of how to read financial statements; it is quite another thing to be able to communicate that understanding to other members of the management team. In each chapter, we have provided examples of how to explain what you have just read about to other managers, employees, and friends who have similar interests in understanding more about the business.

In the introduction, we provide a framework for helping managers understand the business through financial information. We look at a firm in terms of a business strategy, management control, and shareholder accountability cycle or loop. Based on our experiences working in executive development programs, we see that managers find the idea of a strategy/control/accountability loop to be a useful way of thinking about financial information. They see the benefits of using financial information to become more effective managers without having to first become a professional accountant or financial analyst.

In Part One of this book, we are going to show you how to make sense out of the information found in a firm's financial statements using two business strategy models: a Strategic Profit Model and a Strategic Financing Model. From working with managers in executive management seminars, we know that these models are extremely effective in developing a shared understanding of the business and a common language for all managers to use when talking about the financial aspects of their business.

In Part Two, we are going to show you how to make sense out of the key measures of financial performance that reflect the market's assessment of a firm's past and expected future performance. We define and explain the meaning of these key performance measures as we work through the mechanics of how the market values a firm's debt and common stock. After explaining how the market valuation process works, we revisit the Strategic Profit Model and extend that model to include information about the market valuation process.

To reinforce how the information found in the financial statements and market information about the firm relates to a firm's overall business strategy, we focused our analysis on one firm: Wal-Mart. As the world's largest retailer, managers from the United States and around the world know of Wal-Mart. If you read this book cover to cover, you will see how all of the pieces of financial information fit together for one firm. An alternative way to use this guide to financial statement analysis is to analyze your own firm's financial statements as you read the book.

The two parts of this book represent a journey to understanding the business through financial information — a journey that comes full circle in the last chapter and ends back where we started: visualizing the firm through the Strategic Profit Model. The first trip through the material provides the foundation for developing a management understanding of how to use financial statements. By taking a second trip through the book, you will be able to gain additional insights into Wal-Mart and your own company because you will have a better grasp of the financial terminology you learned on the first journey.

In addition to taking individual trips through this book, we recommend taking several group trips through the chapters with members of your management team. The group trips provide a chance for everyone to practice their communication skills. As mentioned above, it takes practice to see if you can translate what you have learned into words.

Acknowledgments

The following organizations have played a significant role in helping us write this book from a management perspective.

Penn State Executive Programs has provided us with the opportunity to actually help managers understand a business through financial information. The organization of the chapters and the materials presented in each chapter reflect their feedback on the best way to learn how to understand the business through financial information. In particular, we wish to thank Al Vicere and Virginia Tucker for their continued support and encouragement.

The Financial Executives Research Foundation (FERF) has provided us with the opportunity to study the changing roles of financial management in major U.S. corporations. Over the last ten years, we have had the opportunity to interview senior corporate executives and financial and nonfinancial managers at all levels throughout our case study firms. The strong emphasis on management communications throughout the book is based primarily on our interviews with all of the executives and managers at the case study firms. In particular, we wish to thank Bob Moore, Roland Laing, Jim Lewis, and Bill Sinnett for supporting our research efforts.

Stephen F. Jablonsky would also like to thank the W. K. Kellogg Foundation and the Kellogg National Fellowship program for providing him with fellowship support to develop a different, more people-oriented approach to teaching and doing research in accounting and finance. Although the practices of accounting and finance are technically grounded, the importance of these disciplines is grounded in how they affect human behavior. The Kellogg fellowship experience is reflected in our emphasis on "insight and understanding" versus "prediction and control." We wish to thank Larriaine Matusak and the fellows and advisors of KNFP Group IV for all of their commitment to helping individuals like myself to expand our horizons beyond our traditional academic disciplines.

Noah P. Barsky would like to thank the University of Connecticut Ph.D. Program for providing support and an intellectual environment conducive to personal and professional growth. In particular, the insights of Mo Hussein, Garry Marchant, Doug Heckathorn, and Stan Biggs have been instrumental in the development of my approach to thinking about business and social issues.

Introduction

People often refer to accounting as the "language of business." Like any language, when we understand accounting, we can communicate with anyone else who speaks that language. Knowledge of any language offers unlimited opportunities to communicate with other people.

Communicating is imparting information by speaking, writing, or visual representation. Communication implies the exchange of information through face-to-face interaction or through more impersonal channels such as written reports or computerized data exchange. Communicating is structuring information to promote a shared understanding between speaker and listener, author and reader. The words, and in our case numbers, must be meaningful to everyone involved in the communications process.

In his autobiography, Sam Walton includes communication as one of his ten rules for running a successful company.

> RULE 4: COMMUNICATE everything you possibly can to your partners. The more they know, the more they'll understand. The more they understand, the more they'll care. Once they care, there's no stopping them. If you don't trust your associates to know what's going on, they'll know that you don't really consider them partners. Information is power, and the gain you get from empowering your associates more than offsets the risks of informing your competitors.[1]

This book has been written in the spirit of open communications underlying Sam Walton's quote.

In his book *The Great Game of Business*, Jack Stack, CEO of Springfield Remanufacturing Corp. (SRC), expresses a similar commitment to increasing understanding through open communications.

The more people know about a company, the better that company will perform. This is an iron-clad rule. You will *always* be more successful in business by sharing information with the people you work with than by keeping them in the dark.

Information should not be a power tool — it should be a means of education. Don't use information to intimidate, control, or manipulate people. Use it to teach people how to work together to achieve common goals and thereby gain control over their lives. When you share the numbers and bring them alive, you turn them into tools people can use to help themselves as they go about their business every day. That's the key to open-book management.[2]

In explaining SRC's approach to managing the business, Stack contrasts its open-book management philosophy with closed-book management.

After all, numbers are simply a way of telling stories about people, as well as a means of keeping score. If you're keeping score, there must be a game going on somewhere. The only issue is whether or not the players know it. (That's the absurdity of traditional closed-book management: it's based on getting people to play a game without telling them.)[3]

As discussed more fully later in the chapter, it is one thing to extol the virtues of open communications; it is another thing to actually create an environment of open communications within a business. As inspirational and uplifting as *The Great Game of Business* may be, Stack stops short of providing specific tools for helping people understand the business through financial information.

In order to make the transition from inspiration to implementation, managers need to know how their actions affect the overall financial performance of their firms. They need tools for translating theory into practice. That is where this book comes into play. Some universal tools for helping managers understand their business through financial information are provided in this book.

Fortunately, we do not have to worry about having enough raw material to help managers begin to understand their business through financial information. In a market economy populated by publicly held corporations, there is more than enough information available to begin the process. Every publicly held corporation is required to include a complete set of financial statements in its annual report to shareholders. These annual reports may be obtained on request by writing or calling the firm's investor relations department. For many firms, all of the information needed to start understanding the business may be accessed through the firm's World Wide Web site.

Financial statements, particularly the balance sheet and the income statement, provide a touchstone for understanding any business. These statements summarize the financial performance of the firm at a particular time (the balance sheet) and over some time period (the income statement). Whether managers know it or not, the score is kept through these financial statements. After working through the material presented in each chapter of this book, managers should have a better understanding of the relationship between their actions, the outcomes reported in the financial statements, and their firm's overall business strategy.

Managers know that a score is being kept for their firms. They also know that they are involved in their firm's economic game plan. What they lack is a better understanding of how the score relates back to the game plan. They want to know how to adjust their actions in order to generate a better performance score for themselves and their firm. This book has been developed to fill the gap between playing the game and generating a better performance score.

Most managers are quite happy that they are not accountants. Managers, particularly nonfinancial managers, are quick to point out that they do not want to become accountants or financial analysts. Managers want to understand how to use financial information to improve the financial performance of their firm. They do not want to become preparers of financial information. They want to learn the language of business to become more effective in their current and future positions, but stop well short of becoming accountants and financial analysts. They are more than happy to leave the technical work to the experts. In developing the approach to understanding the business through financial information presented in this book, we have taken these nonfinancial managers at their word. We have placed understanding in the foreground and moved most of the technical issues into the background.

Accounting is the "language of business." Learning the language of business is like learning any other language. A certain amount of written material is needed to get the process started, but practice improves performance. It is one thing to be able to complete the exercises at the end of each chapter of a Spanish, German, or Japanese language book; it is another thing to engage in a meaningful conversation with individuals who speak the language fluently. Practice makes perfect.

This book has been developed in a manner similar to the model followed in intensive language programs. Even though you will be able to benefit from reading each of the chapters in sequence, you can benefit even more by applying the concepts presented in each chapter to your own company or a company in which you have a personal interest and by practicing your language skills with other managers within your own company or other managers you know on the outside. As stated above, only practice makes perfect.

As we shall see, the financial information included in this book will come from the firm's annual reports to shareholders, *The Wall Street Journal (WSJ)*, the *Value Line Investment Survey (Value Line)*, *Business Week*, and other business periodicals. We will rely exclusively on financial information that is available to the public (either free by request or through public libraries or on a subscription basis through on-line computer services). We encourage every reader to use the tools presented in each chapter to develop a better understanding of their own firm. What better place to start than using the financial statements for your own firm?

Our primary emphasis will be placed on the financial information found in the firm's balance sheets and income statements. This information will then be supplemented by information that can be found in other sections of the firm's annual report, the *WSJ*, *Value Line*, and *Business Week*. This additional information will allow us to look at the financial performance of a firm from a broader economic perspective.

Is a broader economic perspective really necessary? With the advent of Individual Retirement Accounts (IRAs), 401(k) plans, discount brokerage services, and mutual funds, most of the readers of this book will probably be investors in the global economy as well as managers in particular firms. When each of us steps into an investor role, the typical concern is the return (dividends plus stock price appreciation) that has been earned, or can be expected to be earned, by investing in a specific firm or portfolio of firms. We want to know if the managers of the firms we have invested in have created *shareholder value*.

When we play both manager and investor roles, we come full circle. As managers, we need to know what we need to do to create shareholder value. As investors, we want to know if managers have, in fact, created any value. The tools presented in this book allow us to have it both ways.

As managers, we look at the firm in terms of its business strategy. We try to think in terms of what managers have to do to make the firm a success in the future. As investors, we look at the firm in terms of shareholder accountability. We try to think in terms of what management has done for us in the past to create shareholder value. We also want to know what management is doing to create shareholder value in the future.

Going public. Although we have used the approach to understanding the business presented in this book for many years, the interest in going public with this approach was stimulated by our observation of a number of changes that are occurring in the financial management practices of major U.S. corporations. Based on a series of research studies sponsored by the Financial Executives Research Foundation (FERF), we have been able to identify two models of financial management that reflect underlying differences in management operating philosophies.

We use the terms *Business Advocate* and *Corporate Police* to refer to the two models of financial management. This book has been written from a Business Advocate perspective that is consistent with an open-book management operating philosophy. Since the Business Advocate model reflects a management operating philosophy that differs radically from the Corporate Police model, we believe it is worth taking some time to explain the differences between the two models.

BUSINESS ADVOCATES AND CORPORATE POLICE

While studying the financial management practices at six major U.S. corporations (AT&T, Boeing, Citicorp, Ford, Merck, and 3M), we discovered that the work performed by financial professionals could be described in terms of three orientations to financial work:

1. Command and Control
2. Conformance
3. Competitive Team

Even though all of the firms were required to meet similar external financial-reporting requirements (e.g., SEC regulations and Financial Accounting Standards Board pronouncements), the manner in which they met these requirements and met the financial information needs of senior management and line management differed dramatically. No two financial organizations functioned in exactly the same manner, yet each financial organization could be described in terms of some combination of command and control, conformance, and competitive team orientations.

Three Orientations to Financial Work

A short description of the three orientations to financial work is provided in the following list. Even though the descriptions are brief, managers usually have no trouble identifying with the orientation that characterizes their financial organization.

- *Command and control orientation:* This orientation to financial work stresses the vertical flow of financial information up and down the corporate hierarchy. The financial organization serves top management by providing an independent review, evaluation, and commentary on the operating and capital investment plans of the business units.
- *Conformance orientation:* This orientation to financial work stresses the external flow of information prepared in accordance with externally imposed reporting requirements. The financial organization serves regulators, analysts, and other external parties by complying with the rules and regulations established for demonstrating external accountability.
- *Competitive team orientation:* This orientation to financial work stresses the horizontal flow of information among all managers within the firm. The financial organization serves the business units by providing the sophisticated analytical and accounting support necessary for achieving the firm's strategic business objectives.

Two Models of Financial Management

In subsequent studies involving over 2,500 managers (910 financial managers and 1,632 nonfinancial managers), two distinct models of financial management emerged from the research: (1) the Business Advocate model and (2) the Corporate Police model.[4] The Business Advocate model represents a combination of the command and control and competitive team orientations to financial work, while the Corporate Police model represents a combination of the command and control and conformance orientations.

Figure I.1 presents the two models of financial management and three orientations to financial work as a triangle with the command and control orientation at the top. All of the managers we have worked with over the years know that someone has to be in charge. Some formal control structure must be in place if the organization is to function effectively. The question is, do we combine the necessary control function (command and control orientation) with a conformance orientation or a competitive team orientation?

When managers in executive development programs describe the financial management practices of their firms, the differences between the Business Advocate and Corporate Police models of financial management could not be more striking. In a Business Advocate environment, open communications are encouraged and financial information is integrated directly into the fabric of the business operations. In a Corporate Police environment, communications are tied to position in the corporate

Figure I.1   Models of Financial Management: Business Advocates and Corporate Police

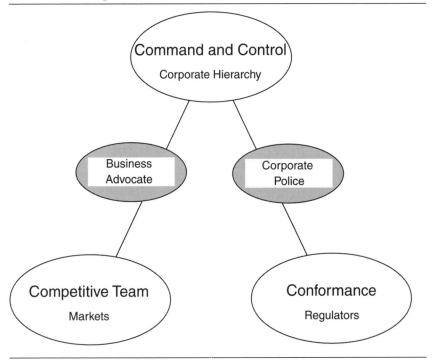

hierarchy on a "need to know" basis, and financial information is used to enforce compliance with corporate policies and procedures.

The differences between the two models are almost as stark as the difference between day and night. The differences may be summarized in terms of the expectations established for the financial professionals working in each type of financial organization.

In the Business Advocate model, financial professionals are expected to

- Know the business and be involved
- Think in terms of service and involvement
- Encourage wide use of financial information
- Integrate business operations throughout the firm
- Provide financial discipline for the business operations

In the Corporate Police model, financial professionals are expected to

- Administer the rules and regulations
- Think in terms of oversight and surveillance
- Limit access to information on a "need to know" basis
- Enforce compliance with policies and procedures
- Monitor the collection and disclosure of information

In a Business Advocate environment, a premium is placed on being able to communicate. A Business Advocate environment is typically a team-based, high-involvement setting. All managers are held mutually accountable for achieving the business objectives and hitting the financial targets set for the business. In this type of environment, everyone needs to know how business strategy, financial control, and shareholder accountability interrelate.

In a Corporate Police environment, "need to know" access to financial information works against open communication. Information is typically restricted to specific budget categories within functional areas of responsibility. Financial personnel are seen as scorekeepers and evaluators rather than educators and integrators. No attempt is made to link business strategy to shareholder accountability through the financial control system.

BUSINESS ADVOCATE PERSPECTIVE

This book has been developed with a vision of the ideal Business Advocate financial organization in mind. In a Business Advocate environment, the concepts contained in this book may be used by individual managers to increase their personal understanding of the business through financial information and by management groups to develop a shared understanding of the business.

Even though we have developed the book with the ideal Business Advocate financial organization in mind, managers from Corporate Police environments are often the most appreciative of our efforts to help them increase their understanding of the business. In these cases, we have been able to make a contribution to their own personal development. However, we have not been able to help them develop a shared understanding of the business along with other members of the management team. Unfortunately, open communication is not a cornerstone of the Corporate Police model.

Figure I.2 presents an overview of the Business Advocate perspective we use to help managers understand the business through financial information. The Business Advocate perspective consists of three major components:

1. Business Strategy
2. Management Control
3. Shareholder Accountability

In a Business Advocate environment, financial information provides the thread that ties the firm's business strategy to shareholder accountability through the firm's management control system.

As we can see from Figure I.2, a gap exists between the worlds of business strategy and shareholder accountability. This gap is filled by people, financial information users. Of all the possible financial information users that may exist in the business environment, we identify most closely with the managers who need to know how to bridge the gap between business strategy and shareholder accountability.

**Figure I.2   Understanding the Business through Financial
Information: The Business Advocate Perspective**

Business Strategy

The *business strategy* component of the framework emphasizes the interrelationships between managers and stakeholders in the firm. *Stakeholders* include customers, suppliers, employees, shareholders, creditors,
taxing authorities, regulators, and the communities where the firm's operations are located. As we shall see throughout this book, business strategy begins with the customer and ends with the shareholders. Customers
provide the primary source of financing for any business, while shareholders own the business and expect a return on their investment. Management is responsible for incorporating the needs of the other
stakeholders into an effective business strategy without losing sight of the
needs of both customers and shareholders. In firms like Wal-Mart and
SRC, keeping employees informed about the performance of the business
is a key part of management's overall strategy.

Other economic events refers to changes in the broader environment
which, although not the result of conscious business strategy, affect the

financial performance of the firm (i.e., floods, earthquakes, war in the Persian Gulf, prolonged economic recession, etc.). Whether managers or other stakeholders in the firm like it or not, the effects of economic events beyond the control of the firm must be included in the financial control system.

The *management control* component of the framework represents the point where information about all of the economic events affecting the firm enters into the firm's operating and financial control systems. In this book, we are concerned primarily with that part of the management control system that generates the information contained in the firm's financial statements.

Auditing is seen as part of a feedback loop that ensures that financial information is reported in accordance with generally accepted accounting principles (GAAP). The penalties for violating GAAP (a qualified opinion or a disclaimer of opinion) are typically so severe that managers are more likely to play the game according to the rules.

The *shareholder accountability* component of the framework emphasizes that financial statements provide a foundation for assessing management's accountability to the firm's shareholders. However, in a market economy, shareholder accountability does not end with the financial statements. Financial statements provide a starting point for assessing management's performance.

As we can see, shareholder accountability also includes market information about the firm's financial performance that does not flow through the firm's management control system. Information about stock prices, dividend yields, interest rates, and so on, along with analyst reports and economic forecasts, are all factored into the assessment process.

Based on our experiences working with managers, we know that it does not take much to become overwhelmed by all of the information found in the financial statements and available from the marketplace. In filling the gap between shareholder accountability and business strategy, we have found that managers need a way of getting their arms around the information so they can put it to good use.

STORYTELLING AND MODEL BUILDING

In a very real sense, this book is about helping managers tell a story about the financial performance of their firm. In order to tell a convincing story, managers need to have some idea of what users of financial information consider to be important performance indicators, and they need to know how their actions affect those performance indicators.

In helping managers develop this storytelling capability, we have found it useful to begin by learning to tell a story about the past performance of a single firm that virtually everyone knows and considers to be highly successful. Over the last several years, we have used Wal-Mart to show managers how to link business strategy to shareholder accountability through financial information. Information about Wal-Mart's financial performance over the last 10 years provides the basis for integrating all of the material presented in this book into a single comprehensive management framework.

Our ultimate goal is to help managers tell a similar story about the financial performance of their own firm, a story that can be told to and shared with other members of their management team. In working your way through chapters 1 through 12, we recommend that you apply these financial statement analysis techniques to your own firm.

ORGANIZATION OF *THE MANAGER'S GUIDE*

This book is organized into two parts. Part One, "Financial Statements and Business Strategy," begins the process of understanding the business through financial information by focusing on the profitability relationships found in the firm's balance sheet and income statement. Our first business strategy model, the Strategic Profit Model (SPM) is used to structure the information found in these two financial statements into a more visually oriented communications framework. As discussed in this section, the SPM is based on the logic underlying the DuPont model, which was first developed and introduced as a major management innovation in the early 1900s. All of the information contained in the balance sheet and income statement is discussed in terms of the margin management, asset management, and financial management concepts embedded within the logic of the SPM.

After using the SPM to understand the relationship between business strategy and profitability, a second business strategy model is introduced, that is, the Strategic Financing Model (SFM). The SFM is used to explore the interrelationships between the firm's long-term investment needs and sources of long-term debt and equity financing.

Profitable firms can get themselves into financial trouble if they do not develop a long-term financing and investment strategy to support their overall business plan. In this discussion, we also address the charge that managers sacrifice the long-run future of the firms in their pursuit of short-term performance measures.

Any discussion of the financial performance of a firm cannot ignore the question of whether management has created value on behalf of the shareholders. In Part Two, "Market Valuation and Business Strategy," we look at the market valuation process in terms of the investors' expectations about interest rates and required returns on investments in common stock. In this section, we show how "time value of money" concepts are applied to the firm's actual and expected future cash flows to determine a current market value for the firm.

After showing how market information and a multiyear time horizon are factored into the market valuation process, we revisit the SPM and extend that model to include market-based performance measures. The SPM, as extended, provides a comprehensive framework for integrating all of the firm- and market-based performance measures into a comprehensive management performance evaluation system.

In Chapter 1, we begin our journey by examining Wal-Mart's financial statements and introducing our first business strategy model, the Strategic Profit Model.

NOTES

1. Sam Walton and John Huey, *Sam Walton, Made in America: My Story* (New York: Doubleday, 1992), 247.

2. *The Great Game of Business* (New York: Currency Doubleday, 1994), 71.

3. *Ibid.*, p. xv.

4. The Business Advocate and Corporate Policeman profiles have been developed from a 29-question research instrument, the Management Communication and Control Systems Diagnostic Questionnaire (DQ5). All 2,542 managers participating in the research studies have completed the diagnostic questionnaire. For more information about the questionnaire, please contact the authors.

PART ONE

Financial Statements and Business Strategy

CHAPTER 1

Financial Statements and Business Strategy

The amount of information available to anyone about publicly held U.S. corporations is staggering. Any one of us can contact the investor relations department at one of these firms and receive a copy of the annual report to shareholders, a proxy statement, and annual and quarterly filings with the Securities and Exchange Commission (SEC). We can also obtain comparative information about hundreds of companies through business periodicals (*Business Week*, *Fortune*, *Forbes*, etc.) and investment advisory services (*Moody's*, *Standard & Poor's*, *Value Line*, etc.). And if this type of information access were not enough, we can go to our firm's World Wide Web site and obtain even more information instantaneously. If we are not careful, we can drown in a sea of financial information.

For many managers, their own firm's annual report to shareholders contains more information than they know what to do with. They do not need more information to become more confused. To a certain extent, their financial statements are about as intelligible as the optical illusion presented in Figure 1.1. On first glance all they see is a black-and-white inkblot with the largest concentration of black appearing on the left side of the image. When asked to identify what they see, they think we are pulling their legs.

We typically respond by saying that they are looking at an animal with the head appearing on the left side of the image. Given this hint, a few managers will begin to see the shape of an animal emerge from the inkblot. For those managers who still have not seen the animal, we provide a second hint. The animal makes the following sound: "moo." With that

Figure 1.1   Ink Blot Test

Source: © 1998 Imaginary Studio.

hint and a little coaching from their colleagues, more managers begin to see the cow.

For those managers who have trouble seeing what the rest of us see, we outline the shape of the cow. The cow's head appears on your left with its body (excluding the hindquarters) extending to the right. The white triangle (in the shape of Africa) is on the cow's head. The cow's left ear extends out of the "northeast coast" of Africa. The cow's right ear is black and can be found just "west" of Africa. The small white dot off of the "southeast coast" of Africa represents the cow's left eye. The white spot somewhat below Africa is on the cow's nose. The very large black spot due east of the cow's face is the cow's left side.

After everyone sees the cow, we point out that most people cannot *not* see the cow in the future. After not seeing the image for some time, it may take someone a few seconds to refocus and see the cow, but they know the cow is there.

To a certain extent, helping managers understand the business through financial statements is like going on this kind of cow hunt. Initially, the financial statements look like our optical illusion. Half of the battle involves convincing managers that the financial statements actually do contain valuable information. The other half of the battle involves helping them see the valuable information contained in those statements.

FINANCIAL STATEMENTS

Our starting point for helping managers understand the business through financial information is the balance sheet and income statement. Although firms are required to include a statement of cash flows and a statement of shareholders' equity in their annual reports to shareholders, the key financial performance indicators that we will use to begin understanding the business are typically found in the balance sheet and income statement.

Throughout this book, we will use Wal-Mart's balance sheets and income statements as our touchstone for understanding the business.

- *Balance Sheet:* The balance sheet lists all of the assets, liabilities, and shareholders' (owners') equity in the company at the end of the year or at the end of a shorter reporting period. *Assets* represent the economic resources controlled by the company. *Liabilities* and *shareholders' equity* represent the claims on the company's assets by creditors (liabilities) and owners (shareholders' equity).
- *Income Statement.* The income statement lists all of the company's revenues, expenses, and net income for the year or shorter reporting period (quarter or month). The net income (or net loss) tells us how well management performed on behalf of the shareholders during the year.

We could have used the income statements and balance sheets for any company to illustrate how managers can analyze a company's financial statement, but we chose Wal-Mart because this company is one of those American success stories and has held the public's attention ever since going public in 1970. By focusing on a single firm like Wal-Mart to introduce the concepts and models presented in this book, we will be able to show how different aspects of the business may be integrated into a comprehensive framework for understanding the entire business.[1]

Figure 1.2 presents Wal-Mart's balance sheets for the fiscal years ended January 31, 1987 and 1997.[2]

Figure 1.2 Wal-Mart Balance Sheets (for the Fiscal Years Ended January 31, 1987 and 1997 — Amounts in Millions)

	1987	1997
Assets		
Current Assets		
Cash and Equivalents	$166	$883
Receivables	$90	$845
Inventory	$2,031	$15,897
Other	$66	$368
Total Current Assets	$2,353	$17,993
Productive Assets		
Property, Plant and Equipment	$2,070	$25,964
Accumulated Depreciation	($394)	($5,640)
Net Productive Assets	$1,676	$20,324
Other Assets	$20	$1,287
Total	$4,049	$39,604
Liabilities and Shareholders' Equity		
Liabilities		
Current Liabilities		
Accounts Payable	$925	$7,628
Current Debt Due	$14	$618
Other	$402	$2,711
Total Current Liabilities	$1,341	$10,957
Long-Term Liabilities		
Long-Term Debt	$179	$7,709
Long-Term Lease Obligations	$764	$2,307
Deferred Income Taxes & Other	$75	$1,488
Total Long-Term Liabilities	$1,018	$11,504
Total Liabilities	$2,359	$22,461
Shareholders' Equity		
Common Stock	$220	$775
Retained Earnings	$1,470	$16,768
Translation Adjustments	$0	($400)
Total Shareholders' Equity	$1,690	$17,143
Total	$4,049	$39,604

Figure 1.3 presents Wal-Mart's statements of income and retained earnings for the fiscal years ended January 31, 1987 and 1997.[3] These statements represent our first financial optical illusion.

Figure 1.3 Wal-Mart Statements of Income and Retained Earnings (for the Fiscal Years Ended January 31, 1987 and 1997 — Amounts in Millions)

	1987	1997
Net Sales	$11,909	$104,859
Total Revenue	$11,909	$104,859
Costs and Expenses		
Cost of Sales	$9,053	$83,663
Operating Expenses	$2,008	$16,788
Interest Expense	$86	$845
Other Income	($84)	($1,287)
Total Costs and Expenses	$11,063	$100,009
Income before Income Taxes	$846	$4,850
Provision for Income Taxes		
Current Portion	$374	$1,974
Deferred Portion	$22	($180)
Total Provision	$396	$1,794
Net Income	$450	$3,056
Dividends	($48)	($481)
Adjustments to Retained Earnings		($201)
Retained Earnings, Beginning Balance	$1,068	$14,394
Retained Earnings, Ending Balance	$1,470	$16,768

In virtually every annual report sent to shareholders, the current year's financial performance is compared to the previous year's performance (on the balance sheet) and previous two years' financial performance (on the income statement). As we can see from Figures 1.2 and 1.3, we have chosen to extend the time horizon to ten years by using the financial statements for the fiscal years ended January 31, 1987 and 1997. With a ten-year gap between statements, we can look at both the short- and long-term aspects of running a business like Wal-Mart.

In order to develop a better understanding of what the words and numbers included in the financial statements mean, we will focus on how Wal-Mart performed for the fiscal year ended January 31, 1987, and for the fiscal year ended January 31, 1997. In the process of learning how to analyze individual balance sheets and income statements, we will also begin to look at how management grew the business between 1987 and 1997. As we shall see in Part Two of this book, investors reward companies for profitable growth by bidding up the price of the company's common stock.

BEGINNING THE ANALYSIS

The definitions of a balance sheet and income statement presented earlier, provide accurate descriptions of those financial statements. However, these definitions do not emphasize a management perspective. In order to help managers understand a business through financial information, we have found it helpful to ground the balance sheet and income statement in the underlying economics of the business.

We begin the financial statement analysis process from a management perspective by stressing the following three points:

Point 1. The balance sheet presents the financial relationships between the resources (assets) under management's control and management's responsibility to creditors (liabilities) and owners (shareholders' equity).

In trying to understand the business through the balance sheet, we alternate between looking at a firm in terms of the *things* owned or controlled by the firm (assets, liabilities, and shareholders' equity) and economic *relationships* between the firm (as represented by management and employees) and external parties (suppliers, customers, creditors, taxing authorities, and shareholders).

Point 2. The income statement shows the amount of net income (assets – liabilities) that management has earned on the owners' behalf during the year.

The net income reported in the income statement represents management's contribution to the overall success of the firm on behalf of the shareholders. All things considered, shareholders would prefer management to generate a higher versus lower net income.[4]

Point 3. By linking the financial performance measures in the income statement to the balance sheet, we can get a pretty good handle on how well management has performed on behalf of the shareholders. The balance sheet and income statement may be meaningfully integrated through the concept of return on shareholders' equity (return on equity, or ROE).

We use the concept of ROE to help managers (1) develop a basic understanding of how all aspects of the firm's business operations may be integrated into a simple yet comprehensive performance measurement system and (2) link the financial performance of a specific firm to the broader global capital markets for debt and equity financing.

We will begin the process of understanding the business through financial information by taking a closer look at the balance sheet (Point 1), then move on to the income statement (Point 2), and then integrate the balance sheet and income statement through the concept of ROE (Point 3).

Balance Sheets

The balance sheet (also referred to as a statement of financial position) provides a snapshot of where the firm stands at a particular point in time. The relationship between the resources under management control and the firm's obligations to creditors and shareholders is expressed in the following financial control equation:

Assets = Liabilities + Shareholders' Equity

In exchange for the right to determine how the firm's resources are used, management promises to be responsible to the creditors and shareholders who have provided the money needed to run the business. That is,

Resources = Obligations

Rights = Responsibilities

In the case of creditors such as lenders, management promises to pay interest and repay principal on the amounts borrowed. In the case of suppliers and employees, management promises to pay amounts owed for goods and services received by the firm. In the case of shareholders, management promises to be held accountable for earning a return on the shareholders' investment.

For the fiscal years ended 1987 and 1997, Wal-Mart's balance sheet equations appear as

Assets = Liabilities + Shareholders' Equity

1987: $4.049B = $2.359B + $1.690B

1997: $39.604B = $22.461B + $17.143B

At the end of 1987, management controlled $4.0 billion of assets on behalf of creditors and shareholders. By the end of 1997, the assets under management control increased to $39.6 billion. Between 1987 and 1997, assets under management control increased by 878%, a 25.6% compound annual growth rate. During that same period of time, liabilities increased at a 25.3% compound annual growth rate and shareholders' equity increased at a 26.1% growth rate. (See the Appendix at the end of the chapter for a discussion of how compound annual growth rates are computed.)

As seen, even the limited amount of information contained in a firm's balance sheet equations can allow us to make a number of descriptive (and most likely boring) statements about a firm. Fortunately, the importance of financial information lies in its use in the performance-evaluation process, not in its use in merely describing the business.

The only trouble with trying to understand the business from two balance sheets is that we know very little about the economic journey management took to get from point A (1987) to point B (1997). Without additional information, it is hard to tell from the balance sheets whether management has been a success or failure over the last ten years. That's where the income statements come into play.

Income Statements

The amounts reported in the firm's balance sheets do not just happen, they result from management formulating and implementing a business strategy and then competing against other firms in the global marketplace. The financial success or failure of that business strategy is captured in the income statement.

While the balance sheet provides us with a snapshot of the firm at a particular point in time, the income statement tells us how well management has performed on behalf of the shareholders during the year. Like the balance sheet, the relationships captured in an income statement are best summarized in the following financial control equation form:

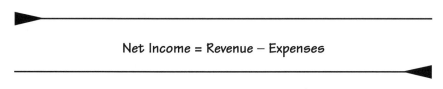

Net Income = Revenue − Expenses

and

Net Earned Assets = Net Income

Given the standard format of a typical income statement, many managers are somewhat familiar with the first financial control equation, but not the second equation. However, it is the second equation that puts teeth into the first equation. Net income equals the amount of net assets (economic resources) that management earned on behalf of the shareholders during the year.

For the fiscal years ended 1987 and 1997, Wal-Mart's income statement equations were:

$$\text{Net Income} = \text{Revenue} - \text{Expenses}$$
$$1987: \$450M = \$11.909B - \$11.459B$$
$$1997: \$3.056B = \$104.859B - \$101.803B$$

In 1987, Wal-Mart generated $11.9 billion in revenue and incurred $11.5 billion in expenses. The net income of $450 million represents the increase in net assets (assets − liabilities) *earned* by management on behalf of the shareholders during the year. In 1997, Wal-Mart generated $104.9 billion in revenue while incurring $101.8 billion in expenses. In 1997, management *earned* $3.1 billion in net assets on behalf of the shareholders.

Generating net assets through the earnings process is the name of the management performance game. Over these ten years, Wal-Mart's net income increased at a 21.1% compound annual growth rate, a feat very few firms, especially large firms, have been able to match in recent history.

As impressive as Wal-Mart's increase in net income was during this period, that growth did not keep up with the growth in revenue and expenses. Between 1987 and 1997, revenue (net sales) grew at a 24.3% compound rate while expenses grew at a 24.4% compound rate. When expenses grow at a faster rate than revenue, net income is bound to suffer. A difference of a mere 0.1% in compound annual growth rates for revenue and expenses had a very dramatic impact on Wal-Mart's net income. Over this ten-year period, the 0.1 percentage point difference had a cumulative effect of 3.2 percentage point difference between the growth in revenue (24.3%) and the growth in net income (21.1%).[5] In Wal-Mart's case, 3.2 percentage points translates into a difference of billions of dollars in net income.

Like our analysis of the balance sheet equation, the analysis of the income statement equation can provide some interesting initial insights into the business (if you are a financial type who likes numbers). Unfortunately, most managers with operating responsibilities are still looking for the cow. They need a more tangible or visceral way of grasping the significance of numbers.

That's where the ROE calculation comes into play. It represents a simple, straightforward point of reference for making our way through the sea of words and numbers found in balance sheets and income statements.

Understanding the Business through the Concept of ROE

We use the concept of ROE to help managers understand a firm's overall business strategy in terms of the information found in income statements and balance sheets. By dividing net income (taken from the income statement) by shareholders' equity (taken from the balance sheet), we can drive a stake into the ground and begin to develop a more in-depth understanding of the business.

The ROE calculation that links the income statement to the balance sheet is as follows:

Return on Equity (ROE) = Net Income ÷ Shareholders' Equity

Wal-Mart's ROEs for the fiscal years ended 1987 and 1997 were as follows:

ROE = Net Income ÷ Shareholders' Equity
1987: 26.6% = $450M ÷ $1.690B
1997: 17.8% = $3.056B ÷ $17.143B

When asked to explain ROE in their own words, many managers fall into the trap of trying to describe how ROE is calculated rather than explaining what the concept might mean in terms of understanding the business. A typical first attempt to explain ROE goes something like this:

▶
───

ROE is the percentage relationship you get when you divide net income by shareholders' equity.

───
◀

This explanation is about as interesting as our description of the compound growth rates associated with Wal-Mart's balance sheet and income statement equations.

Contrast this initial attempt to explain ROE with an explanation that is a little more action-oriented.

▶
───

In 1987, Wal-Mart generated 26.6¢ in profit for every $1 of shareholders' equity.

In 1997, Wal-Mart generated 17.8¢ in profit for every $1 of shareholders' equity.

If management was able to maintain a 26.6¢ ROE, Wal-Mart would have generated an additional $1.508 billion in net income on shareholders' equity of $17.143 billion.

───
◀

Even at this early stage of learning how to understand the business through financial information, it only seems natural to wonder why Wal-Mart's ROE has fallen by 8.8¢ for every $1 of shareholders' equity. Given this drop in ROE, it would probably not be surprising to learn that Wal-Mart's common stock has not performed very well in recent years, as it did during the years when the company was growing the business at a faster rate and generating higher ROEs.[6]

In the July 7, 1997, issue of *Business Week*, where the ROEs of the top 1,000 publicly held global companies were reported, we can see how Wal-

Mart's 17.8% ROE stacks up against the ROEs of other highly visible companies. Relative to the market, we can begin to ask whether a ROE of 17.8% is good or bad. Is Wal-Mart among the leaders or back in the middle of the pack? Selected ROEs of other firms included in the 1997 *Business Week* Global 1,000 are presented below, along with the average ROE for all 1,000 companies and the average ROE for the 447 U.S. companies included in the global 1,000. Given this information, we can begin to get a sense of how well Wal-Mart stacks up against other top firms and competitors in the retail business.[7]

Global Rank	Company	ROE
	Global 1,000	16.2%
	U.S. Companies	21.5%
1	General Electric	23.2%
2	Coca-Cola	61.3%
5	Microsoft	39.2%
7	Intel	34.0%
20	Wal-Mart	18.3%[8]
27	Pepsico	28.0%
174	Sears, Roebuck	25.5%
181	Caterpillar	35.5%
525	Kmart	5.4%

As we can see, Wal-Mart is generating an ROE somewhat above the average for the 16.2% average ROE for the global 1,000 but substantially below the 21.5% average for the 447 U.S. firms included in the global 1,000. Firms like Coca-Cola (61.3%), Microsoft (39.2%), Intel (34.0%), and Caterpillar (35.5%) are all generating ROEs substantially above Wal-Mart's 18.5%. Within the retail business, Wal-Mart (and virtually everyone else) is doing better than Kmart (5.4%), but compared to Sears, Roebuck (25.5%), Wal-Mart is generating a lower ROE.

In Part Two, we will look *outward* and compare Wal-Mart's financial performance to other publicly traded companies. We will look at the relationship between a firm's ROE and its stock price. For the remainder of Part One, we will look *internally* to see how the concept of ROE can be used to develop a comprehensive understanding of a firm's business operations. In Part Two, we will extend our analysis to develop a comprehensive understanding of a firm's long-term financing and investment activities.

In keeping with our optical illusion analogy, using a simple calculation of ROE (net income ÷ shareholders' equity) might be equivalent to describing the location of the cow's ears. Describing the location of the ears is a step in the right direction, but it does not provide a complete outline of the cow's head and body.

The Strategic Profit Model (SPM) is the communications tool we use to help managers see how all of the firm's economic activity may be interrelated through the concept of ROE. If ROE represents the firm as a whole, then the SPM helps everyone see how the whole in terms of its component parts. We use the quick overview of the SPM (discussed below) to flesh out a complete outline of a firm's financial (cash?) cow.

By breaking ROE up into its component parts, managers can begin to see how they can influence the overall profitability of their firms. They begin to see where they can make immediate contributions in their areas of responsibility. They also begin to see how they can have a greater impact by coordinating their efforts with managers in other functional areas or other lines of business.

THE STRATEGIC PROFIT MODEL: QUICK OVERVIEW

Throughout this book, we will use terms like *quick overview, insight, visualize,* and *as we shall see* to describe the process of understanding the business through financial information. Our emphasis on seeing and visualizing can be traced back to the early years of the 20th century and is captured by the management philosophy underlying DuPont's executive charting system.

Since 1919, the DuPont Company has used a chart system for appraising performance. The charts are designed to present in readily understandable *visual* form the financial results of each of the company's industrial departments and of the company as a whole.

In the use of this formula to bring results before the Executive Committee, the presentation is not based on a step-by-step build up to the ultimate objective of Return on Investment. Instead, the end result is presented first and thereafter the important elements that contribute to it. By doing so, as the chart presentation unfolds, the viewers' attention may be focused clearly on those underlying factors that are responsible for any fluctuation in this end result.

The charts themselves *do not* utilize narrative explanation. There is no opportunity for one reviewing the figures to bog down under the weight of particular words or phrases that might be chosen to explain a given development.

It is comparatively easy *to hold the attention* of an entire group to one item at the same moment.

A given format is adhered to until it becomes clear that a change would make a substantial improvement. *Frequent changes are avoided.* [Emphasis added.][9]

As we shall see, the SPM is the charting tool we use to show how all of the elements found in the balance sheet and income statement contribute to the ROE. We always begin with the whole and then break that whole down into its component parts. If the whole is ROE, then its component parts consist of:

- Profit Margin
- Asset Turnover
- Return on Assets
- Financial Leverage

We can begin to see how the parts fit into an integrated whole using just four elements taken from the income statement and balance sheet:

1. Net Sales
2. Net Income
3. Total Assets
4. Shareholders' Equity

In combination, these four elements will allow us to complete an outline of Wal-Mart's financial performance for 1987 and 1997 centered on the concept of ROE. The four elements we will use to prepare a quick overview of Wal-Mart's financial performance are:

Net sales. The amount of customer financing generated through the sales of the firm's goods and services.

Net income. The amount of net assets generated by management on behalf of the shareholders after covering all expenses incurred during the year.

Total assets. The amount of resources under management control at year-end used to generate a return on the shareholders' behalf.

Shareholders' equity. The amount of money paid-in by the shareholders and the amount earned by management on the shareholders' behalf and retained in the business.

The net sales and net income amounts (in millions) presented below come from Wal-Mart's 1987 and 1997 income statements (Figure 1.3) and the total asset and shareholders' equity amounts (in millions) come from Wal-Mart's 1987 and 1997 balance sheets (Figure 1.2). Taken together, these four elements provide the foundation for taking a more in-depth look at how a firm's business strategy is linked to shareholder accountability through the financial statements.

Elements	1987	1997
Net Sales	$11,909	$104,859
Net Income	$450	$3,056
Total Assets	$4,049	$39,604
Shareholders' Equity	$1,690	$17,143

Figure 1.4 presents a quick overview of Wal-Mart's SPM for 1987 and 1997 based on the net sales, net income, total assets, and shareholders' equity reported in the financial statements for those years. After anchoring our discussion with the ROE percentages reported on the left side of

18

Figure 1.4 Wal-Mart Strategic Profit Model: Quick Overview (for the Fiscal Years Ended January 31, 1987 and 1997 — Amounts in Millions)

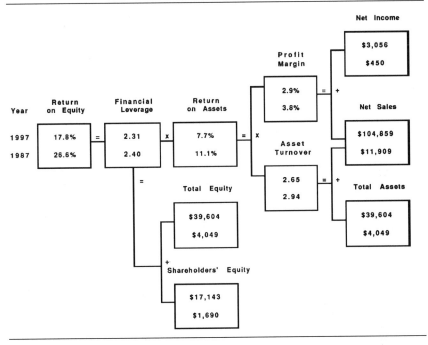

the model, we will work our way through the SPM beginning in the upper right-hand corner.

As stated previously, in dollars ($) and cents (¢) terms,

In 1987, Wal-Mart generated 26.6¢ in profit on every $1 of shareholders' equity; in 1997, Wal-Mart generated 17.8¢.

In the process of growing the business over this ten-year period, Wal-Mart experienced an 8.8¢ drop in ROE. With the quick overview provided by the SPM, we can now take a more in-depth look at the individual components contributing to Wal-Mart's ROE in 1987 and 1997 and the 8.8¢ drop.

Profit Margin

The concept of profit margin establishes the relationship between customers (the principal source of financing for any firm) and the net income (net earned assets) remaining after all expenses and other charges for the period have been taken into consideration.

As we can see from Figure 1.4, the profit margin is calculated by dividing net income by the net sales for the period.

In 1987, Wal-Mart earned 3.8¢ in profit for every $1 of net sales; in 1995, Wal-Mart earned 2.9¢ in profit.

Between 1987 and 1997, Wal-Mart experienced pressure on its margins. In other words, in pursuing its overall business strategy, Wal-Mart was not able to maintain the 3.8¢ on every $1 of net sales.

The 0.9¢ decline in profit margin translates into $944 million of net income (0.9¢ × $104.859 billion in net sales).

In Chapter 2, we will blow up the profit margin component of the SPM to see how margin management fits into Wal-Mart's overall business strategy. For the time being, we will leave you with one of Sam Walton's ten rules for running a successful company.

RULE 9: CONTROL your expenses better than your competition. This is where you can always find the competitive advantage. For twenty-five years running—long before Wal-Mart was known as the nation's largest retailer—we ranked number one in our industry for the lowest ratio of expenses to sales. You can make a lot of different mistakes and still recover if you run an efficient operation. Or you can be brilliant and still go out of business if you're too inefficient.[10]

If Wal-Mart is still the most efficient retailer in the business, why has the profit margin fallen over the last ten years?

Asset Turnover

The concept of asset turnover establishes the relationship between the customer as the principal source of financing (net sales) and the economic resources (assets) utilized to run the business.

As we can see from Figure 1.4, asset turnover is calculated by dividing net sales by total assets.

In 1987, Wal-Mart generated $2.94 in revenue for every $1 of total assets; in 1997, Wal-Mart generated $2.65.

All things considered, management (and shareholders) would prefer to generate more dollars in net sales per $1 of assets than less. The greater the asset turnover, the greater the amount of customer financing management has generated with a given amount of assets. Effective managers are constantly attempting to get the most bang for their investment buck, to do more with less, to increase their turns. Within the context of the SPM, the asset turnover ratio is just one way of visualizing what doing more with less might mean.

In Wal-Mart's case, the asset turnover actually decreased between 1987 and 1997. For every $1 of assets, Wal-Mart generated 29¢ less in net sales in 1997 than it generated in 1987. The 29¢ decline in asset turnover translates into $11.485 billion in net sales on the 1997 asset base of $39.604 billion (29¢ × $39.604B in assets). Stated differently, if Wal-Mart had maintained a $2.94 asset turnover in 1997, it would only have required $35.666 billion in assets ($104.859B ÷ $2.94). The difference of $3.938 billion ($39.604B − $35.666B = $3,938B) represents money that shareholders would not have had to tie up in the business if management had been able to maintain the $2.94 turnover.

In Chapter 3, we will blow up the asset turnover component of the SPM to see how asset management fits into Wal-Mart's overall business strategy. As we shall see, Wal-Mart's overall business strategy differs with respect to the utilization of current assets and productive assets. Wal-Mart's business strategy (as reflected in the financial performance measures) represents a combination of efficient operations and global expansion.

Return on Assets

The concept of return on assets (ROA) establishes the relationship between the net income earned by management and the total assets under management control. If we were only concerned with making the ROA calculation as efficient as possible, we would divide net income by total assets and omit any intermediate steps.

ROA = Net Income ÷ Total Assets

The trouble with efficient calculations is that they can get in the way of effective communications. In Figure 1.4, we can see how ROA is the product of the combination of profit margin and asset turnover.

In 1987, Wal-Mart earned 11.1¢ in profit for every $1 of total assets; in 1997, Wal-Mart earned 7.7¢.

In terms of the imagery presented in Figure 1.4, management can increase ROA by taking a "northern route" and improving its profit margin and/or by taking a "southern route" by increasing asset turnover and utilizing assets more efficiently. A comprehensive management strategy would focus on the most effective way to increase net sales while keeping expenses down and controlling the growth of the asset base.

In Wal-Mart's case, with both profit margin and asset turnover declining between 1987 and 1997, ROA has nowhere to go but down. As management was growing the business, ROA suffered a 3.4¢ decline. If management could have maintained the 11.1% ROA achieved in 1987, Wal-Mart would have generated an additional $1.347 billion in net income on the $39.604 billion asset base under management control in 1997 (3.4¢ × $39,604B).[11]

At this point in our journey toward using the SPM to understand the business, it might be a little more enjoyable if we learn to sing the Strategic Profit Model song. The first three verses of Wal-Mart's 1997 song go like this:

For every $1 of assets, Wal-Mart generated $2.65 in net sales.

For every $1 of net sales, Wal-Mart earned 2.9¢ in profit.

Multiplying the profit margin by the asset turnover; for every $1 of assets, Wal-Mart generated 7.7¢ in profit in 1997.

The 1987 version of Wal-Mart's SPM song was somewhat more joyous and may provide a battle cry for management to improve future versions of the SPM song. The 1987 versions goes like this:

For every $1 of assets, Wal-Mart generated $2.94 in net sales.

For every $1 of net sales, Wal-Mart earned 3.8¢ in profit.

Multiplying the profit margin by the asset turnover; for every $1 of assets, Wal-Mart generated 11.1¢ in profit in 1987.

In Chapter 4, we will return to a discussion of ROA after we have blown up the margin-management and asset-management components of the SPM.

Financial Leverage

The concept of financial leverage establishes the relationship between the total equity (liabilities + shareholders' equity) of the firm and the amount provided by (and earned by management on behalf of) the shareholders.

As we can see from Figure 1.4, financial leverage is calculated by dividing total equity by shareholders' equity.

In 1987, Wal-Mart utilized $2.40 in total equity for every $1 of shareholders' equity; in 1997, Wal-Mart utilized $2.31.

The $1.40 difference between total equity and shareholders' equity in 1987 ($1.31 in 1997) represents Wal-Mart's total liabilities.

Since total equity equals total assets, you could think of financial leverage as the total amount of assets under the control of management relative to the amount of the shareholders' investment in the company.

In 1987, management was responsible for controlling $2.40 in total assets for every $1 of shareholders' equity; in 1997, management was responsible for $2.31.

The "lever" in financial leverage refers to the impact of using someone else's (creditors') money to run the business. In 1987, the $2.40 financial lever turned an 11.1¢ ROA into a 26.6¢ ROE (2.40 × 11.1%). In 1997, a $2.31 lever turned a 7.7¢ ROA into a 17.8¢ ROE. If management had maintained the 1987 level of financial leverage in 1997, Wal-Mart's ROE would have been 18.5¢ (2.40 × 7.7%). By decreasing financial leverage, management increased the decline in ROE by 0.7¢ per $1 of shareholders' equity.

In Chapter 5, we will blow up the financial-leverage component of the SPM to see how financial management fits into Wal-Mart's overall business strategy. As we shall see, Wal-Mart has been growing the business through a combination of long-term debt and retained earnings. Between 1987 and 1997, Wal-Mart issued very few shares of additional common stock.

Return on Equity: Closing the Loop

After walking through a quick overview of Wal-Mart's SPM, anyone can begin to see the cow hidden in Wal-Mart's financial statements. The quick overview is equivalent to taking a half-day Berlitz course in understanding the business through financial information. We can now order simple meals off of the menu and ask for directions to the restroom. *"Donde está el baño?"* Taking care of the basics makes it a lot easier to sit through the afternoon session and feel good about coming back to class the next day.

With a little help, managers are now able to sing (or at least hum to themselves) all of the verses to the SPM song. The 1987 version goes like this:

For every $1 of assets, Wal-Mart generated $2.94 in net sales.

For every $1 of revenue, Wal-Mart earned 3.8¢ in profit.

Multiplying the profit margin by the asset turnover; for every $1 of assets, Wal-Mart generated 11.1¢ in profit.

When we multiply ROA by the $2.40 in total assets management controlled for every $1 of shareholders' equity, we see that Wal-Mart generated 26.6¢ in profit for every $1 of shareholders' equity invested in the business.

The 1997 version of Wal-Mart's SPM song is not quite as joyful, but it goes like this:

For every $1 of assets, Wal-Mart generated $2.65 in net sales.

For every $1 of net sales, Wal-Mart earned 2.9¢ in profit.

Multiplying the profit margin by the asset turnover, we know that for every $1 of assets, Wal-Mart generated 7.7¢ in profit.

When we multiply ROA by the $2.31 in total assets management controlled for every $1 of shareholders' equity, we see that Wal-Mart generated 17.8¢ in profit for every $1 of shareholders' equity invested in the business.

We believe that the summary version of the SPM helps managers begin to see the benefits of opening up the communications process within their own firms. To our way of thinking, the SPM (which helps visualize and humanize the financial communications process) is a key component of a Business Advocate model of financial management. If firms want to make everyone aware of the financial implications of their decisions and actions, introducing the SPM throughout the firm would be a good place to start.

When used within a Business Advocate environment, the SPM helps senior management balance the need for individual autonomy and effective control within the firm. Sam Walton quotes captures this thought quite nicely.

> We decided a long time ago to share so much information about the company with our associates, rather than keep everything secretive.

> We share everything with them: the cost of their goods, the freight costs, the profit margins. We let them see how their store ranks with every other store in the company on a constant, running basis, and we give them incentives to want to win.

> We're always trying for that fine balance between autonomy and control.[12]

In the next four chapters, we will take a closer look at the margin management, asset management, ROA, and financial management components of the SPM.

NOTES

1. We have included the financial statements of other major U.S. corporations as case studies in the Appendixes. The concepts developed in each chapter may be applied to these financial statements to reinforce the learning experience. However, as mentioned in the Introduction, one of the best ways to learn how to understand a business is to apply the concepts to (1) your own firm's financial statements and/or (2) the financial statements of a firm you might be thinking of investing in. Nothing reinforces the learning experience more than self-interest.

2. A number of accounts shown in the balance sheets have been collapsed together to simplify the discussion of key concepts. The operating expenses shown on the income statements include operating, selling, general, and administrative expenses.

3. We refer to the statement of income and retained earnings as simply the income statement to simplify the discussion of key concepts. From a practical perspective, the statement of income and retained earnings provides us with two important pieces of financial information: (1) the amount of dividends that were declared during the year, and (2) the amounts of any charges or

credits that were made to retained earnings that bypassed the income statement.

4. Even though some financial advisory services (Standard & Poor's, Moody's, Dun and Bradstreet, etc.) and some business periodicals (*Business Week*, *Fortune*, *Forbes*, etc.) exclude some elements of net income in reporting on particular aspects of the business, *each* of these users provides an explanation for making these adjustments. In assessing the profitability of a firm, everyone begins with the amount reported as net income.

5. For these compound growth rates, other income has been excluded from total revenue and included as an offset to the total costs and expenses. More on this point later in the chapter.

6. The market valuation process is discussed more fully in Part Two of this book. For the current discussion, all we want to do is generate interest in learning more about how ROE can help us in understanding the business through financial information.

7. The rankings are based on the total market value of the firm's common stock.

8. The *Business Week* calculations are based on Wal-Mart's financial performance through April 30, 1997. Wal-Mart's financial performance during the first quarter of the year increased ROE by 0.5 percentage points.

9. "Executive Committee Control Charts: A Description of the DuPont Chart System for Appraising Operating Performance," AMA no. 6, 1950.

10. Sam Walton and John Huey, *Sam Walton, Made in America: My Story* (New York: Doubleday, 1992), 248–249.

11. In Wal-Mart's 1996 annual report to shareholders, CEO David Glass stated that ROA was going to play a more significant role in the company's overall business strategy.

12. Sam Walton and John Huey, *Sam Walton, Made in America: My Story* (New York: Doubleday, 1992), 227.

Appendix 1A: Compound Annual Growth Rates

When the current year's financial information is compared to the previous year, the percentage increase (or decrease) for the year is determined by dividing the change from one year to the next by the amount reported for the earlier year. For example, Wal-Mart's total assets increased from $37.541 billion at January 31, 1997 to $39.604 billion at January 31, 1997, an increase of $2.063 billion, or 5.5% ($2.063B ÷ $37.541B).

Over the ten-year period January 31, 1987 through January 31, 1997, total assets increased from $4.049 billion to $39.604 billion, an increase of $35.555 billion, or 878%. While this is an accurate description of the total percentage increase, most managers and investors have a hard time relating to a number like 878%. The increase or decrease in total assets over two or more years is much easier to understand when it is expressed as an annual percentage change or compound annual growth rate (CAGR).

Wal-Mart's 878% increase in total assets translates into a 25.6% CAGR. Expressed in this manner, it becomes quite easy for managers to compare the growth in assets to the growth in other measures of company performance, that is, liabilities, shareholders' equity, sales, net income, and so on. Compound annual growth rates also provide a convenient way for managers to compare themselves against the competition and against other investment opportunities.

Most software spreadsheet packages (Excel, Lotus) contain the mathematical formula for computing CAGRs. All you do is enter the starting amount ($4.049 billion in total assets), the ending amount ($39.604 billion), and the number of periods or years (ten years) and the computer calculates the rate needed to grow the starting amount to equal the ending amount.

The actual year-to-year increase in total assets is compared to the hypothetical increase if total assets increased at a uniform 25.6% per year.

Wal-Mart Total Assets (Amounts in Millions)

Year	Actual	25.6% CAGR*
1987	$4,049	$4,049
1988	$5,132	$5,086
1989	$6,360	$6,389
1990	$8,198	$8,025
1991	$11,389	$10,081
1992	$15,443	$12,663
1993	$20,565	$15,907
1994	$26,441	$19,981
1995	$32,819	$25,099
1996	$37,541	$31,528
1997	$39,604	$39,604

*Compound Annual Growth Rate

In Part One of this book, CAGR calculations will be used to help explain various aspects of Wal-Mart's business strategy. In Part Two, CAGRs will be used to help explain how investors and financial analysts evaluate companies from a capital market perspective.

CHAPTER 2

Strategic Profit Model: Margin Management

The quick overview of the Strategic Profit Model (SPM) presented in Chapter 1 showed how return on shareholders' equity (ROE) can be visualized in terms of its component parts: profit margin, asset turnover, return on assets (ROA), and financial leverage. By exploring the interrelationships among the parts, we can begin to see how each of the components of the SPM must be managed in order for the firm to be a success. As we shall see, success begins with the customer and ends with the shareholders.

The concept of profit margin (net income ÷ net sales) can be brought to life for most managers by talking about what they are doing currently to increase or maintain their firm's profit margin. Or, if their firm's profit margin has declined in recent years (like Wal-Mart's), managers can be asked to describe what they are doing to get the profit margin back to past performance levels, or how the new reduced profit margin fits into their firm's current business strategy. In either case, we ask managers to think of the financial numbers in terms of their *actions*. From an action perspective, profit margin becomes the performance indicator that links the customer to the ongoing operations of the firm that must be managed on a day-to-day basis.

Firms must meet the customers' needs at a cost that allows them to generate a profit. Customers provide the money the firm needs to cover current expenses and generate a profit on behalf of the owners. How to pursue customer dollars at a profit is where business strategy starts. According to Sam Walton,

Everything we've done since we started Wal-Mart has been devoted to this idea that the customer is our boss. The controversies it has led us into have surprised me, but they've been easy to live with because we have never doubted our philosophy that the customer comes ahead of everything else.[1]

A blow-up of the margin management component of the SPM allows us to see how this emphasis on the customer (net sales) is related to the costs, expenses, and net income reported in the income statement. The income statement is where we go to see if the firm has operated at a profit in the pursuit of customer satisfaction.

Wal-Mart's statements of income and retained earnings for the fiscal years ended January 31, 1987 and 1997, presented in Chapter 1, are represented in Figure 2.1.[2] We will be exploring the interrelationships among the elements found in these income statements with the knowledge that Wal-Mart generated a profit margin (net income ÷ net sales) of 3.8% in 1987 and 2.9% in 1997.

In 1987, Wal-Mart earned 3.8¢ in profit for every $1 of net sales; in 1997, Wal-Mart earned 2.9¢ in profit.

Given this prior knowledge, we will want to use the margin management component of the SPM to develop a better understanding of Wal-Mart's business operations than are captured in an income statement.

Before taking a more in-depth look at the margin-management component of the SPM, we would like to reinforce the substantive meaning of the term *net income*.

Net income equals the increase in net assets (assets – liabilities) earned by management on behalf of the shareholders during the year.

In 1987, management earned $450 million on behalf of the shareholders; in 1997, management earned $3.056 billion.

Figure 2.1 Wal-Mart Statements of Income and Retained Earnings (for the Fiscal Years Ended January 31, 1987 and 1997 — Amounts in Millions)

	1987	1997
Net Sales	$11,909	$104,859
Total Revenue	$11,909	$104,859
Costs and Expenses		
Cost of Sales	$9,053	$83,663
Operating Expenses	$2,008	$16,788
Interest Expense	$86	$845
Other Income	($84)	($1,287)
Total Costs and Expenses	$11,063	$100,009
Income before Income Taxes	$846	$4,850
Provision for Income Taxes		
Current Portion	$374	$1,974
Deferred Portion	$22	($180)
Total Provision	$396	$1,794
Net Income	$450	$3,056
Dividends	($48)	($481)
Adjustments to Retained Earnings		($201)
Retained Earnings, Beginning Balance	$1,068	$14,394
Retained Earnings, Ending Balance	$1,470	$16,768

Between 1987 and 1997, Wal-Mart increased net assets through the earnings process at a 21.1% compound annual growth rate (CAGR).[3]

By taking a closer look at the income statement through the lens of the SPM, we can develop a better understanding of what Wal-Mart actually did to generate those results. The margin-management component of the SPM brings the numbers to life in a visual format that makes sense to managers.

Figure 2.2 Wal-Mart Strategic Profit Model: Margin Management (For the Fiscal Years Ended January 31, 1987 and 1997 — Amounts in Millions)

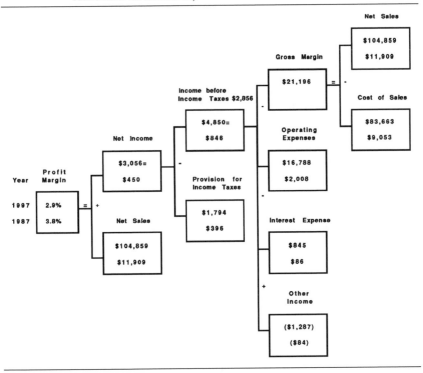

Figure 2.2 presents the margin-management component of Wal-Mart's SPM using the amounts taken from the 1987 and 1997 income statements. Figure 2.3 helps us make the transition from seeing how each of the components of the SPM affects the firm's overall profitability to thinking about how to improve Wal-Mart's financial performance in the future. Figure 2.3(a) converts the income statement from dollars to a percentage of net sales. The percentages for each line item on the income statement will allow us to talk about management's performance in dollars and cents terms.

Figure 2.3(b) converts the changes between 1987 and 1997 into CAGRs. We will use these CAGRs to talk about how management grew the business between 1987 and 1997.

Figure 2.3   Wal-Mart Strategic Profit Model: Margin Management

(a) Percentage of Net Sales

	1987	1997	Change
Net Sales	100.0%	100.0%	0.0%
CGS	76.0%	79.8%	3.8%
Gross Margin	24.0%	20.2%	−3.8%
Operating Expenses	16.9%	16.0%	−0.9%
Interest Expense	0.7%	0.8%	0.1%
Other Income	−0.7%	−1.2%	−0.5%
Income before Income Taxes	7.1%	4.6%	−2.5%
Income Taxes	3.3%	1.7%	−1.6%
Net Income	3.8%	2.9%	−0.9%

(b) Compound Annual Growth Rates (1987–1997)

Net Sales	24.3%
Cost of Sales	24.9%
Gross Margin	22.2%
Operating Expenses	23.7%
Other Income	31.4%
Interest Expense	25.7%
Income before Income Taxes	19.1%
Income Taxes	16.3%
Net Income	21.1%

MARGIN MANAGEMENT

We begin the discussion of the margin management component of the SPM with net sales (the customer financing for the period) and end with net income and the profit margin. In between net sales and net income, we will find all of the costs, expenses, and other income that have to be managed in order for Wal-Mart to be a success.

Net Sales.   Net sales represents the sale of goods and services to customers in exchange for money and/or promises of money.

Since customers are the primary source of financing for any firm, we anchor the discussion of the margin management component of the SPM to net sales. Net sales equals price (P) times quantity (Q). No matter how you cut it, any firm's business strategy can be understood in terms of price and quantity. Firms like Wal-Mart grow the business and increase market share by keeping prices below the competition while increasing volume.

Cost of Sales.   As the name implies, cost of sales represents the dollar cost of the goods sold to customers. The cost of all goods on hand at the beginning of the period plus all purchases made during the period is either recovered through operations (cost of sales) or remains to be recovered and is reported as inventory on the balance sheet.[4]

Like sales, cost of sales equals price times quantity. In fact, the "Q" for both net sales and cost of sales is the same quantity. As a sale is made to a customer, money flows in and goods and services flow out of the business. As the goods and services flow out the door, the cost of those sales is matched to the revenue generated.

Gross Margin.   A firm's gross margin represents the amount of money remaining after recovering the cost of sales made during the period. Gross margin is one of the first performance measures that managers use to monitor the financial health of their firm. If a firm cannot generate an adequate gross margin, it cannot begin to cover its other operating expenses, interest charges, and income taxes, let alone pay dividends and reinvest earnings into the business.

▶────────────────────────────────────

In 1987, Wal-Mart generated a gross margin of $2.856 billion; in 1997, Wal-Mart generated a gross margin of $21.196 billion.

In 1987, Wal-Mart earned a 24.0¢ gross margin for every $1 of net sales; in 1997, Wal-Mart earned a 20.2¢ gross margin.

During that decade, gross margin dollars increased at a 22.2% compound annual growth rate. Over this same period, net sales grew at a 24.3% compound rate and cost of sales grew at a 24.9% compound rate.

────────────────────────────────────◀

The following statement about Wal-Mart's gross margin provides an interesting beginning for trying to understand a firm's business strategy.

> When net sales grows at a different rate than the cost of sales, that difference will be reflected in gross margin dollars.

In Wal-Mart's case, a difference of 0.6 percentage points in the compound growth rates of net sales and cost of sales (24.3% – 24.9%) resulted in a substantially lower growth in gross margin dollars (22.2%). Even though total gross margin dollars have increased, they have not increased as fast as they could have if Wal-Mart was able to maintain its historical relationship between sales and cost of sales.

The difference in growth rates for net sales and cost of sales is captured in the gross margin percentage. In 1987, Wal-Mart was generating 24¢ in gross margin for every $1 of net sales. In 1997, the gross margin had fallen by 3.8¢ for every $1 of net sales (24.0¢ – 20.2¢).

For a firm like Wal-Mart, a drop in gross margin of 3.8¢ per $1 of net sales translates into $4.0 billion gross margin dollars on sales of $104.9 billion. Four billion dollars is a lot of money. Even though management is growing the business through increased sales, the current business is nowhere near as profitable as it was in 1987.

> Question: Is a decline in gross margin as a percentage of net sales dollars necessarily bad for the shareholders?
>
> Answer: It depends.

At first glance, a 3.8¢ decline would appear to be bad. On the one hand, the 3.8¢ decline translates into $4.0 billion in lower gross margin dollars. On the other hand, it is not clear that net sales would have reached $104.9 billion if Wal-Mart had attempted to maintain a higher gross margin percentage. Wal-Mart's strategy of using low gross margins to generate additional sales started very early in the company's history.

Here's the simple lesson we learned . . . say I bought an item for 80 cents. I found that by pricing it at $1.00 I could sell three times more of it than by pricing it at $1.20. I might make only half the profit (gross margin) per item, but because I was selling three times as many, the overall profit was much greater. Simple enough. But this is really the essence of discounting: by cutting your price, you can boost sales to the point where you earn far more for at a cheaper retail price than you would by selling the item at the higher price. In retailer language, you can lower your markup but earn more because you increased volume.[5]

From a management perspective, there might be some benefit to being able to claim that you are the world's largest retailer. However, from the shareholders' perspective, increased size without increased profits is of dubious value. For a decline in gross profit to have no effect on the shareholders, it must be offset by savings or productivity increases in other parts of the business operations. To explore these possibilities, it is necessary to continue our journey toward Wal-Mart's profit margin.

Operating Expenses.   Operating expenses represent all of the costs incurred to operate the distribution centers, sell the goods and services, and run those parts of the business not captured within the gross margin calculation.

In 1987, operating expenses accounted for 16.9¢ of every $1 of net sales; in 1997, operating expenses accounted for 16.0¢ of net sales.

Between 1987 and 1997, operating expenses increased at a 23.7% compound annual growth rate.

When it comes to keeping operating expenses under control, virtually everyone looks to Wal-Mart as the exemplar of superior management performance. By keeping the growth in operating expenses (23.7%) under the growth in cost of sales (24.9%), Wal-Mart was able to partially offset the decline in gross margin.

Since we are only looking at 1987 and 1997, the full impact of Wal-Mart's operating expense performance is not visible. The biggest reductions in operating expenses occurred in 1984. From 1971 until 1983, the operating expenses fluctuated between 18.1¢ and 20.7¢ of every $1 of net sales. After 1983, Wal-Mart's operating expenses have never exceeded 17.6¢ for every $1 of net sales.

The drop in operating expenses can be traced directly to Wal-Mart's 1983 decision to invest in telecommunications technology to support interactive communications with each store and distribution center. After implementing the new computer-based information system, managers and associates (employees) had low-cost, direct access to the information they needed to run the business more efficiently.

In terms of Wal-Mart's overall business strategy, the reduction in operating expenses of 0.9¢ over the last ten years could be used to partially offset the reduction in gross margin percentage and reduce the overall impact of price reductions on the bottom line.

By controlling operating expenses, Wal-Mart was able to "add-back" $944 million in earnings that were "lost" by reducing the gross margin by 3.8¢. With 0.9¢ of the 3.8¢ recovered through operating efficiencies, 2.9¢ remains to be recaptured, if possible.

Since we know that Wal-Mart's overall profit margin actually fell by 0.9¢ between 1987 and 1997 (3.8¢ − 2.9¢), management was only able to come up with an additional 2.0¢ in savings somewhere along the way.

Interest Expense. This expense represents the "charge" Wal-Mart incurs for the use of creditors' money to run the business. Wal-Mart incurs interest charges on its short- and long-term borrowings and capital lease obligations.

In 1987, Wal-Mart incurred an interest expense of 0.7¢ for every $1 of net sales; in 1997, Wal-Mart incurred an interest expense of 0.8¢.

Even though Wal-Mart finances a large part of the growth of the business through debt, interest charges have always remained below 1.0¢ for every $1 of net sales.

As discussed more fully under the financial management component of the SPM, Wal-Mart has required a substantial amount of debt to grow the business. However, interest charges do not use up a significant portion of every sales dollar. Sears Roebuck, on the other hand, was spending between 3.0¢ and 4.0¢ per sales dollar on interest expense during the late 1980s and early 1990s. The high interest costs and related high debt levels contributed, in part, to the "downsizing" of Sears that occurred in the mid 1990s.

Other Income.   Other income represents the amount of revenue that Wal-Mart generates from nonroutine business transactions. For example, the sale of property or equipment may result in a gain or loss, but this gain or loss is not directly related to Wal-Mart's primary business of selling merchandise to customers. In 1987, other income of 0.7¢ could be used to supplement the revenue generated through customer sales. In 1997, 1.2¢ could be used to supplement net sales. The increase in other income offset another 0.5¢ of the 3.8¢ decline in the gross margin.

Income before Income Taxes.   Income before income taxes represents the amount of customer financing remaining after covering all of the costs matched against net sales for the period, other than income taxes. In dollars-and-cents terms, the $846 million in income before income taxes Wal-Mart generated in 1987 represented 7.1¢ of net sales. The $4.850 billion generated in 1997 represented 4.6¢ of net sales.

Every time we create a subtotal for the margin-management component of the SPM, we can consolidate our understanding of the firm's basic business strategy. For Wal-Mart, we have been able to make the following observations. Between 1987 and 1997:

- Net sales increased from $11.909 billion to $104.859 billion, a 24.3% CAGR.
- Cost of sales increased from $9.053 billion to $83.663 billion, a 24.9% CAGR. Cost of sales increased from 76.0¢ to 79.8¢ of every dollar of net sales.
- Gross margin dollars increased from $2.856 billion to $21.196 billion, a 22.2% compound annual growth rate. In terms of dollars of net sales, the gross margin declined by 3.8¢, resulting in $4.859 billion less in gross margin dollars on net sales of $104.859 billion.

- The negative impact on earnings of the 3.8¢ decline in gross margin was offset by the 0.9¢ saved by controlling the rate of growth in operating expenses (23.7%) and the 0.5¢ increase in other income.

- Interest expense remained roughly the same over the ten-year period (a 0.1¢ increase from 0.7¢ to 0.8¢).

- The 3.8¢ decline in gross margin was offset by a net decline of 1.3¢ in operating expenses, interest expense, and other income. The 2.5¢ decline in income before income taxes represented $2.621 billion on net sales of $104.859 billion.

Provision for Income Taxes. This expense represents the income tax expense associated with the firm's performance for a given year. The total provision consists of a current portion and a deferred portion. The income taxes actually due and payable as a result of operating during the year represent the current portion. The income tax effects of timing difference between tax reporting and financial reporting represent the deferred portion.[6]

Wal-Mart's effective tax rate was 46.8% of income before income taxes in 1987 and 37.0% in 1997. Between 1987 and 1997, Wal-mart's effective tax rate fell by almost 21%. The reduction reflects the benefits firms like Wal-Mart received from the tax reform act of 1986.

Stated in terms of sales dollars, the impact of the tax reform act was quite dramatic.

In 1987, income taxes accounted for 3.3¢ for every $1 of sales; in 1997, income taxes accounted for 1.7¢ — a reduction of 1.6¢.

When a change in the law provides a corporation with income tax benefits, management has two basic choices on what to do with the savings: (1) pass the savings along to the shareholders in the form of a higher net income or (2) pass the savings along to the customer in the form of lower prices. Based on our analysis up to this point, we would argue that Wal-Mart chose to pass the tax savings along to its customers as part of its overall strategy to grow the business through increased sales, and in the long run, generate even more net income. The decrease in the effective tax rate of 1.6¢ per $1 of net sales translates into $1.7 billion on $104.9 billion in net sales. It would appear that this 1.6¢ tax savings along with the 1.3¢ savings from controlling operating expenses, went a long way toward minimizing the effects of the 3.8¢ decline in gross margin.

Net Income.   Net Income summarizes the results of all of the economic activity that resulted in a change in the net assets (assets – liabilities) earned by management on behalf of shareholders during the year.

▶

In 1987, management earned $450 million on behalf of the shareholders; in 1997, management earned $3.056 billion.

◀

After discussing each of the elements making up net income within a margin-management perspective, we should have developed a better understanding of Wal-Mart's basic business strategy. At this point, all we need to do is bring the profit margin calculation back into the picture and recouple this analysis to the full SPM.

Profit Margin.   Profit margin represents the amount of each dollar of net sales left over after covering all operating expenses, interest charges, and income taxes for the year.

▶

In 1987, Wal-Mart earned 3.8¢ in profit for every $1 of net sales; in 1997, Wal-Mart earned 2.9¢ in profit.

◀

In Chapter 1, we began the process of understanding the whole (ROE) in terms of its component parts (profit margin, asset turnover, ROA, and financial leverage). In this chapter, we set the whole equal to the profit margin and looked at how each of the parts (sales, cost of sales, etc.) contributed to our understanding of the business.

In Chapter 3, we will set the whole equal to asset turnover to discover how knowledge of each of the parts (cash, receivables, inventory, property, plant and equipment, etc.) adds to our understanding of the business as a whole.

NOTES

1. Sam Walton and John Huey, *Sam Walton, Made in America: My Story* (New York: Doubleday, 1992), 188.

2. The statement of income and change in retained earnings (hereafter, income statement) allows the reader to see all of the elements that have affected the change in retained earnings during the year. Net income increases retained earnings and shareholder dividends decrease retained earnings. In recent years, firms have been showing other adjustments (increases and decreases) to retained earnings that result from the regulatory reporting requirements in force at the time the financial statements are prepared.

3. Growing the firm's asset base by issuing long-term debt and common stock will be explored in Chapters 7 and 8 when we take a look at the firm's long-term *investment* and *financing* activities.

4. In practice, a number of different accounting techniques have been devised for determining the amounts to report as cost of sales (recovered cost) and inventory (unrecovered cost). From a management communications perspective, we are more concerned with the relationship between selling prices, unit costs, and sales volume than with the choice of a particular accounting technique.

5. Sam Walton and John Huey, *Sam Walton, Made in America: My Story* (New York: Doubleday, 1992), 25.

6. For a firm like Wal-Mart, the majority of the timing differences relate to depreciation. Firms write down (depreciate) property, plant, and equipment at a faster rate for tax purposes than they do for financial reporting purposes in order to minimize current income tax payments. The depreciation included in the income statement is based on the asset's useful economic life. The timing differences are reflected in the deferred income tax computation.

CHAPTER 3

Strategic Profit Model: Asset Management

In Chapter 2, we emphasized how the margin-management component of the Strategic Profit Model (SPM) helps us see how expenses are related to net sales through the concept of profit margin. In this chapter, we are going to emphasize how the asset-management component of the SPM helps us focus on how assets are related to net sales through the concept of asset turnover.

In the quick overview of the SPM presented in Chapter 1, we used the concept of asset turnover to visualize the relationship between the firm's net sales for the year (customer financing) and the total assets under management control at year-end. By visualizing the relationship in this manner, we can begin to think about how assets are deployed to generate a return on the shareholders' investment. Within the context of the quick overview provided by Wal-Mart's SPM, we could see the following:

▶

In 1987, management controlled $4.049 billion in total assets; in 1997, management controlled $39.604 billion.

In 1987, management generated $2.94 in net sales for every $1 of assets; in 1997, management generated $2.65.

◀

Initial reaction: Even though Wal-Mart's asset base grew, management generated 29¢ less in net sales for every $1 of assets in 1997 than it did in

1987. On the surface, it would appear that management has become less effective in utilizing the resources under its control.

Has Wal-Mart really become less efficient, or is there some other explanation for the decline? The facts (a 29¢ decline in asset turnover) appear to be inconsistent with Wal-Mart's reputation for operational efficiency. If the asset-management component of the SPM is going to be of any value to us, it should help us understand why asset turnover declined by 29¢ per $1 of assets.

As we shall see, the power of any turnover ratio lies in its ability to help us explore the relationship between *time* and *money*.

For every $1 invested in assets during the year, how fast has management been able to convert those dollars invested in assets into dollars of customer financing?

Management can increase the speed (efficiency) by either generating more net sales dollars from a given asset base or reducing the assets needed to generate a given level of net sales.

In a competitive business environment, all firms are facing the same efficiency imperative. Managers are constantly being required to do more with less. And when a firm like Wal-Mart starts doing less with more, everyone who follows the company wants to know why this is happening and what the implications are for future performance.

Figure 3.1 presents the asset section of Wal-Mart's balance sheets for 1987 and 1997 that we will use to help us understand the business through the asset-management component of the SPM. As we can see, total assets consist of current assets, productive, and other assets.[1] Each of these categories in turn consists of specific types of assets.

Taken at face value, Figure 3.1 fulfills management's responsibility for reporting on the total assets under its control. Unfortunately, as reported in the balance sheets, the information provides us with virtually no understanding of Wal-Mart's business strategy. A context for understanding the business through financial information is missing.

Figure 3.2 presents that missing context in the form of the asset-management component of Wal-Mart's SPM. As we can see, the amounts taken from Wal-Mart's 1987 and 1997 balance sheets have been supple-

Figure 3.1   Wal-Mart Balance Sheets, Asset Section (for the Fiscal Years Ended January 31, 1987 and 1997 — Amounts in Millions)

	1987	1997
Assets		
Current Assets		
Cash and Equivalents	$166	$883
Receivables	$90	$845
Inventory	$2,031	$15,897
Other	$66	$368
Total Current Assets	$2,353	$17,993
Productive Assets		
Property, Plant, and Equipment	$2,070	$25,964
Accumulated Depreciation	($394)	($5,640)
Net Productive Assets	$1,676	$20,324
Other Assets	$20	$1,287
Total	$4,049	$39,604

mented with the net sales of $11.909 billion for 1987 and $104.859 billion for 1997, taken from Wal-Mart's income statements. Figure 3.2 shows how the elements found in the asset section of the balance sheet are interrelated and linked to net sales through the concept of asset turnover. Asset turnover is an indicator of how well management is using the resources under its control to grow the business.

Figure 3.3(a) presents an analysis of the asset section of both balance sheets in terms of days net sales and Figure 3.3(b) presents the compound annual growth rates (CAGRs) over this ten-year period. The days net sales analysis and compound annual growth rates will be used to help tell a story about Wal-Mart's asset management strategy.

The discussion of asset management is divided into three parts before returning to a discussion of asset turnover:

1. Current assets
2. Productive assets
3. Other assets

Figure 3.2 Wal-Mart Strategic Profit Model: Asset Management (for the Fiscal Years Ended January 31, 1987 and 1997 — Amounts in Millions)

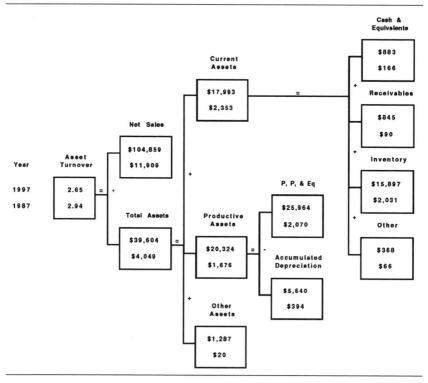

CURRENT ASSETS

Current assets represent resources that will be converted into cash within the firm's operating cycle (usually one year or less). This category includes four financial elements:

1. Cash and Equivalents
2. Receivables
3. Inventory
4. Other Current Assets

Cash and equivalents. Cash and equivalents represents money and short-term investments maturing in 90 days or less. Virtually all firms monitor

Figure 3.3   Wal-Mart Strategic Profit Model: Asset Management

(a) Days Net Sales

	1987	1997	Change
Cash and Equivalents	5.1	3.1	−2.0
Receivables	2.8	2.9	0.2
Inventory	62.2	55.3	−6.9
Other CA	2.0	1.3	−0.7
Current Assets	72.1	62.6	−9.5
Productive Assets	51.4	70.7	19.4
Other Assets	0.6	4.5	3.9
Days Total Assets	124.1	137.9	13.8

(b) Compound Annual Growth Rates CAGR (1987–1997)

Cash and Equivalents	18.2%
Receivables	25.1%
Inventory	22.8%
Other Current Assets	18.7%
Current Assets	22.6%
Productive Assets	28.3%
Other Assets	51.7%
Total Assets	25.6%

their cash balances and short-term financial investments on a daily basis. On the one hand, all firms want to have enough cash on hand to cover current obligations, pay for investments in productive assets, and acquire other businesses. On the other hand, firms do not want to have too much cash on hand. Cash in the bank and cash sitting in a money market fund do not earn a very high return.

Firms walk a fine line between holding enough cash to meet normal business needs and not tying up too much cash in non-interest bearing investments.

Firms like Wal-Mart generate a high level of cash flow from the business but do not let the money sit around in a bank account after it has been generated. Rather than leave the money in the bank, Wal-Mart would prefer to invest in other parts of the business.

▶ In 1987, Wal-Mart had \$166 million invested in cash and equivalents; in 1997, Wal-Mart had \$883 million invested in cash and equivalents. ◀

Even though Wal-Mart's total assets grew at a 25.6% CAGR, management actually used less cash to run the business in 1997 than it did in 1987 relative to the net sales being generated each year. Wal-Mart had fewer days sales tied up in cash in 1997 than it did in 1987.

▶ In 1987, Wal-Mart had 5.1 days net sales tied up in cash and equivalents; in 1997, Wal-Mart had 3.1 days net sales tied up in cash and equivalents. ◀

The days net sales calculations for cash and equivalents (and each of the other current assets) provide a convenient way of seeing how efficiently management is utilizing the resources under its control.

Days net sales for cash and equivalents is computed using the following formula:

▶

$$\frac{\text{Days Net Sales}}{\text{(Cash)}} = \frac{\text{Cash and}}{\text{Equivalents}} \div \text{Net Sales} \times 365 \text{ Days}$$

◀

Wal-Mart's days sales tied up in cash and equivalents for 1987 and 1997 are as follows:

▶

1997: 3.1 Days = \$883M ÷ \$104.859B × 365 Days

1987: 5.1 Days = \$166M ÷ \$11.909B × 365 Days

Between 1987 and 1997, Wal-Mart reduced its investment in cash and equivalents by 2.0 days net sales.

Any time a firm can reduce its investment in a particular asset without having a negative impact on other parts of the business, it becomes more efficient. The reduction of 2.0 days sales invested in cash and equivalents translates into an increase in efficiency of $575 million. The increase in efficiency was calculated as described next.

In 1997, one day of sales equaled $287.3 million.

One Day of Sales = Net Sales ÷ 365 Days
1997: $287.3M = $104.859B ÷ 365 Days

By operating the business with 3.1 days net sales invested in cash and equivalents versus the 5.1 days invested in 1987, the 2.0-day decrease translates into the increase in efficiency of $575 million.

Efficiency Increase = Sales per Day × Days Saved
1997: $575M = $287.3 Million per Day × 2.0 Days

Between 1987 and 1997, it would appear that Wal-Mart made substantial improvements in its cash-management practices.

Receivables. Receivables represent the amount of money owed to the business by customers. Since most of Wal-Mart's sales are made for cash, customer receivables do not represent a large part of the ongoing operations of the business. Receivables do, however, represent a significant portion of current assets.

In 1987, Wal-Mart had $90 million invested in receivables; in 1997, Wal-Mart had $845 million invested in receivables.

Since most of Wal-Mart's sales are for cash, the number of days' net sales tied up in receivables remained relatively stable (2.8 days in 1987 and 2.9 days in 1997). From an overall asset-management perspective, some of the efficiency gains from improved cash-management practices (from 5.1 days to 3.1 days) have to be reduced by the increase in days net sales tied up in receivables (from 2.8 days to 2.9 days).

As the old saying goes, "A bird in the hand is worth two in the bush." Firms extend credit to customers to get the business and develop long-term relationships. However, once extended, customers are expected to pay within the terms of the agreement. Delays in collecting receivables from customers can translate into delays in paying suppliers and creditors.

Inventory. Inventory represents the unrecovered cost of goods purchased and held for resale. Until sold, all product costs are included in inventory. As discussed in Chapter 2, the cost of sales represents the inventory costs that were recovered through sales during the year.

Like cash management, inventory management plays a big role in Wal-Mart's overall business strategy. As mentioned in Chapter 2, Wal-Mart likes to keep selling prices low and generate more gross margin dollars by keeping inventory turnover high. The more Wal-Mart turns its inventory, the more sales it generates relative to its investment in inventory.

To a certain extent, the concept of asset turnover is nothing more than an extension of the logic of inventory turnover to all of the assets under management control.

Between 1987 and 1997, Wal-Mart experienced a decrease in its investment in inventory relative to net sales. As shown below, Wal-Mart invested 55.3 days' net sales in inventory to support its retail operations in 1997. In 1987, Wal-Mart was investing 62.2 days net sales in inventory.

$$\frac{\text{Days' Net Sales}}{\text{(Inventory)}} = \text{Inventory} \div \text{Net Sales} \times 365 \text{ Days}$$

1997:   55.3 Days = \$15.897B ÷ \$104.859B × 365 Days

1987:   62.2 Days = \$2.031B ÷ \$11.909B × 365 Days

If we had chosen to use 1971 instead of 1987 as the base year to compare with 1997, we would have seen an even more dramatic decrease in days net sales tied up in inventory. In 1971, Wal-Mart invested 87.1 days of net sales in inventory. Compared to 1971, Wal-Mart has decreased the days net sales invested in inventory by over a full month (31.8 days to be more exact). Between 1971 and 1987, Wal-Mart reduced its investment in inventory by 24.9 days' net sales. At \$32.6 million in net sales per day, Wal-Mart reduced its investment in inventory by \$812 million.

1987:   \$812M = \$32.6M per Day × 24.9 Days

Between 1987 and 1997, Wal-Mart reduced its investment in inventory by another \$1.982 billion.

1997:   \$1.982B = \$287.3M per Day × 6.9 Days

Since 1971, inventory management has been one of Wal-Mart's greatest strengths, providing it with a competitive edge over other retailers.

Other Current Assets.   Other current assets represent prepaid expenses (primarily pre-opening costs for new stores) that will be charged against earnings during the first full month of operations at the new store.

As with cash and equivalents and inventory, Wal-Mart has dramatically reduced its investment in prepaid expenses associated with opening new stores. By reducing the number of days' net sales from 2.0 days to 1.3 days, management has freed up an additional $20 million to be used in other parts of the business.

1997: $20M = $287.3M per Day × 0.7 Days

If more information was provided about other current assets, we could probably be more specific about the source of those savings. If the number of days sales invested in other current assets had changed by a significant amount, we would probably have been more interested in probing a little deeper into the cause of the change.

Total Current Assets.   Total current assets represent the aggregate investment in cash and equivalents, receivables, inventory, and other current assets. Cash and equivalents, receivables, and inventory are closely identified with the firm's operating cycle and the firm's ongoing business operations.

If we compare Wal-Mart's investment in current assets from 1987 to 1997, we can see a net savings of 9.5 days net sales (72.1 days − 62.6 days). And at $287.3 million per day, management was running the business with $2.7 billion less of an investment in current assets in 1997 as compared to 1987 performance levels.

1997: $2.729B = $287.3M per Day × 9.5 Days

As Wal-Mart has been growing the business, it has become much more efficient in utilizing the current assets under management control. Compared to 1987, Wal-Mart invested relatively less money in current assets in 1997 than it invested in productive and other assets. In 1987, current assets represented 58.1% of total assets; in 1997, current assets represented 45.4% of total assets.

% Current Asset = Current Assets ÷ Total Assets

1997:   45.4% = \$17.993B ÷ \$39.604B

1987:   58.1% = \$2.353B ÷ \$4.049B

The change in the relative mix of current assets, productive assets, and other assets is also reflected in the difference in CAGRs. Between 1987 and 1997, Wal-Mart's investment in current assets increased at a 22.6% CAGR versus the 25.6% growth rate for total assets. This tells us that the growth in Wal-Mart's asset base can be attributed primarily to the net investment in productive assets.

If we only include current assets in Wal-Mart's turnover calculation, we can see management's increased efficiency from another angle.

Current Asset Turnover = Net Sales ÷ Current Assets

1997:   5.83 = \$104.859B ÷ \$17.993B

1987:   5.06 = \$11.909B ÷ \$2.353B

In 1987, Wal-Mart generated \$5.06 in net sales for every \$1 invested in current assets; in 1997, Wal-Mart generated \$5.83 for every \$1 invested in current assets.

Between 1987 and 1997, management grew the business and increased current asset efficiency by 77¢ per \$1 of investment in current assets. Simply stated, Wal-Mart is getting more "bang for the buck" for its investment in current assets.

PRODUCTIVE ASSETS

Productive assets represent the resources held for the long-term support of business operations. This category includes two financial elements that are netted out against each other to create a third element:

- Property, Plant, and Equipment

- Accumulated Depreciation
- Net Productive Assets

Property, Plant, and Equipment. Property, plant, and equipment represent the productive assets under management control.

In the early 1970s, the basis for reporting productive assets in the balance sheet shifted from ownership to control. Under the present financial reporting rules, all assets owned or controlled through capital leases are included on a firm's balance sheet.

Accumulated Depreciation. Accumulated depreciation represents the cost of plant and equipment that has been recovered through charges against net income in past years. The accumulated depreciation shown for Wal-Mart includes the amortization associated with the property, plant, and equipment controlled through capital leases.

Net Productive Assets. From a management perspective, the net productive assets represent the cost of productive assets to be recovered through future business operations.[2]

$$\text{Property, Plant, and Equipment} - \text{Accumulated Depreciation} = \text{Net Productive Assets}$$

In 1987, Wal-Mart's net investment in productive assets equaled \$1.676 billion; in 1997, Wal-Mart's net investment equaled \$20.324 billion.

Between 1987 and 1997, the investment in net productive assets grew at a 28.3% compound annual rate. The growth in net productive assets is out of line when compared to the growth in net sales (24.3%), current assets (22.6%), and total assets (25.6%).

In 1987, net productive assets represented 41.4% of total assets versus 51.3% of total assets in 1997.

% Net Productive Assets = Net Productive Assets ÷ Total Assets

1997:   51.3% = $20.324B ÷ $39.604B

1987:   41.4% = $1.676B ÷ $4.049B

Since turnover is the name of the asset-management game, it might be interesting to see what would happen if we only included net productive assets in our turnover calculation. Just how efficiently is management using its investment in net productive assets?

Productive Asset Turnover = Net Sales ÷ Net Productive Assets

1997:   5.16 = $104.859B ÷ $20.324B

1987:   7.11 = $11.909B ÷ $1.676B

In 1987, for every $1 invested in net productive assets, Wal-Mart generated $7.11 in net sales; in 1997, Wal-Mart generated $5.16.

For every $1 of investment in net productive assets, Wal-Mart generated $1.95 less in net sales in 1997 than it generated in 1987.

OTHER ASSETS

Other assets represent the resources, other than productive assets, that are held for the long-term support of the business operations.

In 1987, Wal-Mart's investment in other assets equaled $20 million; in 1997, Wal-Mart's investment in other assets equaled $1.287 billion.

Between 1987 and 1997, investment in other assets grew at a 51.7% compound annual rate. This growth rate is the most out of line when compared to net sales (24.3%), current assets (22.6%), and net productive assets (28.3%).

In 1987, other assets represented 0.5% of total assets versus 3.3% of total assets in 1997.[3]

% Other Assets = Other Assets ÷ Total Assets

1997: 3.3% = $1.287B ÷ $39.604B

1987: 0.5% = $20 million ÷ $4.049B

The increase from 0.5 to 3.3% will have a negative effect on the overall asset turnover ratio.

If we combine the discussion of other assets with other net productive assets, it would appear that Wal-Mart is doing one of three things, two of which are not good:

1. Paying too much money for the long-term investments it is making
2. Picking locations that are not generating the anticipated sales levels
3. Building a foundation for future growth that will not turn into net sales until some time in the future

TOTAL ASSETS

Total assets represent all of the resources under management control. As mentioned previously, the total assets under management control atWal-Mart grew at a 25.6% compound annual rate between 1987 and 1997.

Based on the discussion of each of the elements making up total assets, we should be more aware of the different issues surrounding the management of current assets, productive assets, and other assets. The overall growth rate for total assets (25.6%) represents a combination of three different growth rates.

1. Current Assets (22.6%)
2. Productive Assets (28.3%)
3. Other Assets (51.7%)

When compared to the growth in net sales (24.3%), Wal-Mart appears to be becoming *more* efficient in managing its current assets while becoming *less* efficient in managing its productive assets and other assets.

Bottom Line: The increases in current asset efficiency have not been large enough to offset the decreases in productive and other asset efficiency.

Net Sales.   Net sales represents all of those dollars of customer financing generated during the year that we have used as a benchmark for trying to understand how Wal-Mart manages its assets. By dividing net sales by the total assets under management control, we have created a powerful tool for helping us understand a major part of any firm's business operations.

Since the customer is the primary source of financing for any firm, it only seems natural to use net sales as a basis for trying to understand the business. On the one hand, Wal-Mart does a good job of turning inventory and receivables into cash and then moving that money out into other parts of the business. On the other hand, Wal-Mart has not been as successful in deploying its productive and other asset dollars to support the overall level of sales.

ASSET TURNOVER

In the quick overview of the Strategic Profit Model, we showed that asset turnover equaled net sales divided by total assets. We also saw that Wal-Mart's asset turnover declined from 2.94 in 1987 to 2.65 in 1997. By taking a closer look at the asset-management component of the SPM, we have now seen that current assets, productive assets, and total assets have all been growing at different rates.

In making the transition to the return-on-asset component the SPM, we would just like to summarize the two different trends that we see when we take a closer look at the assets underlying the turnover calculation.

Current Assets: Between 1987 and 1997, Wal-Mart actually increased its effectiveness in managing current assets. The number of days' sales tied up in current assets dropped from 72.1 days to 62.6 days. In 1997, management ran the business with $2.7 billion less of an investment in current assets as compared to 1987 performance levels.

Productive Assets: Between 1987 and 1997, Wal-Mart generated substantially fewer dollars of net sales per $1 invested in productive assets. The number of days sales tied up in productive assets increased from 51.4 days to 70.7 days. In 1997, management ran the business with $5.5 billion more of an investment in productive assets as compared to 1987 performance levels.

Total Assets: Taken in total, the efficiencies that management achieved in the area of current asset management were more than offset by the decline in net sales per dollar of investment in productive (and other) assets.

For those among us who are new to understanding the business through financial information, you can rest assured that Wal-Mart's management team is aware of the need to improve their productive and other asset-management practices. Financial analysts and investors who track the performance of Wal-Mart's common stock are quick to remind management of the problems it is facing. The real trick is to come up with a strategy that will correct the situation.

In Chapter 4, we will broaden the lens, so to speak, by looking at how asset-management and margin-management issues are integrated through the concept of return on assets (ROA). In order to generate a profit on behalf of the shareholders, management must turn the assets under its control and make sure that every $1 of assets turned includes an adequate margin of profit. Turns and margins represent the financial heart of the business.

As mentioned in Chapter 1, Wal-Mart's CEO, David Glass, indicated that ROA will be playing a more significant role in Wal-Mart's overall business strategy. As we shall see, the concept of ROA provides us with an additional opportunity to understand the business through financial information.

NOTES

1. We have followed the convention used in the *Value Line Investment Survey* of subdividing current assets into cash and equivalents, receivables, inventory, and other current assets. Productive assets include property, plant, and equipment and capital leases. The combination of the elements making up productive assets will have no material effect on the material in this chapter.
2. Within the context of the asset-management component of the SPM, the distinctions between gross productive assets and accumulated depreciation do not add much to our understanding of the business. As we shall see, these distinctions play a much larger role in looking at the business through the lens of the Strategic Financing Model to be discussed in Chapters 7 and 8.
3. Since Wal-Mart provides no further breakdown of other assets, it is impossible to tell what is accounting for the disproportionate growth compared to current assets and productive assets. For Wal-Mart, other assets represent a relatively small portion of total assets. For some companies (especially companies that have acquired other firms in the past), other assets may represent a material portion of total assets.

CHAPTER 4

Strategic Profit Model: Return on Assets

In this chapter, we use the concept of return on assets (ROA) to integrate our understanding of the margin-management and asset-management issues discussed in Chapters 2 and 3.

As mentioned in Chapter 1, our approach to understanding the business through financial information is grounded in the management philosophy underlying the DuPont executive charting system developed in the early years of the 20th century. In the American Management Association (AMA) monograph describing the DuPont system, all of the parts of the model were integrated together through the concept of ROA. Within the context of the Strategic Profit Model (SPM), these same parts are integrated together through the concept of ROA.[1]

Since the DuPont management philosophy underlies our approach to understanding the business through financial information, it seems appropriate to restate the principles presented in the original AMA monograph.

1. The charts are designed to present in readily understandable visual form the financial results of each of the company's industrial departments and of the company as a whole.

2. The presentation is not based on a step-by-step buildup to the ultimate objective of Return on Investment. Instead, the end result is presented first and thereafter the important elements that contribute to it.

3. The charts themselves do not utilize narrative explanation.

4. It is comparatively easy to hold the attention of an entire group to one item at the same moment.[2]

Converting financial information into management action is where the SPM comes into play. The ROA component of the model helps managers see how profit margins and asset turnovers interact to produce the firm's ROA. By combining what they see with what they know (from experience), they can begin to think in terms of what they will have to do to increase the ROA.

Figure 4.1 presents the ROA component of Wal-Mart's SPM using the amounts taken from the 1987 and 1997 income statements and balance sheets presented in the previous two chapters. As we can see from this figure, ROA is presented as the combined result of Wal-Mart's margin-management and asset-management strategies discussed in the last two chapters. By combining margin management and asset management through the concept of ROA, we can summarize our observations about both aspects of Wal-Mart's business operations and look for additional insights into the business that result from widening the lens we use to understand the business.

Up through the ROA component of the SPM, we are trying to use financial information to understand a firm's basic business operations (industrial departments in the DuPont case). The financial results are visualized and contain no narrative explanations. Once the financial results are visualized, through the SPM, we try to understand what the numbers mean from a business strategy perspective.

In 1987, management earned $450 million on total assets of $4.049 billion; in 1997, management earned $3.056 billion on total assets of $39.604 billion.

In 1987, Wal-Mart earned 11.1¢ on every $1 of assets invested in the business; in 1997, Wal-Mart earned 7.7¢.

Even though net income increased in absolute terms, Wal-Mart generated 3.4¢ less profit per $1 of assets in 1997 than it did in 1987.

Figure 4.1   Wal-Mart Strategic Profit Model, Return on Assets (for the Fiscal Years Ended January 31, 1987 and 1997 — Amounts in Millions)

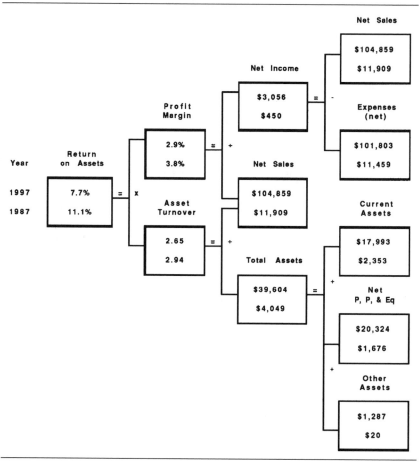

On the one hand, managers and investors need to know that ROA has fallen by 3.4¢ for every $1 of assets invested in the business. On the other hand, this knowledge is not of much use if it cannot be converted into actions that will result in improved performance in the future.

Figure 4.2(a) presents the absolute percentage change in profit margin, asset turnover, and ROA between 1987 and 1997 and Figure 4.2(b) presents the compound annual growth rates (CAGRs) over this ten-year pe-

Figure 4.2 Wal-Mart Strategic Profit Model: Return on Assets

(a) Percentage Change (1987–1997)

Profit Margin	−22.9%
Asset Turnover	−10.0%
Return on Assets	−30.6%

(b) Compound Annual Growth Rates (1987–1997)

Net Sales	24.3%
Expenses (net)	24.4%
Net Income	21.1%
Current Assets	22.6%
Productive Assets	28.3%
Other Assets	51.7%
Total Assets	25.6%

riod. The percentage changes and CAGRs will be used to help tell a story about Wal-Mart's combined margin-management and asset-management strategy. By looking at ROA in terms of its component parts, we can see that the 3.4¢ decline from 1987 to 1997 resulted from a decline in both the profit margin and assets turnover.

In 1987, Wal-Mart generated 3.8¢ in net income for every $1 of net sales; in 1997, Wal-Mart generated 2.9¢.

In 1987, Wal-Mart generated $2.94 in net sales for every $1 of assets; in 1997, Wal-Mart generated $2.65.

At first glance, a 0.9¢ decline in profit margin and a 29¢ decline in asset turnover may not appear to be very high. However, when the decline in profit margin is combined with the decline in asset turnover, the effects on ROA are magnified.

In 1987, Wal-Mart earned 11.1¢ on every $1 of assets invested in the business; in 1997, Wal-Mart earned 7.7¢

and

A 3.4¢ decline in ROA translates into $1.3 billion less net income being earned on a $39.6 billion asset base.

Stated in a slightly different way,

Between 1987 and 1997, Wal-Mart's profit margin decreased by 22.9% and asset turnover decreased by 10.0%. The combined effect of a decrease in profit margin and asset turnover resulted in a 30.6% decrease in ROA.

and

A 30.6% decline in ROA translates into $1.3 billion less net income being earned on a $39.6 billion asset base.

As we can see from the ROA component of the SPM, the key performance measures (profit margin, asset turnover, and ROA) provide a convenient way to help us understand Wal-Mart's business.

RETURN ON ASSETS

In using ROA to help us understand the business:

- We start by summarizing what we know about the growth in Wal-Mart's net sales.
- We then take a "northern route" (as visualized in Figure 4.1) to summarize what we know about Wal-Mart's margin-management strategy.
- We then take a "southern route" to summarize what we know about Wal-Mart's asset-management strategy.
- We can then begin to look at the interactive effects of combining margin-management and asset-management strategies to increase Wal-Mart's ROA.

Net Sales: Growing the Business

As mentioned in the previous three chapters, any story we tell about Wal-Mart has to be built on a foundation of growing the business. Between 1987 and 1997, total revenue increased at a 24.3% CAGR. In 1990, Sam Walton set a goal of becoming a $125 billion company (as measured in terms of net sales) by the year 2000. Given this commitment to continue growing the business from the shareholders' perspective, the question becomes one of growing the business at a profit.

Profit Margin: The Northern Route

Since 1987, Wal-Mart has been experiencing pressure on its profit margins. "Experiencing pressure" is a nice way of saying that Wal-Mart has not been able to maintain its historical spread between net sales and net expenses. As shown in Figure 4.2 (b), net sales grew at a 24.3% compound annual rate between 1987 and 1997 as compared to 24.4% compound annual growth rate for net expenses. This seemingly small difference between the growth in net sales and net expenses (24.3% − 24.4% = −0.1%), compounded over ten years, translates into a substantially slower compound growth rate in net income (21.1%) and a correspondingly lower profit margin (2.9% versus 3.8%).

At $104.859 billion net sales, a 0.1% difference in CAGRs for sales and expenses translates into a 0.9¢ decline in profit margin over the ten-year period, and a 0.9¢ decline in profit margin translates into $944 million less net income.

Unless that reduction can be offset by improved performance in other parts of Wal-Mart's operations, the effects of a lower profit margin will flow all the way through to a reduction in ROA and ROE.

As discussed in Chapter 2, low prices (P) relative to the competition translate into more gross margin dollars when a firm can increase quarterly (Q). Unfortunately, this pricing strategy does not work when competitors match your low prices. When you multiply a lower price (P) times the same quantity (Q), you end up with fewer gross margin dollars and no additional market share. As far as the customers are concerned, they are more than happy to reap the benefit of lower prices. In a highly competitive environment, customers may win and the shareholders may lose if the lost gross margin dollars are not offset by reductions in total expenses.

As discussed more fully in Chapter 2, Wal-Mart's gross margin fell from 24.0¢ to 20.2¢ from 1987 to 1997. This 3.8¢ decline was offset in part by a 0.9¢ decrease in operating expenses and a 1.6¢ decrease in income taxes per dollar of net sales. During this ten-year period, Wal-Mart was using savings in operating expenses and lower taxes to support its strategy of "everyday low pricing." However, if lower prices do not result in increases in volume, it may be time to pass any savings along to shareholders in the form of higher profit margins.

Asset Turnover: The Southern Route

When successful, taking the southern route may be characterized as getting more bang for each buck invested in total assets.

Wal-Mart's southern route strategy has focused on utilizing current assets more efficiently while expanding the productive and other asset base to support future sales growth. As discussed in Chapter 3, the decline in asset turnover from $2.94 in 1987 to $2.65 in 1997 reflects the combined effects of focusing on efficiency and expansion.

The efficiency aspect of Wal-Mart business strategy is captured by the difference in compound growth rates between net sales (24.3%) and current assets (22.6%). Between 1987 and 1997, Wal-Mart grew the business while reducing its investment in current assets relative to net sales. If shareholders only used the relationship between current assets and net sales to evaluate management, Wal-Mart's management team would receive high marks. Current asset turnover increased from $5.06 per $1 of current assets in 1987 to $5.83 per $1 of current assets in 1997 (see discussion in Chapter 3). For the current asset management aspects of the business, Wal-Mart receives high marks.

Unfortunately, these high marks cannot be extended (at least at the present time) to management's productive and other asset management practices. Compared to the growth in total revenue (24.3%) and in total assets (25.6%), the growth in productive and other assets is out of line (productive assets 28.3%; other assets 51.7%).

Since we do not know very much about the composition of other assets, we will focus on Wal-Mart's productive-asset strategy. In 1987, Wal-Mart was generating $7.11 in net sales per $1 of productive assets. By 1997, productive asset turnover had fallen to $5.16, or $1.95 fewer net sales per $1 of productive assets in 1997 versus 1987.

Based on these observations about Wal-Mart's asset management practices, any change in business strategy would appear to have to be targeted to Wal-Mart's productive asset management practices.

Return on Assets: Going Both Routes

In keeping with the management philosophy underlying the DuPont executive charting system, ask yourself the following questions:

1. If you had to explain the decline in Wal-Mart's ROA between 1987 and 1997 in three sentences, what would you say?

2. Devise a five-year plan to take Wal-Mart forward from its 1997 performance, what would you say in three sentences?

In other words, given all of the financial information we have reviewed, how would you go about providing a concise answer that is consistent with the facts that we see right before our eyes?

We have found that making a connection between what we see and what we say is an integral part of understanding any business through financial information. The old adage "those that do not learn from the past are bound to repeat it" captures the essence of the practice of saying what we see.

Our attempt to say what we thought we saw and speculate about the future is provided below.

EXPLAINING PAST PERFORMANCE

- Between 1987 and 1997, Wal-Mart was able to grow the business, but was not able to maintain its profit margin and asset turnover compared to past performance.
- The decline in gross margin per $1 of net sales was not offset by savings in operating expenses and reductions in income taxes.
- The efficiency gains related to the increase in net sales generated per $1 invested in current assets more than offset the expansionary effects related to declines in net sales generated per $1 invested in productive (and other) assets.

SPECULATING ABOUT THE FUTURE

- Profitable growth cannot occur through reducing prices since competitors will match price reductions to avoid losing market share.
- Any reductions in operating expenses and income taxes need to be passed along to the shareholders in the form of higher profit margins.
- Management needs to focus on growing the productive assets base in locations that will generate higher levels of net sales per $1 of investment in total assets.

If asked to justify our position, we would return to the more detailed discussion of the margin-management and asset-management components of the SPM.

If you have been applying our approach to understanding the business through financial information to your own company, we suggest you try to describe your firm's past performance and possible future performance in six questions or less. After you have come up with your own assessment, we suggest that you compare your assessment to those of your co-workers. The ensuing conversations are likely to prove very stimulating.

In the words of Warren Buffett, there are only five ways of increasing a firm's return on equity (or in our case, explain a decrease). A firm can

1. Increase asset turnover
2. Widen operating margins
3. Pay lower taxes
4. Increase leverage
5. Use cheaper leverage[3]

Of the five ways to increase return on equity, four ways are captured by the concept of ROA:

1. Increasing asset turnover
2. Widening operating margins
3. Paying lower taxes
4. Using cheaper leverage (i.e., paying lower interest rates)

With four of the five ways of increasing profitability captured through ROA, we have 80% of the information we need to explain increases and decreases in ROE. The remaining 20% of the information we need is captured by increasing (or decreasing) financial leverage.

In Chapter 5, we will blow up the financial management component of the SPM and see how financial leverage fits into Wal-Mart's overall business strategy.

NOTES

1. The SPM is more comprehensive in the sense that it goes beyond the DuPont charting system by including the financial management aspects of the business that are needed to reach ROE, but up to the ROA presentation, the model is virtually identical to the DuPont model.

2. "Executive Committee Control Charts: A Description of the DuPont Chart System for Appraising Operating Performance," *AMA* no. 6, 1950.
3. Robert G. Hagstrom, Jr., *The Warren Buffett Way* (New York: John Wiley & Sons, 1994), 58.

CHAPTER 5

Strategic Profit Model: Financial Management

In this chapter, we use the concept of financial leverage to show how a firm's relationships with its creditors and shareholders are linked to the management issues captured by the concept of return on assets (ROA).

In the quick overview of the Strategic Profit Model (SPM) presented in Chapter 1, we used the concept of financial leverage to link return on equity (ROE) back to the return on the total assets under management control. As we could see from the quick overview, financial leverage had a positive effect on Wal-Mart's ROE in both 1987 and 1997. As discussed more fully in this chapter, the total liabilities included in the firm's capital structure provided the lever that increased the shareholders' return.

Figure 5.1 presents the liabilities and shareholders' equity section of Wal-Mart's balance sheets for the fiscal years ended January 31, 1987 and 1997, that will be used to explore the concept of financial leverage in more depth. As we can see from Figure 5.1, current liabilities and long-term liabilities equal total liabilities. Shareholders' equity consists of common stock, retained earnings, and translation adjustments.[1]

In setting the stage for looking at the financial management aspects of a firm's business strategy, we often refer to the liability and shareholders' equity (total equity) section of the balance sheet as the "invisible" side of the business. There are no *things* like inventory and productive assets in this section of the balance sheet. All we find under liabilities and shareholders' equity are *promises* — promises made by management to pay suppliers and employees for goods and services received in the past, promises to repay lenders principal and interest on money borrowed in the past, and promises made to shareholders to earn a return on their investment.

**Figure 5.1 Wal-Mart Balance Sheets, Liabilities and Shareholders'
Equity Section (for the Fiscal Years Ended January 31,
1987 and 1997 — Amounts in Millions)**

	1987	1997
Liabilities and Shareholders' Equity		
Liabilities		
Current Liabilities		
Accounts Payable	$925	$7,628
Current Debt Due	$14	$618
Other	$402	$2,711
Total Current Liabilities	$1,341	$10,957
Long-Term Liabilities		
Long-Term Debt	$179	$7,709
Long-Term Lease Obligations	$764	$2,307
Deferred Income Taxes and Other	$75	$1,488
Total Long-Term Liabilities	$1,018	$11,504
Total Liabilities	$2,359	$22,461
Shareholders' Equity		
Common Stock	$220	$775
Retained Earnings	$1,470	$16,768
Translation Adjustments	$0	($400)
Total Shareholders' Equity	$1,690	$17,143
Total	$4,049	$39,604

Like the other concepts embedded within the concept of ROE (i.e., profit
margins, asset turnover, and ROA), the concept of financial leverage is useful because it allows us to see important aspects of managing the business
that might otherwise go unnoticed. As discussed under the quick overview
of the SPM, the concept of financial leverage allows us to shift gears and
move from management's responsibilities to all parties who have a financial interest in the firm to its specific responsibilities to shareholders.

Figure 5.2 presents the financial-leverage component of the SPM using
the amounts taken from the 1987 and 1997 liability and shareholders'
equity sections of Wal-Mart's balance sheets.

Figure 5.2 Wal-Mart Strategic Profit Model: Financial Leverage (for the Fiscal Years Ended January 31, 1987 and 1997 — Amounts in Millions)

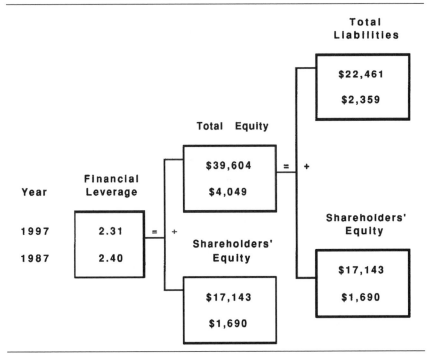

Figure 5.3(a) presents the percentage breakdown of total liabilities and shareholders' equity in 1987 and 1997, and Figure 5.3(b) presents the compound annual growth rates (CAGRs) over this ten-year period. The percentage breakdowns and CAGRs will be used to help tell a story about Wal-Mart's financial-management strategy. (The CAGR for net sales has been included for comparison purposes.)

The material presented in this chapter will unfold in the following manner:

- We begin by discussing how the concept of financial leverage allows us to move from looking at the firm as a whole to looking at the firm from the shareholders' perspective.
- We then take a closer look at the composition of Wal-Mart's total liabilities and total shareholders' equity.

73

Figure 5.3   Wal-Mart Strategic Profit Model: Financial Leverage

(a) Percent of Total Liabilities and Shareholders' Equity

	1987	1997
Total Liabilities	58.3%	56.7%
Shareholders' Equity	41.7%	43.3%
Total Liabilities and Shareholders' Equity	100.0%	100.0%

(b) Compound Annual Growth Rates (1987–1997)

Net Sales	24.3%
Total Liabilities	25.3%
Shareholders' Equity	26.1%
Total Liabilities and Shareholders' Equity	25.6%

• We then summarize the key financial management issues from a business strategy perspective.

FINANCIAL LEVERAGE

As shown in Figure 5.2, the financial leverage component of the SPM provides us with an opportunity to see how management's responsibilities to *all* creditors and shareholders is transformed into management's *specific* responsibilities to shareholders.

▶────────────────────────

In 1987, Wal-Mart utilized $2.40 in total equity for every $1 of shareholders' equity in running the business; in 1997, Wal-Mart utilized $2.31.

In 1987, total liabilities accounted for 58.3% of total equity; in 1997, total liabilities accounted for 56.7% of total equity.

────────────────────────◀

The decreasing role played by total liabilities relative to shareholders' equity is also reflected in the difference in compound growth rates. Total liabilities grew at a 25.3% compound rate between 1987 and 1997 versus a 26.1% compound rate for shareholders' equity.

In terms of overall business strategy, a change or difference in financial leverage can be measured in terms of its impact on ROE, as discussed in Chapter 1.

The $2.40 in financial leverage increased the 11.1% ROA to a 26.6¢ ROE in 1987. The $2.31 in financial leverage increased the 7.7¢ ROA to an 17.8¢ ROE in 1997.

Relative to 1987 performance levels, the decrease in financial leverage had a negative impact on the 1997 ROE. If management had maintained a financial leverage of 2.40 in 1997, ROE would have been 0.7% higher (2.40 −7.7% = 18.5%; 18.5% −17.8% = 0.7%).

On a shareholders' equity base of $17.143 billion, 0.7¢ translates into $120 million in lower returns to shareholders from using less debt to run the business.

To a certain extent, borrowing money to finance the business seems somewhat at odds with Sam Walton's underlying business philosophy.

From the time I took out my first bank loan—the $1,800 to buy that ice cream machine for the Ben Franklin down in Newport—I was never really comfortable with debt. But I recognized it as a necessity of doing business, and I had gotten pretty good at accumulating it.[2]

Debt has its advantages and disadvantages. Firms like Wal-Mart are no different than the rest of us. If we have a goal or objective we want to realize (e.g., own our own home) and we do not have the money, paying 20% up front and borrowing the remaining 80% looks pretty good. However, if we lose our job, those principal and interest payments can wipe out our life's savings or force us into bankruptcy.

The same type of thinking holds for Wal-Mart. If Wal-Mart needs more money to grow than it can generate through the business, borrowing money provides the fuel for growth. However, there is always the danger (or risk) that Wal-Mart might not be able to meet its principal and interest payments in the future.

As we shall see, Sam Walton and his successor, CEO David Glass, have become "pretty good" at accumulating debt over the years. As we shall also see beginning in Chapter 9, Wal-Mart has an excellent credit rating and can borrow money at very favorable interest rates compared to its competitors.

Within the context of the SPM, our primary objective is to see how management maintains a balance between liabilities and shareholders' equity, and how the elements making up liabilities and shareholders' equity change in response to management's overall business strategy.

We will begin our discussion with total liabilities and then move on to shareholders' equity. Total liabilities will be discussed in terms of current liabilities and long-term liabilities. Shareholders' equity will be discussed in terms of common stock, retained earnings, and translation adjustments.

TOTAL LIABILITIES: A CLOSER LOOK

Figure 5.4 presents a blow-up of Wal-Mart's total liabilities for 1987 and 1997. As we can see from Figure 5.4, the distinctions between current and long-term liabilities will be used to help us understand the financial-management aspects of running the business.[3]

Figure 5.5(a) presents an analysis of current liabilities in terms of days' net sales, and Figure 5.5(b) presents the CAGRs over this ten-year period. The days' net sales analysis and CAGRs will be used to help tell a story about the liability component of Wal-Mart's financial-management strategy.

Current Liabilities

Current liabilities represent obligations or management responsibilities to creditors that must be satisfied within the year or within the firm's normal operating cycle, whichever is longer. This category includes three finan-

Figure 5.4   Wal-Mart Strategic Profit Model: Financial Management Liabilities (for the Fiscal Years Ended January 21, 1987 and 1997 — Amounts in Millions)

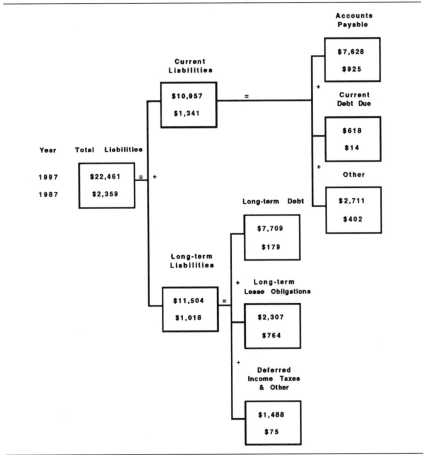

cial elements: (1) accounts payable, (2) current debt due, and (3) other current liabilities.

Accounts Payable.   Accounts payable represent the outstanding promises to pay suppliers for goods and services received. Since accounts payable are directly related to the firm's ongoing business activities, the days' net sales calculations provide a convenient way of seeing how the firm is managing its relationships with suppliers.

Figure 5.5   Wal-Mart Strategic Profit Model: Financial Management Liabilities

(a) Days' Net Sales

	1987	1997	Change
Accounts Payable	28.4	26.8	−1.8
Current Debt Due	0.4	2.2	1.7
Other	12.3	9.4	−2.9
Current Liabilities	41.1	38.1	−3.0

(b) Compound Annual Growth Rates (1987–1997)

Net Sales	24.3%
Current Liabilities	23.4%
Long Term Liabilities	27.4%
Total Liabilities	25.3%

In 1987, accounts payable represented 28.4 days net sales; in 1997, the number of days sales associated with accounts payable was 26.6 days, a decrease of 1.8 days between 1987 and 1997.

1997:   26.6 Days = \$7.628B ÷ \$104.859B × 365 Days

1987:   28.4 Days = \$925M ÷ \$11.909B × 365 Days

Part of the conventional wisdom in running a business is to collect your accounts receivable as soon as possible and pay your accounts payable as late as possible; in that way, a firm can maximize the amount of cash it has to use in other parts of the business. The only trouble with conventional wisdom is that firms can get into trouble if everyone plays the same game.

In a broader business context, one firm's accounts payable are another firm's accounts receivable. By paying as late as possible, customers are creating asset-management problems for their suppliers. By paying suppliers 1.8 days faster in 1997 than it did in 1987, Wal-Mart went against the conventional wisdom. At a 1997 rate of $287.3 million in net sales per day, paying suppliers 1.8 days faster resulted in a $517 million benefit for Wal-Mart's suppliers.

1997: $517M = $287.3 Million per Day × 1.8 Days

Building relationships with suppliers is a key element in Wal-Mart's overall business strategy. The "people" side of Wal-Mart's business strategy includes suppliers along with customers and associates.

Current Debt Due.   Current debt due represents the current portion of long-term debt coming due within the next year. Between 1987 and 1997, Wal-Mart's current debt due has increased by 1.8 days net sales.

1997:   2.2 Days = $618M ÷ $104.859B × 365 Days

1987:   0.4 Days = $14M ÷ $11.909B × 365 Days

The long-term debt a firm incurs must eventually be repaid. When the original long-term debt is due to be repaid within the year, it is reclassified as a current liability.

Other Current Liabilities.   Other current liabilities represent all other short-term obligations that will have to be met in the coming year. In Wal-Mart's case, a substantial portion of the other current liabilities is represented by accrued liabilities and accrued income taxes.

In 1987, other current liabilities represented 12.3 days' net sales; in 1997, the number of days' sales associated with other current liabilities was 9.4 days, a decrease of 2.9 days over 1987.

1997:   9.4 Days = $2.711B ÷ $104.859B × 365 Days

1987:   12.3 Days = $402M ÷ $11.909B × 365 Days

◀

The 2.9-days decrease in other current liabilities equals $1.488 billion of additional short-term financing relative to the 1987 level of short-term financing.

▶ ───

1997: $833M = $287.3 Million per Day × 2.9 Days

◀

Current Liabilities: Summary.   Overall, Wal-Mart's current obligations decreased by 3.0 days between 1987 and 1997. The decrease consists of two offsetting management practices. On the one hand, Wal-Mart decreased the time it takes to pay regular suppliers, employees (i.e., accrued liabilities), and the government (accrued income taxes). Between 1987 and 1997, accounts payable and other current liabilities decreased by 4.7 days. On the other hand, the amount of long-term debt coming due within 1997 has increased by 1.7 days.

The 3.0-day decrease in current liabilities is also reflected by the difference in compound growth rates between net sales (24.3%) and current liabilities (23.4%). As with current assets (22.6% CAGR), management kept the growth in current liabilities below the growth in net sales.

Long-Term Liabilities

Long-term liabilities represent management's obligations to creditors and scorekeeping differences between financial reporting and income tax reporting that extend beyond the year or normal business operating cycle.[4] This category includes three financial elements:

1. Long-Term Debt
2. Capital Lease Obligations
3. Deferred Income Taxes and Other Long-Term Liabilities.

At this stage of trying to understanding the business through financial information, our discussion of long-term liabilities will be somewhat brief.

We will return to a more in-depth analysis of these financial elements when we begin our discussion of financing the business beginning in Chapter 7.

Long-Term Debt. Long-term debt represents the amounts owed to lenders that will come due beyond one year. Between 1987 and 1997, Wal-Mart's long-term debt increased from $179 million to $7.7 billion.

Long-Term Lease Obligations. Long-term lease obligations are similar to long-term debt in that they represent amounts owed to lessors that will come due beyond one year. They differ in that the lease obligations are directly related to the productive assets controlled by management through capital lease agreements. Between 1987 and 1997, Wal-Mart's long-term leases increased from $764 million to $2.3 billion.

Deferred Income Taxes and Other Long-Term Liabilities. Deferred income taxes and other long-term liabilities represent a firm's long-term obligations not included in long-term debt and long-term lease obligations. Deferred income taxes represent the cumulative effects of timing differences that occur in computing the firm's actual income tax obligation and the hypothetical calculation used for financial reporting to shareholders. Although deferred income taxes typically appear with other long-term liabilities on the balance sheet, some users of financial statements reclassify deferred income taxes as part of shareholders' equity.[5]

For 1997, Wal-Mart's other long-term liabilities included minority interest of $1.025 billion. Minority interest represents the ownership interest of Wal-Mart's joint venture partners. In the discussion and analysis of operations included in the 1997 annual report, management indicated that these joint ventures are immaterial to total company operations.

Wal-Mart's deferred income taxes and other long-term liabilities increased from $75 million in 1987 to $1.5 billion in 1997.

Long-Term Liabilities: Summary. Since the discussion of long-term liabilities will receive more attention beginning in Chapter 7, the primary concern at this point is to understand how total long-term liabilities have changed relative to current liabilities.

Between 1987 and 1997, Wal-Mart's long-term liabilities increased at a 27.4% CAGR versus the 23.4% growth rate for current liabilities.

The increasing role played by long-term debt in Wal-Mart's overall business strategy is also reflected in the percentage of total liabilities represented by long-term liabilities. In 1987, long-term liabilities represented 43.2% of total liabilities; in 1997, long-term liabilities represented 5.12%.

After discussing the elements making up shareholders' equity, we will see how long-term liabilities fit into Wal-Mart's overall business strategy.

SHAREHOLDERS' EQUITY

Figure 5.6 presents a blow-up of Wal-Mart's shareholders' equity for 1987 and 1997. As we can see, shareholders' equity consists of three financial elements:

1. Common Stock
2. Retained Earnings
3. Translation Adjustments

Figure 5.7(a) presents the percentage breakdown of the elements making up shareholders' equity in 1987 and 1997, and Figure 5.7(b) presents the CAGRs over this ten-year period. The percentage breakdowns and CAGRs will be used to help tell a story about the shareholders' equity component of Wal-Mart's financial-management strategy. (The CAGR for net sales has been included for comparison purposes.)

Common Stock. Common stock represents the money received by management from issuing common stock to shareholders. In effect, management promised to be held accountable by the shareholders in exchange for the right to control the future of the firm.

Figure 5.6 **Wal-Mart Strategic Profit Model: Financial Management —
Shareholders' Equity (for the Fiscal Years Ended January
31, 1987 and 1997 — Amounts in Millions)**

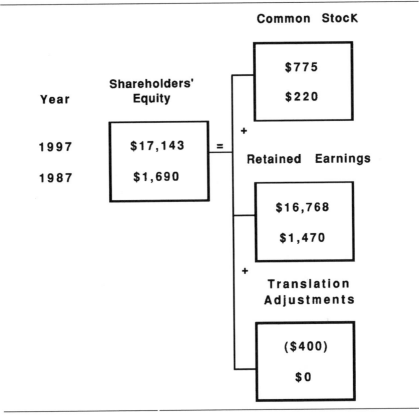

In 1987, Wal-Mart had $220 million in common stock outstanding; in 1997, common stock outstanding equaled $775 million.

Between 1987 and 1997, common stock grew at a 13.4% compound annual rate.

Compared to all of the other compound growth rates we have been discussing throughout this book, the 13.4% compound annual growth rate for

Figure 5.7 Wal-Mart Strategic Profit Model: Financial Management — Shareholders' Equity

(a) Percent Shareholders' Equity

	1987	1997
Common Stock	13.0%	4.5%
Retained Earnings	87.0%	97.8%
Translation Adjustments	0.0%	−2.3%
Shareholders' Equity	100.0%	100.0%

(b) Compound Annual Growth Rates (1987–1997)

Net Sales	24.3%
Common Stock	13.4%
Retained Earnings	27.6%
Translation adjustments	NM*
Total Shareholders' Equity	26.1%

(*Not meaningful)

common stock is exceptionally low. This low growth rate is also reflected in the declining percentage of total shareholders' equity.

In 1987, Wal-Mart's common stock represented 13.0% of total shareholders' equity; in 1997, common stock represented 4.5%.

As we can see, issuing additional shares of common stock has not been a big part of Wal-Mart's business strategy since 1987.

Retained Earnings.   These earnings represent management's cumulative contribution to growing the business on the shareholders' behalf. Aside from some minor charges to retained earnings for the repurchase of some shares of common stock outstanding, the year-end balances represent Wal-Mart's cumulative net income less dividends paid to shareholders.

In 1987, Wal-Mart had $1.470 billion in retained earnings; in 1997, retained earnings equaled $16.768 billion. Management grew retained earnings at a 27.6% compound rate over this ten-year period.

In 1987, retained earnings equaled 87.0% of total shareholders' equity; in 1997, retained earnings equaled 97.8%.

We typically refer to firms with such a high percentage of shareholders' equity accounted for by retained earnings as a business that has been "financed by management." That is, management relies primarily on its own efforts to grow the business through shareholders' equity.

Translation Adjustments.   These adjustments represent the cumulative effects of translating foreign operations into U.S. dollars that have not been included in the determination of net income.

In 1987, Wal-Mart was not involved in international operations to any great extent. As of 1997, global expansion had become part of Wal-Mart's overall business strategy. Based on changes in global exchange rates, the $400 million translation adjustment is likely to fluctuate up and down in the future.

Shareholders' Equity: Summary

Keeping our analysis to within total shareholders' equity, the difference in compound growth rates between common stock (13.4%) and retained earnings (27.6%) speaks for itself. Between 1987 and 1997, Wal-Mart's management continued to increase its contribution (through retained earnings) to growing the business on the shareholders' behalf rather than asking the shareholders for additional funds.

If we went back to the early 1970s, after Wal-Mart had just gone public, retained earnings only accounted for 40% of shareholders' equity, with common stock accounting for the other 60%. Between 1970 and 1997, management truly financed the growth in the business through retained earnings.[6]

FINANCIAL MANAGEMENT PERSPECTIVE

As discussed at the beginning of the chapter (and seen in Figure 5.2), Wal-Mart's financial leverage decreased from $2.40 in 1987 to $2.31 in 1997. Based on a comparison of the compound growth rates in total liabilities and shareholders' equity, we could see that total liabilities were growing at a slower rate than shareholders' equity. However, at that point in our discussion, we could not see the dynamics occurring within those two categories.

Figure 5.8 presents a broader view of the financial leverage component of Wal-Mart's SPM. This extended view allows us to see the dynamics occurring with total liabilities and shareholders' equity.

Figure 5.9(a) presents an extended version the percentage breakdown of total equity (liabilities and shareholders' equity) in 1987 and 1997, and Figure 5.9(b) presents the CAGRs over this ten-year period. The percentage breakdowns and CAGRs will be used to help tell a story about Wal-Mart's overall financial-management strategy.

Based on our current understanding of the elements making up total liabilities and shareholders' equity, we can make the following observations about how Wal-Mart's financial management practices fit into management's overall business strategy:

- Between 1987 and 1997, financial leverage decreased from $2.40 to $2.31. This decrease resulted from total liabilities growing at a slower CAGR than total shareholders' equity (25.3% versus 25.6%).
- Within total liabilities, current liabilities grew at a slower rate (23.4%) than long-term liabilities (27.4%). In addition, current liabilities grew slower than net sales (24.3%). This slower growth rate is reflected in the fact that current liabilities represented 38.1 days sales in 1997 versus 41.1 days sales in 1987.
- Between 1987 and 1997, long-term liabilities grew to represent a greater percentage total equity. In 1987, long-term liabilities represented 25.1% of total equity versus 29.0% in 1997. Long-term debt financing (to be discussed more fully in Chapter 7) represents a significant part of Wal-Mart's overall business strategy.
- Between 1987 and 1997, Wal-Mart did not issue significant amounts of common stock to grow the business (13.4% CAGR). At the end of

**Figure 5.8   Wal-Mart Strategic Profit Model: Financial Leverage —
Extended View (for the Fiscal Years Ended January 31,
1987 and 1997 — Amounts in Millions)**

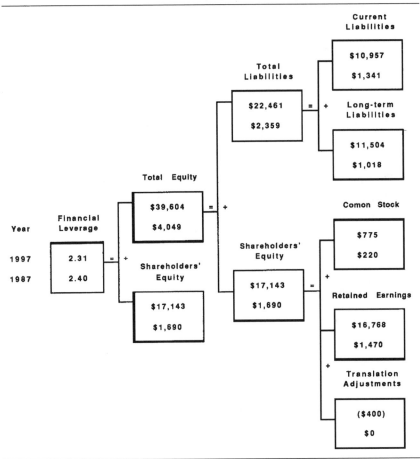

1987, common stock represented 5.4% of total equity. By the end of
1997, common stock represented only 2.0% of total equity.

- Between 1987 and 1997, retained earnings increased at a 27.6% compound annual rate, the fastest growth rate for all of the elements making up total equity. Given the increase from 36.3% to 42.3% of total
equity between 1987 and 1997, retained earnings represents the single
largest source of financing for the business.

Figure 5.9   Wal-Mart Strategic Profit Model: Financial Leverage

(a) Percent Total Equity

	1987	1997
Current Liabilities	33.1%	27.7%
Long-Term Liabilities	25.1%	29.0%
Common Stock	5.4%	2.0%
Retained Earnings	36.3%	42.3%
Translation Adjustments	0.0%	−1.0%
Total equity	100.0%	100.0%

(b) Compound Annual Growth Rates (1987–1997)

Net sales	24.3%
Current Liabilities	23.4%
Long-Term Liabilities	27.4%
Common Stock	13.4%
Retained Earnings	27.6%
Translation Adjustments	NM*
Total Equity	25.6%

(*Not meaningful)

- In summary, from 1987 to 1997, management grew the business through its own contribution (retained earnings) and the contribution from long-term creditors (long-term liabilities). The decrease in financial leverage from $2.40 to $2.31 is due, in large part, to the fact that retained earnings represents the largest percentage of total equity (42.3% in 1997) and has been increasing at the fastest CAGR (27.6%).

As we can see from this summary, by working our way through the financial management component of the SPM, we have added to our list of insights into Wal-Mart's overall business strategy.

In Chapter 6, we will put all of the individual pieces (of insight) we have been accumulating back together in our attempt to develop a more comprehensive understanding of the profitability aspects of Wal-Mart's overall business strategy.

NOTES

1. We have followed the convention used in the *Value Line Investment Survey* of subdividing current liabilities into accounts payable, current debt due, and other current liabilities. Long-term liabilities include long-term debt, long-term lease obligations, and deferred income taxes. The combination of the elements making up current liabilities and long-term liabilities will have no material effect on the discussion in this chapter.

2. Sam Walton and John Huey, *Sam Walton, Made in America: My Story* (New York: Doubleday, 1992), 92.

3. In Chapter 7 when we introduce our second business strategy model, the Strategy Financing Model, the distinction between current liabilities and long-term liabilities will help us develop the concept of "working capital" (current assets – current liabilities) needed to talk about a firm's long-term financing and investment activities.

4. At this stage of trying to understand the business through financial information, our discussion of long-term liabilities will be somewhat brief. We will return to a more in-depth discussion of these financial elements beginning in Chapter 7.

5. We will return to the issue of how to treat deferred income taxes in Chapter 7.

6. Beginning in Chapter 7, we will focus more specifically on how management finances the business from internal and external sources of funds. At that time, we will return to the role retained earnings plays in growing the business.

CHAPTER 6

Strategic Profit Model: Comprehensive Management

In taking the amounts reported in Wal-Mart's income statements and balance sheets and recasting them within the framework of the Strategic Profit Model (SPM), we have been engaging in a process of "double description." We have taken the exact same information used to describe the firm in income statement and balance sheet terms and described the firm in a second way, through the visual framework provided by the SPM.

The term "double description" comes from the work of Gregory Bateson.[1] According to Bateson, "an increment of insight is provided by a second language of description without the addition of any extra so-called objective information."[2] The financial statements provide a way of looking at the firm that emphasizes management's stewardship responsibility for safeguarding assets and the fair presentation of financial information. The SPM emphasizes management's responsibility for generating a return on the shareholders' investment in the firm. The two ways of describing the firm's business activities complement each other. The financial statements emphasize formal accountability to shareholders; the SPM emphasizes substantive accountability. The combination of formal and substantive accountability provides a strong foundation for understanding any business through financial information.

Before returning to Wal-Mart's SPM to summarize what we have learned about the business, we would like to reemphasize the importance of working from the financial statements to understand the firm's overall business strategy.

INTEGRITY OF FINANCIAL STATEMENTS

Our approach to understanding the business through financial information is based on two principles.

---

1. Charity

2. Due Diligence

Our ability to rely on the first principle in trying to understand any business is based on the assertions made by both management and the firm's external auditors that are included in the annual report to shareholders. In those few instances where we have had to fall back on the principle of due diligence, we have not felt comfortable in accepting the assertions made by either party.

SHAREHOLDER ACCOUNTABILITY

The annual reports to shareholders of public companies typically include a statement of management's responsibility for financial statements. The wording of these statements has become standardized over the years. The statement of responsibility includes four assurances on behalf of the company.

1. Management is responsible for the integrity and objectivity of the financial statements and information included in the annual report.
2. The financial statements have been prepared in conformity with generally accepted accounting principles and include certain estimates and judgments made by management in light of current conditions and circumstances.
3. Management maintains a system of accounting and controls that is designed to protect assets from being used improperly and that the accounting records provide a reliable basis for the preparation of financial statements.

4. The board of directors, through the activities of its audit committee consisting solely of outside directors, participates in the process of reporting financial information.

From our perspective, these assurances provide the basis for moving from the financial statements to the quick overview version of the SPM. Then in the process of trying to understand the business in more depth, we can tack back and forth between each component of the SPM and particular elements of financial information found in the income statements and balance sheets.

If anyone feels uncomfortable relying on the assurances of management, the report of the independent auditors provides additional assurances to establish the foundation for thinking about how shareholder accountability may be linked to business strategy through financial information.

REPORT OF INDEPENDENT AUDITORS

To further assure investors about the integrity of the financial statements, public firms' annual reports include a report from the independent auditors. Over the years, the independent auditors have also standardized the wording of their report to the board of directors and shareholders. The audit report includes the following assertions about the firm's financial statements:

1. The financial statements are the responsibility of management. The independent auditor's responsibility is to express an opinion on these statements based their audit performed in accordance with generally accepted auditing standards.
2. The standards require the auditors to plan and perform the audit to obtain reasonable assurance that the financial statements are free of material misstatement.
3. In their opinion, the financial statements present fairly, in all material respects, the financial position (balance sheet) of the company for the last two years and the consolidated results of operations for the previous three years.

If you have already begun the process of trying to understand the business operations of your own firm, take a moment to assure yourselves of the integrity of senior management and the independent auditors. Management's statement of responsibilities and the report of the independent auditors is typically found at the end of the notes to the financial statements.

FROM FORMAL TO SUBSTANTIVE ACCOUNTABILITY

Even though all annual reports of publicly traded companies must include assurances about the integrity of the information found in the financial statements, not all firms have been equally successful in creating value on behalf of the shareholders.

If we had used the financial statements for Kmart or Sears to illustrate the process of understanding the business through financial information, our discussion of management's business strategy would be quite different. At the current time, Kmart is selling off noncore businesses and closing down underperforming stores. Sears has recently sold off or spun off Caldwell Banker (real estate), Dean Witter (brokerage), and Allstate (insurance) as management attempts to refocus on its core business (retailing). A second description of a Kmart or a Sears using the SPM would provide a binocular view of what would be different in terms of management's success in creating value for the shareholders.

Strategic Profit Model Revisited

Figure 6.1 presents the same SPM for Wal-Mart that was presented in Figure 1.4 as the quick overview.

Figure 6.2 presents the compound annual growth rates (CAGRs) associated with each of the elements of the summary version of the SPM.

After working our way through the material presented in Chapters 2 through 5, this summary version of the SPM should trigger a much deeper understanding of Wal-Mart's business than we had when we began this journey to understanding the business through financial information. The information contained in Figures 6.1 and 6.2 can be used to pull together everything we have learned about Wal-Mart's business up to this point.

We have organized our summary under two headings: return on assets (ROA) and return on equity (ROE). Under the ROA heading, we summarize what we know about Wal-Mart's margin-management and asset-management strategies. Under the ROE heading, we summarize what we

Figure 6.1 **Wal-Mart Strategic Profit Model: Summary Version (for the Fiscal Years Ended January 31, 1987 and 1997 — Amounts in Millions)**

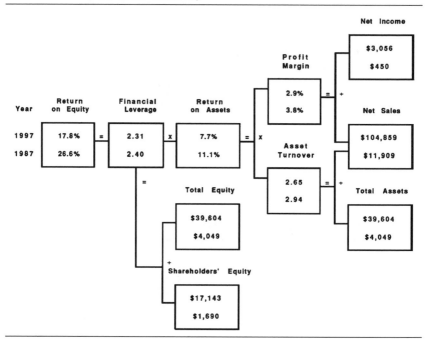

Figure 6.2 **Wal-Mart Strategic Profit Model: Summary Version (for the Fiscal Years Ended January 31, 1987 and 1997)**

Compound Annual Growth Rates (1987–1997)	
Income Statement	
Net Sales	24.3%
Expenses (net)	24.4%
Net Income	21.1%
Balance Sheet	
Assets	25.6%
Liabilities	25.3%
Shareholders' Equity	26.1%

know about Wal-Mart's financial management practices. We would not have been in a position to prepare this summary without working our way through the materials presented in Chapters 2 through 5.

RETURN ON ASSETS

Margin Management.   Between 1987 and 1997, Wal-Mart experienced pressure on its margins. The 0.9¢ decline in profit margin resulted from management's inability to use reductions in operating expenses and savings in income tax reductions to offset the decrease in gross margin. The 3.8¢ decline in gross margin per $1 of net sales could not be completely offset be the 0.9¢ decline in operating expenses, the 1.6¢ decline in income taxes, and 0.5¢ increase in other income.

▶

The 0.9¢ decline in profit margin translates into $944 million less net income on net sales of $104.859 billion in 1997.

◀

Asset Management.   Between 1987 and 1997, Wal-Mart became "more efficient" and "less efficient" in utilizing the total assets under management's control. By reducing the number of days' net sales tied up in current assets (62.6 days in 1997 versus 72.1 days in 1987) management was able to generate more net sales per $1 of investment in current assets in 1997 than it did in 1987. The overall decline in asset turnover of 29¢ from 1987 to 1997 can be attributed to the growth in productive and other assets. Over this ten-year period, productive assets increased as a percentage of total assets and the net sales generated per $1 of productive assets decreased substantially.

▶

The 29¢ decline in asset turnover translates into $3.938 billion in additional assets in 1997 needed to generate $104.859 billion in net sales.

◀

Combined Effects. Given the pressure from competitors, it is unlikely that Wal-Mart will be able to increase market share by lowering prices. If Wal-Mart is to improve its profit margin, future operating efficiencies will have to be passed along to the shareholders in the form of higher net income.

Since Wal-Mart increased the efficiency of its current asset management practices between 1987 and 1997, any improvement in asset turnover will likely have to come from improved productive asset management. Whether management is paying too much for new properties or it is overestimating the revenue that can be generated from these properties, some action must be taken to reverse the decline in revenue per dollar of productive assets.

▶───────────────────────────────────────

If management could have maintained the 11.1% ROA achieved in 1987 versus the actual ROA of 7.7%, Wal-Mart would have generated an additional $1.347 billion in net income on the $39.604 billion asset base under management control in 1997.

───────────────────────────────────────◀

In recent years, and in situations where firms cannot grow the business as fast as they have in the past, many companies have increased their emphasis on increasing ROA.

RETURN ON EQUITY

Financial Management. Between 1987 and 1997, management decreased the amount of debt it used to run the business. The decrease in 9¢ per $1 of shareholders' equity invested in the business reflects changes in both total liabilities and shareholders' equity.

Liabilities. Between 1987 and 1997, current liabilities expressed in terms of days net sales decreased by 3.0 days. That decrease reflects a 1.8-day decrease in accounts payable (26.6 days in 1997 versus 28.4 days in 1987), a 2.9-day decrease in other current liabilities, and a 1.7-day increase in current debt coming due within the year.

Like the relationship between current assets and productive assets, Wal-Mart's long-term liabilities (27.4% CAGR) have been growing at a faster rate than current liabilities (23.4%). Next to retained earnings, long-term liabilities have accounted for the largest increase in Wal-Mart's total equity.

Shareholders' Equity. Between 1987 and 1997, shareholders' equity grew primarily through increasing retained earning (27.6% CAGR) with only a small amount of the growth coming from the issuance of additional common stock (13.4% CAGR). As of January 31, 1997, retained earnings accounted for 97.8% of shareholders' equity and 42.3% of total equity.

Combined Effects. The decrease in Wal-Mart's financial leverage from $2.40 to $2.31 (a 3.8% decline), combined with the 3.4 percentage point decrease in ROA (11.1% − 7.7%) contributed to the overall decrease in ROE from 26.6% to 17.8%. However, even if Wal-Mart had maintained a financial leverage of $2.40, ROE would have still declined to 18.5%.

Given management's emphasis on increasing ROA as part of Wal-Mart's overall business strategy, we would not expect financial leverage to change dramatically over the next several years. Based on the insights developed by using the SPM to help us understand Wal-Mart's business, we would suspect that management will be taking a real close look at how it can increase its gross margin on sales while growing the business and managing the productive assets under its control.

DRAWING YOUR OWN CONCLUSIONS

In this summary of our understanding of Wal-Mart's business through the SPM, we have ventured a little further away from explanation and more toward speculation than we have done in the past. We have done so in the hopes of stimulating you to engage in the same sort of speculation process as you attempt to understand more about your own business through use of the SPM.

Hopefully, by developing a better understanding of the business, you will become a more effective manager and/or investor. Understanding is nice, but the rewards flow to those who take action.

Throughout the remainder of this book, we will follow the same approach that we have followed in developing the full-blown SPM. Translating understanding into action is a three-step process.

1. We have to *see* or visualize the numbers to make them meaningful to us.

2. We have to *say* what we *see* in order to make sure we know what we are talking about.

3. We have to take what we *see* and what we *say* and translate this knowledge into action (*do* it).

In Chapter 7, we will introduce a second business strategy model — the Strategic Financing Model (SFM) — to help us develop a better understanding of how management builds the firm's long-term financing and investment base. In Chapter 8, we'll see how management factors its commitment to grow the business on behalf of the shareholders into the firm's overall business strategy.

NOTES

1. Gregory Bateson is the author of *Mind and Nature* (Bantam Books, 1979) and *Steps to an Ecology of Mind* (Chandler Press, 1972). Trained in cultural anthropology, Bateson provides an approach to biological, psychological, and social systems that emphasizes the "pattern which connects" all of the elements of those systems together into a unified whole.

2. Gregory Bateson, *Mind and Nature* (Bantam Books, 1979), 82.

CHAPTER 7

Strategic Financing Model: Long-Term Investment and Financing

Income statements and balance sheets provide a wealth of information for helping users of financial information understand the business. When we view the information included in those statements through the lens of the Strategic Profit Model (SPM), we are able to see profitability relationships that otherwise might go unnoticed by most people.

If we were limited to just one model in helping managers understand the business, there is no doubt that we would stick with the SPM. The SPM helps everyone see how profitable a firm has been in the past, and it provides a framework for speculating about how the firm might perform in the future. If Wal-Mart earned 17.8¢ on every $1 of shareholders' equity in 1997, what is management likely to earn in 1998, in the year 2000, 2010, or 2025?

As useful as the SPM is in helping us understand how profitable a firm has been in a particular year, it falls a little short in two areas:

1. Understanding how long-term investment and financing decisions fit into the firm's overall business strategy
2. Understanding the relationship between the firm's financial performance as reflected in the financial statements and the market valuation of the firm's common stock

In order to correct for the first shortfall, we restructure the balance sheet and visualize the long-term investment and long-term financing aspects of the business through a second business strategy model, the Strategic Financing Model (SFM). The restructured balance sheet focuses on the firm's long-term capital commitments (to working capital and gross productive/other assets) and on who provided the long-term money to finance those commitments (creditors, shareholders, and management). The SFM then allows us to see how these capital commitments and sources of financing fit together in a manner that makes sense to managers.

This chapter is organized into two parts. In the first part of the chapter, we restructure the balance sheet in order to focus on the long-term investment and long-term financing aspects of the firm's overall business strategy. By taking managers through the process of restructuring the balance sheet, we introduce the additional financial concepts senior executives use when planning for the future.

In the second part of the chapter, we introduce our second business strategy model, the SFM. Like the SPM, the SFM helps managers see how long-term investment and long-term financing decisions fit into the firm's overall business strategy.

RESTRUCTURING THE BALANCE SHEET

For many people, the term *restructuring* conjures up all kinds of negative images. Virtually all of us know of someone who has lost their job as management has restructured the business to become more competitive. To these people, the term "restructuring" conjures up all sorts of negative and unpleasant images.

When we restructure the balance sheet, we have a much more constructive use in mind. We want to see how firms like Wal-Mart have built the long-term investment and long-term financing foundation that supports all of their business operations.[1]

We base our approach to the restructuring process on the guidance provided by Gregory Bateson.

The division of the perceived universe into parts and wholes is convenient and may be necessary, but no necessity determines how it shall be done.[2]

Since we want to understand the long-term investment and financing aspects of the firm's business strategy, we need to restructure the balance sheet to provide a foundation for visualizing or perceiving the firm from a long-term perspective.

Figure 7.1 presents Wal-Mart's balance sheets for 1987 and 1997, which were first presented in Chapter 1. As discussed more fully in that chapter, we indicated that the basic financial control equation underlying the balance sheet is

$$\text{Assets} = \text{Liabilities} + \text{Shareholders' Equity}$$

For the fiscal years ended January 31, 1987 and 1997, Wal-Mart's balance sheet equations appear as:

$$\text{Assets} = \text{Liabilities} + \text{Shareholders' Equity}$$
$$1997: \quad \$39.604B = \$22.461B + \$17.143B$$
$$1987: \quad \$4.049B = \$2.359B + \$1.690B$$

We used that financial control equation to anchor our understanding of all of the information found in a balance sheet.

For example, we saw that total assets equaled current assets plus productive and other assets. We also saw that current assets consisted of cash and equivalents, receivables, inventory, and other current assets. Any mystery or possible misunderstanding surrounding the meaning of any of the elements making up the balance sheet (and the income statement) was eliminated as we looked at each of these elements within the context of the SPM.

When we move to a restructured balance sheet, the financial control equation shifts from

$$\text{Assets} = \text{Liabilities} + \text{Shareholders' Equity}$$

to

Figure 7.1   Wal-Mart Balance Sheets (for the Fiscal Years Ended January 31, 1987 and 1997 — Amounts in Millions)

	1987	1997
Assets		
Current Assets		
Cash and Equivalents	$166	$883
Receivables	$90	$845
Inventory	$2,031	$15,897
Other	$66	$368
Total Current Assets	$2,353	$17,993
Productive Assets		
Property, Plant, and Equipment	$2,070	$25,964
Accumulated Depreciation	($394)	($5,640)
Net Productive Assets	$1,676	$20,324
Other Assets	$20	$1,287
Total	$4,049	$39,604
Liabilities and Shareholders' Equity		
Liabilities		
Current Liabilities		
Accounts Payable	$925	$7,628
Current Debt Due	$14	$618
Other	$402	$2,711
Total Current Liabilities	$1,341	$10,957
Long-Term Liabilities		
Long-Term Debt	$179	$7,709
Long-Term Lease Obligations	$764	$2,307
Deferred Income Taxes and Other	$75	$1,488
Total Long-Term Liabilities	$1,018	$11,504
Total Liabilities	$2,359	$22,461
Shareholders' Equity		
Common Stock	$220	$775
Retained Earnings	$1,470	$16,768
Translation Adjustments	$0	$400)
Total Shareholders' Equity	$1,690	$17,143
Total	$4,049	$39,604

Total Long-Term Investment = Total Long-Term Financing

A restructured balance sheet differs from a regular balance sheet in three ways:

1. The long-term investment section of the restructured balance sheet is made up of *working capital, gross productive assets,* and *gross other assets.*
2. The long-term financing section is made up of *external debt financing, external equity financing,* and *internal equity financing.*
3. *Internal equity financing* equals retained earnings plus several score-keeping adjustments that have been added-back to retained earnings.

The process of learning how long-term investment and financing activities fit into the firm's overall business strategy begins with understanding the reasons for restructuring the balance sheet to promote long-term thinking.

Figure 7.2 presents the same information found in Wal-Mart's balance sheets for 1987 and 1997, only restructured to account for the three differences mentioned above. The amounts shown in italics represent the changes that occurred between 1987 and 1997.

The new financial control equation underlying the restructured balance sheet emphasizes the relationship between Wal-Mart's cumulative long-term investment and long-term financing decisions.

Total Long-Term Investment = Total Long-Term Financing
1997: $34.287B = $34.287B
1987: $3.102B = $3.102B

As we can see from a comparison of the 1987 and 1997 control equations, Wal-Mart increased its long-term investment from $3.1 billion to $34.3 billion. On the financing side of the equation, we see the mirror im-

Figure 7.2 Wal-Mart Restructured Balance Sheets (for the Fiscal Years Ended January 31, 1987 and 1997 — Amounts in Millions)

	1987	Change	1997
Long-Term Investment			
Current Assets			
Cash and Equivalents	$166	$717	$883
Receivables	$90	$755	$845
Inventory	$2,031	$13,866	$15,897
Other	$66	$302	$368
Total Current Assets	$2,353	$15,640	$17,993
Current Liabilities			
Accounts Payable	$925	$6,703	$7,628
Current Debt Due	$14	$604	$618
Other	$402	$2,309	$2,711
Total Current Liabilities	$1,341	$9,616	$10,957
Working Capital	$1,012	$6,024	$7,036
Gross Productive Assets			
Property, Plant, and Equipment	$2,070	$23,894	$25,964
Gross Other Assets			
Other Assets	$20	$1,267	$1,287
Total Long-Term Investment	$3,102	$31,185	$34,287
Long-Term Financing			
External Debt Financing			
Long-Term Debt	$179	$7,530	$7,709
Long-Term Lease Obligations	$764	$1,543	$2,307
Total External Debt	$943	$9,073	$10,016
External Equity Financing			
Common Stock	$220	$555	$775
Total External Equity	$220	$555	$775
Internal Equity Financing			
Retained Earnings	$1,470	$15,298	$16,768
Accumulated Depreciation	$394	$5,246	$5,640
Deferred Income Taxes and Other	$75	$1,413	$1,488
Translation Adjustments	$0	($400)	($400)
Total Internal Equity	$1,939	$21,557	$23,496
Total Long-Term Financing	$3,102	$31,185	$34,287

age of the investment side of the equation. Over this ten-year period, Wal-Mart increased its long-term financing and long-term investment by $31.2 billion.

Even though we might not be able to provide a detailed description of Wal-Mart's long-term investment and financing strategy at this time, we do know that they invested $31.2 billion for the long-term and management had to come up with $31.2 billion of long-term financing to match that investment. Given this start, we can begin to develop a more in-depth understanding of the long-term aspects of Wal-Mart's overall business strategy.

We will explain the differences between a regular balance sheet and a restructured balance sheet in the process of describing Wal-Mart's restructured balance sheets, presented in Figure 7.2.

LONG-TERM INVESTMENT

Working Capital. Current liabilities are subtracted from current assets to arrive at Wal-Mart's working capital for the fiscal years ended January 31, 1987 and 1997. Working capital represents the long-term investment in the business that must be maintained in order to run the day-to-day operations of the business.

When we shift gears and move from the regular balance sheet to the restructured balance sheet, current assets and current liabilities become part of the firm's long-term investment base. Using the language of investing and financing, current assets represent short-term investments related to the firm's operating cycle (cash, receivables, inventory, etc.), while current liabilities represent short-term financing provided by suppliers and other short-term creditors (accounts payable, current debt due to creditors, and other current liabilities).

When the amount of short-term financing provided by current liabilities is subtracted from the short-term investment in current assets, any balance must be financed from long-term sources of funds. As discussed more fully within the context of the SFM, most firms cannot survive without some level of long-term investment in working capital.

▶────────────────────────────────

In 1987, Wal-Mart had $1.012 billion invested in working capital; in 1997, Wal-Mart had $7.036 billion invested in working capital.

Over the ten-year period, Wal-Mart increased its long-term investment in working capital by $6.024 billion.

◄

The language of investment and financing that underlies the restructured balance sheet helps us develop a different frame of reference for understanding the business.

►

Did Wal-Mart really need to increase its investment in working capital by $6.024 billion during this ten-year period?

If so, where did the money come from to finance this $6.024 billion increase in long-term investment?

◄

Gross Productive Assets. When we want to see how much money has been invested in new stores, distribution centers, and other long-term commitments, we look at the firm's gross productive assets.

When we compare the restructured balance sheet to the regular balance sheet, we see that accumulated depreciation has not been subtracted from property, plant, and equipment. Accumulated depreciation has been added back to retained earnings (to be discussed more fully below).

►

In 1987, Wal-Mart had $2.070 billion invested in gross productive assets; in 1997, that investment equaled $25.964 billion.

Over the ten-year period, Wal-Mart increased its long-term investment in gross productive assets by $23.9 billion.

◄

As discussed in Chapter 4 under the asset-management component of the SPM, the growth in net productive assets (property, plant, and equipment less accumulated depreciation) was out of line compared to the growth in current assets. Within the context of a restructured balance sheet, we can see that the investment in gross productive assets was three times as great as the growth in working capital.

Gross Other Assets. For a firm like Wal-Mart, the *gross productive assets* shown on the restructured balance sheets are the same as the *other assets* reported on the regular balance sheet. However for some companies, the difference can be quite large.[3]

▶

In 1987, Wal-Mart had $20 million invested in gross other assets; in 1997, that investment equaled $1.287 billion.

Over the ten-year period, Wal-Mart increased its long-term investment in gross other assets by $1.3 billion.

◀

Total Long-Term Investment. As we can see from Figure 7.2, Wal-Mart has only three places to puts its long-term investment dollars: (1) working capital, (2) gross productive assets, and (3) gross other assets.

▶

In 1987, Wal-Mart had $3.102 billion invested for the long term; in 1997, the total long-term investment equaled $34.287 billion.

◀

Based on the logic of the financial-control equation underlying the restructured balance sheets, if Wal-Mart had $34.287 billion invested for the long term, it had to have come up with an equivalent amount of long-term financing.[4]

LONG-TERM FINANCING

When it comes to financing the long-term future of the business, the money can only come from one of three sources: external debt financing (creditors), external equity financing (shareholders), or internal equity financing (management).

External Debt Financing. In Wal-Mart's case, external debt financing comes from long-term notes, bonds, and capital lease obligations.

In 1987, Wal-Mart employed $943 million of external debt financing for the long-term; in 1997, external debt financing equaled $10.016 billion.

Over the ten-year period, external debt financing increased by $9.073 billion.

When we compare the restructured balance sheet to the regular balance sheet, we see that deferred income taxes have been added back to retained earnings and are not included as a part of external debt financing. Deferred income taxes, like depreciation charges, represent scorekeeping adjustments that reflect the timing differences between financial reporting and income tax reporting. Until the income taxes are actually due and payable, the deferred income taxes are part of management's (internal) contribution to financing the future of the business.[5]

External Equity Financing. Since Wal-Mart has only common stock outstanding, its external equity financing consists solely of the money received for the common stock issued and outstanding.[6]

Over the ten-year period, external equity financing increased from $220 million to $775 million.

As discussed more fully within the context of the SFM, we see that external equity financing was not a major factor in financing the business during this ten-year period.

Internal Equity Financing. Internal equity financing can be defined passively as a residual amount or actively as management's positive contribution to financing the future of the firm.

Defined passively, internal equity financing equals retained earnings plus amounts added back for accumulated depreciation, deferred income taxes, and translation adjustments. As we can see from the amounts reported for 1997 (in Figure 7.1), $5.640 billion was added back to retained earnings for accumulated depreciation, $1.488 billion added back for deferred income taxes, and $400 million subtracted for translation adjustments.

In 1987, Wal-Mart employed $1.939 billion of internal equity financing for the long term; in 1997, internal equity financing equaled $23.496 billion.

Within the context of the SFM, we will emphasize a more active and positive definition of internal equity financing. We will assume that if we were working within the firm, we could monitor the level of internal equity financing generated by management without having to make all of these scorekeeping adjustments to retained earnings.

Between 1987 and 1997, the internal equity financing contributed by management increased by $21.557 billion.

Total Long-Term Financing. When it comes time to finance the business for the long term, management has only three places to go to get the money: (1) long-term creditors (external debt financing), (2) shareholders (external equity financing), or (3) to themselves (internal equity financing).

$$\begin{array}{c}\text{External Debt}\\\text{Financing}\end{array} + \begin{array}{c}\text{External Equity}\\\text{Financing}\end{array} + \begin{array}{c}\text{Internal Equity}\\\text{Financing}\end{array} = \begin{array}{c}\text{Total}\\\text{Long-Term}\\\text{Financing}\end{array}$$

Since Wal-Mart had $34.287 billion invested for the long term, we know that the total long-term financing had to equal that same amount, which it did, as shown in Figure 7.2.

As mentioned previously, a restructured balance sheet differs from a regular balance sheet in three ways:

1. The long-term investment section of the restructured balance sheet is made up of *working capital, gross productive assets,* and *gross other assets.* As of January 31, 1987, Wal-Mart had $3.1 billion invested for the long term. By January 31, 1997, that long-term investment had increased to $34.3 billion.

2. The long-term financing section is made up of *external debt financing, external equity financing,* and *internal equity financing.* Between January 31, 1987, and January 31, 1997, Wal-Mart's long-term financing increased from $3.1 billion to $34.3 billion, exactly equaling the increase in long-term investment.

3. *Internal equity financing* equals retained earnings plus several score-keeping adjustments that have been added back to retained earnings. As of January 31, 1987, Wal-Mart's internal equity financing equaled $1.9 billion. By January 31, 1997, internal equity financing had increased to $23.5 billion.

Even though managers need to understand the language of long-term investment and long-term financing, they are really more interested in knowing how long-term investment and financing decisions affect their lives. That is where the SFM comes into play. The SFM helps managers see what senior management is doing to structure the firm's finances in order to be successful in the future.

STRATEGIC FINANCING MODEL

If the SPM helped us see the profitability "cow" in Wal-Mart's income statements and balance sheets, then the SFM should help us see the financing and investment "bull" in Wal-Mart's restructured balance sheets. As we all know, it takes both cows and bulls to make a herd. Without a well thought-out long-term investment and financing strategy, even highly profitable firms can get themselves into financial difficulty.

We use the SFM to help managers develop a better understanding of how a firm matches a long-term financing strategy with its long-term investment plan, and how the long-term financing and investment strategy is driven, in part, by the amount of internal equity financing generated by management on the shareholders' behalf.

Long-term investing and financing activities do not just happen. Senior management must decide on how fast to grow the business (including whether growth is even a realistic possibility) and how to finance that growth. The first component of the SFM shows how the long-term financing aspects of the business are matched to the firm's long-term investment strategy. The second component of the SFM looks at the firm's long-term business strategy from the internal perspective of the managers responsible for generating a return on the shareholders' behalf.

Figure 7.3 presents the long-term financing and long-term investment foundation for Wal-Mart's SFM using the amounts taken from the 1987 and 1997 restructured balance sheets.

Figure 7.4(a) presents a percentage breakdown of Wal-Mart's long-term financing and long-term investment base, and Figure 7.4(b) presents the related compound annual growth rates (CAGRs) for the ten-year period. The percentage breakdowns and CAGRs will be used to help us understand the long-term financing and investment aspects of Wal-Mart's overall business strategy.

As we did with the SPM, the narrative explanation of Wal-Mart's business strategy follows the visual representation of the business.

Long-Term Financing = Long-Term Investment (LTF = LTI)

No matter how much a firm's long-term investment base increases or decreases, it will always have to be matched by an equivalent increase or decrease in long-term financing.

In 1987, Wal-Mart's long-term financing and investment base equaled $3.102 billion; in 1997 the long-term base equaled $34.287 billion.

Between 1987 and 1997, Wal-Mart's long-term financing and investment foundation increased by $31.185 billion, a 27.2% CAGR.

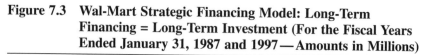

Figure 7.3 **Wal-Mart Strategic Financing Model: Long-Term Financing = Long-Term Investment (For the Fiscal Years Ended January 31, 1987 and 1997 — Amounts in Millions)**

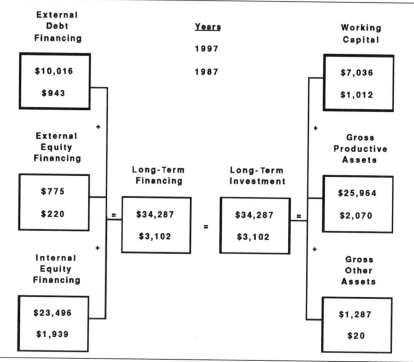

As mentioned above, the logic of financial control underlying the restructured balance sheet requires the long-term financing to equal the long-term investment. However, logic does not require Wal-Mart to grow at a 27.2% compound annual rate. The decision on how fast to grow the business resides with senior management in consultation with the board of directors.

In looking back over Wal-Mart's past performance, the SFM should help us see how management has matched its long-term investment needs with the three sources of long-term financing as part of the firm's overall business strategy.

In discussing the long-term aspects of a firm's business strategy, we begin with Wal-Mart's working capital.

**Figure 7.4   Wal-Mart Strategic Financing Model: Long-Term
Financing = Long-Term Investment**

(a) Percent Total Financing and Total Investment

	1987	1997
External Debt Financing	30.4%	29.2%
External Equity Financing	7.1%	2.3%
Internal Equity Financing	62.5%	68.5%
Total Long-Term Financing	100.0%	100.0%

	1987	1997
Working Capital	32.6%	20.5%
Gross Productive Assets	66.7%	75.7%
Gross Other Assets	0.6%	3.8%
Total Long-Term Investment	100.0%	100.0%

(b) Compound Annual Growth Rates (1987–1997)

External Debt Financing	26.7%
External Equity Financing	13.4%
Internal Equity Financing	28.3%
Total Long-Term Financing	27.2%
Working Capital	21.4%
Gross Productive Assets	28.8%
Gross Other Assets	51.7%
Total Long-Term Investment	27.2%

LONG-TERM INVESTMENT

Working Capital.   Working capital represents Wal-Mart's long-term investment in the day-to-day operations of the business, which must be financed from long-term sources.

In 1987, Wal-Mart's investment in working capital equaled $1.012 billion; in 1997, the investment in working capital equaled $7.036 billion.

Between 1987 and 1997, the investment in working capital increased at a 21.4% compound annual rate compared to the 28.8% growth rate for gross productive assets.

To a certain extent, the fact that working capital grew at a slower rate than gross productive assets should come as no surprise. As discussed in Chapter 3, the days' net sales tied up in current assets decreased from 72.1 days in 1987 to 62.6 days in 1997. From the discussion in Chapter 5, we know that the days' net sales tied up in current liabilities decreased from 41.1 days in 1987 to 38.1 days in 1997.

When current liabilities are subtracted from current assets, we can see that Wal-Mart's long-term investment in working capital decreased from 31.0 days' net sales in 1987 to 24.5 days in 1997.

	Days' Net Sales	
	1987	1997
Current Assets	72.1	62.6
Current Liabilities	41.1	38.1
Working Capital	31.0	24.5

Between 1987 and 1997, Wal-Mart was able to reduce its long-term investment in working capital by 6.5 days' net sales. At $287.3 million of net sales per day (see Chapters 3 and 5 for a more complete discussion of days' net sales), Wal-Mart reduced the working capital portion of its total long-term investment by $1.867 billion in 1997 when compared to 1987 performance levels.

In 1987, working capital equaled 32.6% of the total long-term investment. By 1997, the investment in working capital had dropped to 20.5%.

No matter how you measure Wal-Mart's long-term investment in working capital (the compound growth rate, days net sales invested in working capital, and percentage of total long-term investment), Wal-Mart still maintained or improved its working capital management practices over the ten years between 1987 and 1997, resulting in a $1.867 billion reduction in long-term investment.

Gross Productive Assets.   Gross productive assets represent Wal-Mart's cumulative long-term investment in property, plant, and equipment owned by the firm or controlled through capital lease arrangements.

Between 1987 and 1997, Wal-Mart's investment in gross productive assets increased from $2.070 billion to $25.964 billion, a CAGR of 28.8%.

Since the investment in gross productive assets grew at a much faster rate than the growth in working capital (21.4%), we should probably modify our explanation of what Wal-Mart is doing with its "savings" from reductions in the number of days net sales invested in working capital.

It appears that between 1987 and 1997, Wal-Mart was able to reallocate the $1.867 billion in working capital savings to accelerate the growth of its investment in gross productive assets.

Compared to 1987 performance levels, Wal-Mart had made a significant increase in its investment in property, plant, and equipment by 1997. If management had been able to maintain the 2-to-1 mix of gross productive assets to working capital from 1987 into 1997, the long-term investment in gross productive assets would have been $14.072 billion versus the actual investment of $25.964 billion, a $11.982 billion difference.

$11.892B = 2 × $7.036B (working capital in 1997)
$11.892B = $25.964B − $14.072B

It would appear that Wal-Mart, like other large firms, has been a victim of its past success. When the $11.982 billion "overinvestment" calculation is combined with the decrease in net sales per $1 of investment in productive assets (discussed in Chapters 3 and 4), we can see that Wal-Mart's long-term investments in productive assets were not delivering the same bang for the buck in 1997 that they delivered back in 1987.

Gross Other Assets. As mentioned above, the investment in gross other assets increased by $1.267 billion on a base of $20 billion in 1987. Given the lack of details about the composition of other assets, about all we can say is that they constituted 3.8% of the long-term investment base in 1997 versus 0.6% in 1987.

Long-Term Investment. Between 1987 and 1997, Wal-Mart reduced its investment in working capital while increasing its investment in gross productive and other assets.

In 1987, Wal-Mart utilized $2.07 in gross productive and other assets to run the business for every $1 working capital; in 1997, Wal-Mart utilized $3.83 in gross productive and other assets for every $1 of working capital.

Between 1987 and 1997, Wal-Mart almost doubled the intensity of gross productive and other assets used to run the business relative to its investment in working capital ($1.76 = $3.83 − $2.07).

When firms like Wal-Mart allow the ratio of gross productive and other assets to increase at a disproportionate rate, we can speculate that management has fallen victim to a common business affliction.

Sales growth for the sake of sales growth.

If we recall the discussion in Chapters 3 and 4 about asset turnover and return on assets (ROA), we can come to the same conclusion within the context of the SFM. Growing the business through increasing sales is of no benefit to the shareholders if the growth requires a disproportionate growth in long-term investment.

Improvements in working capital management practices are to be admired. However, to turn around and overinvest in gross productive and other assets does not produce benefits to shareholders.

LONG-TERM FINANCING

External Debt Financing. External debt financing represents the amount of money raised from long-term creditors that is used to finance the total long-term investment in the business.

In 1987, Wal-Mart utilized $943 million of external debt financing to run the business; in 1997, Wal-Mart utilized $10.016 billion.

Between 1987 and 1997, external debt financing increased at a 26.7% CAGR.

In 1987, external debt financing represented 30.4% of total long-term financing; in 1997, external debt financing represented 29.2%.

As discussed more fully in Chapter 10, Standard & Poor's and Moody's give Wal-Mart their highest credit rating relative to risk-free government bonds. With a strong credit rating, firms like Wal-Mart can take advantage of the leverage effects of debt financing (see Chapter 5). However, like any other firm that finances its business with long-term debt, it is subject to interest rate risk (changes in interest rates). If interest rates go up, the interest costs associated with issuing new debt and/or refinancing old debt will also go up. If that happens, Wal-Mart will experience additional pressure on its margins, with interest charges consuming a greater portion of every net sales dollar (see Chapter 3).

External Equity Financing. External equity financing represents the amount of money raised by issuing common stock to shareholders less any amounts paid out to reacquire outstanding shares.

▶

In 1987, Wal-Mart utilized $220 million of external equity financing to run the business; in 1997, Wal-Mart utilized $775 million.

Between 1987 and 1997, external equity financing increased at a 13.4% CAGR.

In 1987, external equity financing represented 7.1% of total long-term financing; in 1997, external equity financing represented 2.3%.

◀

Aside from minor amounts of common stock issued through the exercise of stock options, external equity financing has not been a major source of long-term financing for Wal-Mart. In fact, in recent years (1994 through 1997), Wal-Mart has been reacquiring shares on the open market to meet its obligations to employees who are exercising their options to acquire common stock.

Internal Equity Financing. Internal equity financing represents management's contribution to financing the long-term future of the firm.

▶

In 1987, Wal-Mart utilized $1.939 billion of internal equity financing in the business; in 1997, Wal-Mart utilized $23.496 billion.

Between 1987 and 1997, internal equity financing increased at a 28.3% CAGR.

In 1987, internal equity financing represented 62.5% of total long-term financing; in 1997, internal equity financing represented 68.5%.

As discussed more fully in Chapter 8, a significant part of management's overall business strategy must focus on how the future of the firm is to be financed from internal sources. In Wal-Mart's case, management generates high ROEs, pays low dividends, and finances a substantial portion of the firm's growth through internal equity financing.

Long-Term Financing. Between 1987 and 1997, Wal-Mart reduced its reliance on long-term creditors (external debt financing) and shareholders (external equity financing) in growing the business and increased its reliance on internal equity financing.

	Percent Long-Term Financing		
	1987	1997	Change
External Debt Financing	30.4%	29.2%	–1.2%
External Equity Financing	7.1%	2.3%	–4.8%
Internal Equity Financing	62.5%	68.5%	6.0%

The 6.0 percentage point increase in internal equity financing has been offset by the 1.2 percentage point decrease in external debt financing and the 4.8 percentage point decrease in external equity financing.

As we can see from the 1987 and 1997 percentages of total long-term financing, internal equity financing has been and continues to be the primary driver for financing the future of the firm. This internal equity financing has been and continues to be supplemented by a significant amount of external debt financing.

Even though our discussion in this chapter has focused on what happened at Wal-Mart between 1987 and 1997, we hope that you would agree that we now have a pretty good foundation for speculating about Wal-Mart's future performance. Firms cannot change their culture overnight, and we are firm believers that knowledge of past performance is a good place to start in assessing possible future performance.

In Chapter 8, we are going to extend our analysis of the long-term investment and long-term financing aspects of Wal-Mart's overall business strategy by bringing the customer into play and focusing on the primary role played by internal equity financing in growing the business.

NOTES

1. Restructuring information found in a firm's financial statements is a practice followed by virtually every investment advisory service (Standard & Poor's, Moody's, Dun and Bradstreet, etc.) and management consulting firm (McKinsey & Company, Inc., Stern, Stewart and Co., Ernst & Young, Marakon Associates, Alcar, etc.). For whatever reason, these users of financial information believe that they can gain additional insights into the business by restructuring the information found in the financial statements. In this respect, we are no different than these other financial advisors. We believe there are additional insights to be gained through the restructuring process. The restructured balance sheets discussed in this chapter reflect the most common adjustments made by the advisory services and consulting firms mentioned above. The investment advisory services typically provide a multi-year summary of selected information. In effect, they provide the reader with a partial balance sheet. The management consulting firms typically ignore scorekeeping adjustments for depreciation, amortization, deferred income taxes, and changes in accounting methods in their restructuring of the financial statements. As each of you becomes more comfortable with the process of restructuring the balance sheet, please feel free to experiment with other types of restructurings.

2. Gregory Bateson, *Mind and Nature* (Bantam Books, 1979), 39.

3. If one company bought another company and incurred "goodwill" (i.e., paid more for the company than the fair market value of its assets and liabilities), the goodwill will typically be included in the balance sheet under other assets. Over time, the goodwill is amortized and the accumulated amortization is treated the same as accumulated depreciation. If Wal-Mart had reported any goodwill and accumulated amortization, the accumulated amortization would have been added back to retained earnings on the restructured balance sheet.

4. In making the transition from *total assets* to *total long-term investment*, we subtracted current liabilities from current assets to focus on the long-term investment in working capital, and we added back the accumulated deprecia-

tion to retained earnings to focus on the investment in gross productive assets and gross other assets.

5. For the purpose of learning how to understand the business through financial information, no attempt has been made to separate the other long-term liabilities included in "deferred income taxes and other" from the part that is only deferred income taxes.

6. In 1994 through 1997, Wal-Mart repurchased shares of common stock on the open market and charged retained earnings for a portion of the repurchase price. For the purpose of this analysis, the adjustments are not material. If this adjustment and other adjustments were considered to be material, we would have to include additional steps to the restructuring process.

CHAPTER 8

Strategic Financing Model: Financing the Business

In using the Strategic Financing Model (SFM) to develop a better understanding of the long-term aspects of a firm's business strategy, we get an opportunity to practice using the language of financing and investing. Even though we may not yet be fluent speakers, the discussion of the restructured balance sheet in Chapter 7 provided us with the basic vocabulary of long-term investing and financing. We know that the firm's long-term investment base consists of working capital, gross productive assets, and gross other assets. We also know that the long-term investment can only be financed from one of three long-term sources: (1) external debt financing (creditors), (2) equity financing (shareholders), and (3) internal equity financing (management).

In this chapter, we are going to add an "action" component to the SFM and link the long-term aspects of the firm's business strategy directly back to the customer, the primary source of financing for any firm. In order to see a firm's long-term business strategy in action, we will focus on the *changes* between the restructured balance sheets for the fiscal years ended January 31, 1987 and 1997.

In order to focus on the strategic implications of the changes in the components of the restructured balance sheets between the fiscal years ended January 31, 1987 and 1997, we create one additional financial statement—the financial flow statement:

1. Only includes the amounts reported for each of the major categories reported for the two restructured balance sheets

2. Presents the long-term financing information before the long-term investment information

3. Includes a history and summation of the net sales made 1988 through 1997

With this information in hand, we can begin to understand how Wal-Mart built and financed its long-term investment base between 1987 and 1997.

Figure 8.1 presents Wal-Mart's financial flow statement for the ten-year period ended January 31, 1997. The financial flow statement includes two sections. The top section of the statement provides a summary, by major category, of the information found in Wal-Mart's restructured balance sheets discussed in Chapter 7 (see Figure 7.2). As mentioned above, the one notable difference is that the information about Wal-Mart's long-term financing activities is presented above the information about Wal-Mart's long-term investment activities. The lower section of Figure 8.1 presents Wal-Mart's net sales for the fiscal years ended January 31, 1987 through 1997.

In Chapter 7, we discussed the reasoning behind restructuring the balance sheet. Now we can concentrate on how management actually financed the increase in long-term investment. As we can see from Figure 8.1, the "change" column, which extends down to include Wal-Mart's net sales for the years 1987 through 1997, has been presented in italics. By focusing on the changes that have occurred over this ten-year period, we are able to increase our understanding of the long-term financing and investment aspects of Wal-Mart's overall business strategy.

The logic of financial control underlying the financial flow statement is represented as a self-balancing equation similar to the self-balancing equations underlying the balance sheet, the income statement, and the restructured balance sheet.

Total Long-Term Financing = Total Long-Term Investment

LTF = LTI

From Figure 8.1, we can see that between January 31, 1987, and January 31, 1997, Wal-Mart increased its long-term financing by $31.2 billion.

Figure 8.1   Wal-Mart Financial Flow Statement (for the Ten Years Ended January 31, 1997 — Amounts in Millions)

Long-Term Financing	1987	*Change*	1997
External Debt Financing	$943	*$9,073*	$10,016
External Equity Financing	$220	*$555*	$775
Internal Equity Financing	$1,939	*$21,557*	$23,496
Total Long-Term Financing	$3,102	*$31,185*	$34,287

Long-Term Investment	1987	*Change*	1997
Working Capital	$1,012	*$6,024*	$7,036
Gross Productive Assets	$2,070	*$23,894*	$25,964
Gross Other Assets	$20	*$1,267*	$1,287
Total Long-Term Investment	$3,102	*$31,185*	$34,287

Year	Net Sales (in millions)
1988	*$15,959*
1989	*$20,649*
1990	*$25,811*
1991	*$32,602*
1992	*$43,887*
1993	*$55,484*
1994	*$67,344*
1995	*$82,494*
1996	*$93,627*
1997	*$104,859*
Ten Year Total	*$542,716*

That increase in long-term financing was used to meet Wal-Mart's long-term investment needs, which equal $31.2 billion. However, like all of the other financial statements we have looked at in Chapters 1 through 7, it is not easy to tell a story about how management went about growing the business. That is where the "financing the business" component of the SFM comes into play.

STRATEGIC FINANCING MODEL: FINANCING THE BUSINESS

The financing the business component of the SFM allows us to see how management has combined its external debt and equity financing and internal equity financing to grow the business. As discussed more fully below, a firm only has three sources of long-term financing: external debt financing, external equity financing, and internal equity financing.

The total long-term financing, no matter what source it came from, can only be invested in one of the three components of long-term investment — working capital, gross productive assets, or gross other assets. From a communications perspective, the question becomes one of arranging the information found in Figure 8.1 in a way that makes sense to managers.

In order to increase our understanding of how Wal-Mart management financed the business between 1987 and 1997, we follow a three-step process:

1. Align the net sales provided by customers over the ten-year period with the internal equity financing generated by management.
2. Relate the internal equity financing generated by management to the change in long term over the ten-year period.
3. Determine the additional external debt and equity financing, if any, that was needed to meet Wal-Mart's strategic business objectives.

Figure 8.2 presents our way of helping managers make sense out of the long-term financing and investment information found in Figure 8.1. The percentages shown below the dollar amounts are based on the total net sales for the ten-year period. For example, internal equity financing represented 4.0% of the total net sales from 1987 through 1997.

MANAGEMENT'S CONTRIBUTION TO FINANCING THE BUSINESS

The primary purpose of business operations is to grow shareholder wealth through profitable operations. Management's contribution to growing a company's investment base provides a good starting point for looking at

Figure 8.2   Wal-Mart Strategic Financing Model: Financing the Business (for the Period January 31, 1987 through 1997 — Amounts in Millions)

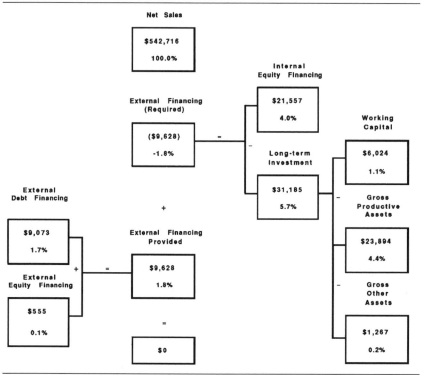

Wal-Mart's long-term financing and investment activity over the 1987–1997 period. Before we focus in on management's contribution, we need to take one step back and take a look at net sales, the primary source of financing for any business.

Net Sales.   One way of trying to understand the long-term aspects of a firm's business strategy is to anchor all of the financial relationships back to the customer. Since the customer is the primary source of financing, it would only seem logical to keep the customer in mind when we think about positioning the firm for success in the future.

126

> Between 1987 and 1997, Wal-Mart generated $542.716 billion in customer financing through the sale of merchandise to customers.

Since we are emphasizing the long-term aspects of a firm's business strategy, it only seems natural to use a time horizon that is consistent with taking a longer-term perspective. Even though Wal-Mart's net sales of $104.859 billion in 1997 are quite impressive, the fact that Wal-Mart generated $542.7 billion in net sales between 1987 and 1997 reinforces the need to keep the customer in the forefront of thinking about the firm's future.

Given that Wal-Mart has demonstrated the ability to generate over half a trillion dollars through sales to customers, the question now becomes one of understanding how Wal-Mart has used these dollars of customer financing to run the business and grow the company over this ten-year period.

If we look at the elements presented in the SFM in terms of total net sales for the ten-year period, we can ask the following question:

> For every $1 of net sales generated from customers, what did management do with the money?

Internal Equity Financing. Internal equity financing represents management's contribution to growing the business. It consists of the money "left over" after covering all operating costs, interest, income taxes, and shareholder dividends.

> Between 1987 and 1997, management generated $21.557 billion of internal equity financing.
>
> The $21.557 billion represented 4.0¢ of every $1 of net sales generated by management.[1]

127

Since we have to account for every cent of every dollar of net sales received from customers, it might be nice to know what happened to the other 96.0¢ of customer financing. Between 1987 and 1997, management spent $521.159 billion to cover operating costs, interest, income taxes, and shareholder dividends.

If any firm wants to increase the money generated from internal operations to finance the future of the business, it must reduce the amount of money spent on running the day-to-day operations of the firm.

▶

If Wal-Mart could have generated an additional 1.0¢ of internal equity financing from the business over the period between 1987 and 1997, management would have had an additional $5.427 billion to invest in the business for the long term.

◀

Even before we look at the remainder of the action component of the SFM, we know that we have three options for using the internal equity financing generated by management. The money can be used to:

1. Grow the business by increasing the long-term investment in working capital, gross productive assets, and gross other assets
2. Reduce the level of external debt financing
3. Reduce the level of external equity financing

As we work through the remainder of the action component of the SFM, the number of possibilities decrease as management makes specific, strategic commitments to financing the future of the firm.

LONG-TERM INVESTMENT

As we can see from Figure 8.2, Wal-Mart increased its long-term investment base by $31.185 billion. The increase in long-term investment represents the total net change in working capital, gross productive assets, and gross other assets. In discussing each element of Wal-Mart's long-term investment, we will develop a better understanding of how management has grown Wal-mart's long-term investment base.

Working Capital. The investment in working capital represents the money spent to support the ongoing operations of the firm.

Between 1987 and 1997, Wal-Mart spent $6.024 billion to increase the investment in working capital.

For every $1 of net sales, management spent 1.1¢ to increase its investment in working capital.

As discussed in Chapter 7, Wal-Mart has kept the growth of working capital well below the growth in gross productive assets and gross other assets. However, all firms have to invest *some* amount of money in working capital to support the business.

Between 1987 and 1997, 27.9% of internal equity financing generated by management was invested in working capital (27.9% = $6.024B ÷ $21.557B).

Investment in Gross Productive Assets. This investment represents the money spent to expand the business and modernize operations.

Between 1987 and 1997, Wal-Mart spent $23.894 billion to increase the investment in gross productive assets.

For every $1 of net sales, management spent 4.4¢ to increase its investment in productive assets.

Between 1987 and 1997, 111.3% of internal equity financing generated by management was invested in gross productive assets (111.3% = $23.894B ÷ $21.557B).

Investment in Gross Other Assets. This investment represents the money spent on unspecified long-term commitments.

Between 1987 and 1997, Wal-Mart spent $1.267 billion to increase the investment in gross other assets.

For every $1 of net sales, management spent 0.2¢ to increase its investment in other assets.

Between 1987 and 1997, 116.7% of internal equity financing generated by management was invested in gross productive assets and gross other assets (116.7% = [$23.894B + $1.267B] ÷ $21.557B).

Even without considering the long-term investment in working capital, Wal-Mart seems to be running into a bit of a problem. Any time you spend more money than you generate from internal operations, management must go outside the firm to raise money from creditors and shareholders.

Total Long-Term Investment. When we combine the long-term requirements for working capital with the requirements for gross productive assets and gross other assets, we see that management has more than exhausted all of the internal equity financing generated between 1987 and 1997.

Between 1987 and 1997, Wal-Mart spent $31.185 billion to increase the total long-term investment in the firm.

For every $1 of net sales, management spent 5.7¢ to increase the total long-term investment.

Given this information about Wal-Mart's long-term investment expenditures, we can make the following observations about the long-term aspects of Wal-Mart's business strategy:

- If Wal-Mart is spending 5.7¢ of every $1 of net sales on building the long-term investment base, management is obviously putting all of the internal equity financing it is generating (4.0¢) back into the business.

- The total long-term investment equals 144.6% of the internal equity financing generated between 1987 and 1997. Of that 144.6%, 27.9% represents the investment in working capital and 116.9% represents the investment in gross productive assets and gross other assets.
- When a firm's long-term investment needs cannot be met from money generated internally, management has to go outside the business to raise the additional money.

Based on these three observations, we have information that reinforces some of the insights gained from looking at the business through the Strategic Profit Model (SPM) and provides a somewhat different perspective on the business.

The difference between the 4.4¢ being spent on gross productive assets and gross other assets versus the 1.1¢ being spent on working capital reinforces previous observations about Wal-Mart's asset-management practices. Wal-Mart is spending 4.18 times as much on gross productive assets and gross other assets than it is spending on working capital (4.18 = $25.161 billion ÷ $6.024 billion). On the one hand, Wal-Mart is becoming more efficient in managing working capital. On the other hand, Wal-Mart is not getting the same number of net sales dollars out of its investment in gross productive assets and gross other assets as it was in the 1970s and early 1980s.

The new insight provided by this action component of the SFM is that no matter where Wal-Mart is putting its long-term investment dollars, management cannot finance the increased investment entirely from internally generated funds. Between 1987 and 1997, the shortfall equaled $9.6 billion. From the logic of the financial control equation underlying the financial flow statement, we know that management must have gone outside the business to raise the additional money from external sources (creditors and shareholders).

EXTERNAL FINANCING

External Financing (Required). External financing required represents the shortfall or gap between what management has been able to provide from internal sources to grow the business and the total long-term investment.

Between 1987 and 1997, Wal-Mart generated $21.557 billion in internal equity financing and invested $31.185 billion to increase the firm's long-term investment base.

For every $1 of net sales, the 4.0¢ in internal equity financing fell short of the 5.7¢ invested in the business for the long term.

The shortfall of $9.628 billion equaled 1.8¢ of every $1 of net sales generated over the period between 1987 and 1997.

Since Wal-Mart has been, and still is, committed to growing the business, it is not surprising that additional external financing has been required. If we had used this component of the SFM to understand a firm with little or no growth possibilities, it is quite possible that management would be generating more money than it was reinvesting in the business and actually reducing the amount of external debt and equity financing employed in the business.

Depending on whether the external financing is required (a negative amount) or not required (a positive amount), management is faced with different choices:

1. If external financing is required, management must decide whether to borrow more money and/or issue additional common stock.
2. If external financing is not required, management must decide whether to pay down the debt financing or repurchase some of the outstanding common stock and thereby pay down the external equity financing.

Since the long-term financing reported in the financial flow statement equals the long-term investment (see Figure 8.1), we know that the shortfall was covered. The question that remains is one of seeing how management used some combination of debt and equity financing to cover the shortfall.

External Financing (Required) = External Financing Provided

Aside from monitoring the level of return on equity (ROE) within the context of the firm's overall business strategy, senior management is responsible for deciding whether to grow the business and how to finance that growth. When management goes outside the firm to raise additional money, it must consider if the firm can meet the expectations of the creditors and shareholders who are providing the additional money.

Between 1987 and 1997, Wal-Mart required an additional $9.628 billion to meet its long-term investment needs. That long-term need was met by raising $9.628 billion in external financing.

The shortfall of 1.8¢ of internal equity financing was made up by a net increase of 1.8¢ of external financing being provided by creditors and shareholders.

Whether we are talking about $1, $1 million, or $9.6 billion, the logic of financial control dictates that the amount of external financing required must equal the amount provided.

External Financing Required = External Financing Provided
$9.628B = $9.628B

Or as visualized through Figure 8.2,

External Financing (Required) + External Financing Provided = $0
($9.628B) + $9.628B = $0

If we had to identify one responsibility that senior management cannot delegate to other managers, it would be determining the amount of external financing that will be needed to run the business and decide on the amounts to be raised from creditors and shareholders.

By the time we work our way to the "external financing provided" part of the SFM, a number of strategic choices have already been made. Management has:

- Committed all of the internal equity financing it has generated to grow the business
- Decided to grow the business at a faster rate than could be supported by the amount of internal equity financing provided
- Chosen to go outside the firm to raise the additional money needed to grow the business

The only choice left for management to make is deciding how much money to raise from creditors and how much to raise from shareholders.

External Debt Financing.   This source of external financing represents the amount of money raised from creditors to grow the business.

Between 1987 and 1997, Wal-Mart raised $9.073 billion in external debt financing. The external debt financing represented 94.2% of the total financing raised from external sources during this ten-year period.

For every $1 of net sales, Wal-Mart raised an additional 1.7¢ from long-term creditors.

Since we have already considered the effects of internal equity financing on growing the business, the importance of Wal-Mart's debt-financing strategy in growing the business becomes even more evident. As we can see, the vast majority of the external financing (94.2%) has come from long-term creditors.

Since we know that Wal-Mart raised 1.7¢ of its external financing needs through debt financing, the additional 0.1¢ had to be raised from external equity financing.

External Equity Financing.   This source of financing represents the amount of money raised from shareholders through the issuance of common stock.

Between 1987 and 1997, Wal-Mart raised $555 million in external equity financing. The external equity financing represented 5.8% of the total external financing raised during this period.

For every $1 of net sales, Wal-Mart raised an additional 0.1¢ from shareholders.

Aside from some minor stock repurchases in 1994 through 1997, the increase in external equity financing came about primarily through the exercise of stock options by employees and management. Like any number of other firms committed to increasing the value of the shareholders' investment in the firm, external equity financing has not been a prime source of funds for large firms. Since large firms like Wal-Mart attract the attention of numerous financial analysts, any increase in external equity financing not accompanied by a proportional increase in earnings or cash flow per share (earnings plus depreciation and other noncash adjustments) will likely have a negative impact on the firm's stock price (more on this issue in Chapters 11 and 12).

THE SFM AND UNDERSTANDING THE BUSINESS

As mentioned in Chapter 7, the SFM supplements the SPM by focusing on the long-term financing and investment aspects of the firm's overall business strategy. In restructuring the balance sheet, we make two basic adjustments that support taking a long-term view of the firm. First, we subtract current liabilities from current assets to arrive at the long-term investment in working capital. Second, we add back the scorekeeping adjustments for depreciation, deferred income taxes, and translation adjustments to retained earnings to create a long-term financing and investment perspective.

By focusing on the changes in each of the major categories in the restructured balance sheet, we can create a financial flow statement that allows us to build an action component for the SFM.

In visualizing these restructured balance sheets and the financial flow statement through the lens of the SFM, we can gain additional insights into the long-term aspects of the firm's overall business strategy. In Wal-

Mart's case, we were able to make the following observations about the long-term aspects of management's overall business strategy.

Long-Term Financing = Long-Term Investment

- Between 1987 and 1997, Wal-Mart's long-term investments were heavily weighted toward gross productive assets versus working capital. Consistent with the insights we gained through the SPM during this ten-year period, Wal-Mart was becoming more efficient in its working capital management practices and appeared to have become less efficient in managing its investment in gross productive assets. During this period, 76.6% of the total long-term investment dollars went into gross productive assets, with only 19.3% of those investment dollars going into working capital and 4.1% going into gross other assets.

- Between 1987 and 1997, external debt financing played a prominent role in Wal-Mart's overall business strategy while external equity financing played a less important role. During this period, external equity financing represented only 5.8% of total external financing. On the other hand, external debt financing represented 94.2% of total external financing.

- Between 1987 and 1997, the bulk of Wal-Mart's long-term financing came from internal operations. Internal equity financing was 2.24 times as great as the total external debt and equity financing.

- Between 1987 and 1997, the $21.557 billion of internal equity financing generated by management equaled 4.0¢ of every $1 of net sales.

- All of the internal equity financing (and then some) was used to grow the long-term investment base—$9.628 billion of the increase in long-term investment of $31.185 billion could not be financed from internal sources. The 5.7¢ increase in long-term investment per $1 of net sales resulted in a 1.8¢ shortfall that had to be financed from external sources.

- The $9.628 billion needed to cover the shortfall from internal equity financing came primarily from long-term creditors. Long-term creditors provided $9.073 billion or 1.7¢ of long-term financing for every $1 of net sales. External debt financing accounted for over 94.2% of the external financing raised between 1987 and 1997.

- The role played by external equity financing in the period between 1987 and 1997 was negligible. The $555 million increase in external equity financing represented 0.1¢ of every $1 of net sales, or 5.8% of the total external financing needed to grow the business.

In Part Two of this book, beginning in Chapter 9, we will attempt to increase our understanding of the business a bit further by adding market information into our thinking about business strategy. We will cross the boundaries of the firm (as represented by the information found in the financial statements) and add information about interest rates, inflation rates, stock prices, and risk measures to the framework we have been developing throughout Part One. We will consider how the market value of debt and equity securities fit into the firm's overall business strategy.

NOTE

1. If we restructured Wal-Mart's income statements to determine the amount of internal equity financing included in Figure 8.2, we would make the following adjustments to net income:

   Net Income + Depreciation + Change in Deferred Income Taxes + Translation Adjustments − Shareholder Dividends = Internal Equity Financing

   Based on our experiences working with managers in executive education programs, restructuring the income statement creates more problems than it solves. Instead of trying to understand the business, we typically end up trying to understand how the reconciliation process works. It is much easier to talk our way through the reconciliation process. Internal equity financing equals net income less shareholder dividends plus or minus adjustments for depreciation, deferred income taxes, and translation adjustments.

PART TWO

Market Valuation and Business Strategy

CHAPTER 9

Market Valuation: Market Performance Measures

In Part One (Chapters 1 through 8), we concentrated on the relationship between business strategy and the information found in the firm's financial statements. As we saw, the Strategic Profit Model (SPM) and the Strategic Financing Model (SFM) provided a systematic framework for seeing how all of the parts of the business fit into an integrated whole. Within the boundaries provided by the financial statements, the SPM and the SFM have proven to be powerful tools for helping managers understand the business through financial information.

But what happens when we have to cross the boundaries provided by the financial statements and start to factor additional market information into the firm's business strategy?

> If we want to understand the business through financial information, we cannot stop at the boundaries of the firm. We must also incorporate market information into the management communications process.

As soon as we acknowledge that we must factor market information into our understanding of the business, the firm becomes part of a greater whole known as the global capital marketplace. In global capital markets, firms are evaluated in terms of the value they create for their share-holders.

Many managers of publicly traded companies own shares of their firm's common stock directly or indirectly through their company's pension plan and individual 401(k) plan. These same managers, along with millions of other investors, typically invest in the common stock of other companies individually or through mutual fund investments. As investors, these managers have a personal interest in seeing the value of their investment port-folio grow over time.

In helping managers see how market information is linked to business strategy, all we do is ask them to remember that they wear two hats — a management hat *and* an investor hat. If the firm has developed a market-oriented business strategy, the interests of managers and investors should be similar. Both managers and investors will be interested in seeing the market value of their company's common stock increase.

To get managers to start thinking like investors, we typically ask the following two questions:

1. As an investor, would you buy stock in your own company?
2. As a manager, what are you doing to increase the value of your (shareholder's) investment in your company?

To a large extent, Chapters 9 through 12 are devoted to helping managers think like investors and providing them with a way of integrating this investor perspective into the SPM we developed in Part One. The purpose of this chapter is to familiarize managers with the language of the market valuation process. Defining the basic terms used in discussions about market valuation is an important first step in helping managers see how their actions can affect the value of the shareholders' investment in the firm.

In the first part of this chapter, we will add some information about the market value of Wal-Mart's common stock to the summary version of the SPM. In keeping with the management philosophy underlying the Du-Pont executive charting system discussed in Chapter 1, we will look to see what the market is telling us about its perceptions of Wal-Mart's financial performance.

In the second part of the chapter, we will look at Wal-Mart within the context of the broader capital marketplace. We will compare Wal-Mart's common stock performance to a "market basket" of other firms, as represented by the Standard and Poor's index of 500 firms (S&P 500).

In Chapters 10 and 11, we will take a closer look at the mechanics of how the market values a firm's debt and equity securities. In Chapter 12, we will return to the SPM and expand the model to incorporate key measures of market performance within a single management communications framework.

MARKET VALUATION AND THE STRATEGIC PROFIT MODEL

Figure 9.1 presents the summary version of Wal-Mart's SPM for the fiscal years ended January 31, 1987 and 1997, with one additional piece of financial information: the average market price of Wal-Mart's common stock for the fiscal years ended January 31, 1987 and 1997.

Figure 9.2 presents the compound annual growth rates (CAGRs) for the ten-year period, including the growth rate for Wal-Mart's common stock. The CAGRs will be used to help us understand the capital market aspects of Wal-Mart's overall business strategy.

As we can see from the stock price information that has been added to Figure 9.1, the market value of one share of Wal-Mart's common stock increased from $5.15 in 1987 to $23.70 in 1997. From Figure 9.2, we can see that the market value of one share of Wal-Mart's common stock increased at a 16.5% CAGR.

On the surface, a 16.5% CAGR looks pretty good relative to other investments in the marketplace, but looks can be deceiving. As we can see from Figure 9.2, all of the other CAGRs associated with the income statement and balance sheet are substantially higher (net sales, 24.3%; net income, 21.1%; assets, 25.6%; shareholders' equity, 26.1%). Between 1987 and 1997, Wal-Mart's market performance did not keep up with its management performance, as reflected in the management measures of performance.

When we combine stock market performance measures with management performance measures, we are combining an orientation to past performance, as captured in the financial statements, with an orientation toward the future, as captured in the market value of the firm's common stock. In very general terms, if the market value of the firm's common stock is growing at a slower rate than the management performance measures, investors do not expect the firm to grow as fast in the future as it

Figure 9.1 **Wal-Mart Strategic Profit Model: Summary Version, Including Stock Price Performance (for the Fiscal Years Ended January 31, 1987 and 1997 — Amounts in Millions)**

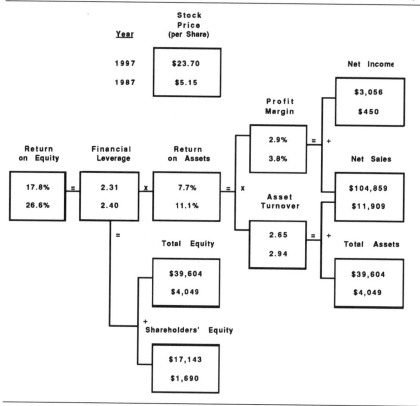

has grown in the past. Likewise, if the market value is growing at a faster rate than the management performance measures, investors expect the firm to grow at a faster rate in the future.

In Wal-Mart's case, this logic seems to make good common sense. Between 1987 and 1988, net income increased from $450 million to $628 million (a 39.6% increase). Between 1996 and 1997, net income increased from $2.740 billion to $3.056 billion (an 11.5% increase). So even though Wal-Mart is the world's largest retailer, it has not been growing as fast recently as it has grown in the past. Slower growth, coupled with declining returns on investment (ROEs — 26.6% in 1987 compared to 17.8% in 1997) has had a dramatic effect on Wal-Mart's stock price.

Figure 9.2 **Wal-Mart Strategic Profit Model: Summary Version (for the Fiscal Years Ended January 31, 1987 and 1997)**

Compound Annual Growth Rates (1987–1997)

Market Information

Stock Price	16.5%

Income Statement

Net Sales	24.3%
Expenses (net)	24.4%
Net Income	21.1%

Balance Sheet

Assets	25.6%
Liabilities	25.3%
Shareholders' Equity	26.1%

The total market value of Wal-Mart's common stock outstanding also reflects this change in growth opportunities. The total market value (market capitalization of the company) equals the market value of one share of common stock times the total number of shares outstanding.

Market Value = Stock Price × Shares Outstanding

1997: $11.626B = $5.15 × 2.2575B Shares

1987: $54.344B = $23.70 × 2.2930B Shares

For the entire ten-year period, the total market value of Wal-Mart's common stock outstanding increased from $11.6 billion to $54.3 billion, a $42.7 billion increase. However, the rate of increase between 1987 and 1988 was substantially slower than the rate of increase between 1996 and 1997.

Between 1987 and 1988, the total market value of Wal-Mart's common stock increased from $11.626 billion to $17.744 billion (a 52.6% increase). Between 1996 and 1997, the total market value of Wal-Mart's common stock decreased from $55.032 billion to $54.344 billion (a 1.3%

decrease). It would appear that the market is adjusting the value of Wal-Mart's common stock to reflect an environment of slower growth and lower profitability.

In order to support the statements we have just made about Wal-Mart's change in performance between 1987 and 1988 and 1996 and 1997, we need to fill in the blanks for the years not included in Figure 9.1. We need to see how management's performance and the market's assessment of that performance has been changing over time.

Figure 9.3 presents the relationships between the total market value of Wal-Mart's common stock, net income, and shareholder's equity as reported in Wal-Mart's income statements and balance sheets. As we can see from the bottom of the figure, the total market value of Wal-Mart's common stock increased at a 16.7% CAGR over the entire ten-year period compared to the 21.1% compound annual growth in net income and 26.1% compound annual growth in shareholders' equity.

However, as we can also see from the graphic presentation of Wal-Mart's actual performance over the ten-year period, the growth in market value was not anywhere near as smooth as the growth in net income and shareholders' equity. Up through 1993, the market value of Wal-Mart's common stock was increasing at a 33.8% CAGR while net income was increasing at a 28.2% CAGR and shareholders' equity was increasing at 31.5%. During this period, the market was assigning a premium to Wal-Mart's common stock relative to the growth in net income and shareholders' equity.

To a certain extent, the $12.3 billion decline in market value from 1994 through 1997 represents a correction to a more realistic market valuation — i.e., where the growth in market value is more in line with the growth in net income and shareholders' equity. (*Note:* As of July 1997, Wal-Mart's common stock was trading at a market value of around $36.00 per share, a 32% increase over the average share price of $27.30 for fiscal year ended January 31, 1997. It would appear that the correction-in-progress will bring the market value back in line with both the growth in net income and shareholders' equity.)

PRICE/EARNINGS AND MARKET/BOOK RATIOS

Market analysts frequently link share price information to the information found in the financial statement through two ratios: (1) the price/earnings (P/E) ratio and (2) the market/book (M/B) ratio. These ratios provide yet

Figure 9.3 **Wal-Mart Market and Management Measures of Performance (for the Years Ended January 31—Shares and Dollar Amounts in Millions)**

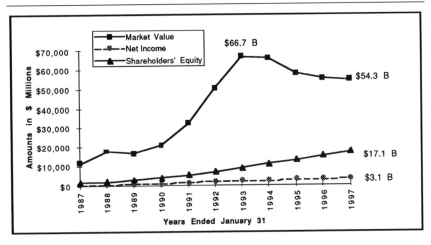

Year Ended January 31	Common Stock Outstanding	Market Value	Net Income	Shareholders' Equity
1987	2,258	$11,626	$450	$1,690
1988	2,260	$17,744	$628	$2,257
1989	2,262	$16,516	$837	$3,008
1990	2,265	$21,173	$1,076	$3,966
1991	2,285	$32,556	$1,291	$5,366
1992	2,298	$50,443	$1,608	$6,990
1993	2,300	$66,688	$1,995	$8,759
1994	2,299	$65,516	$2,333	$10,753
1995	2,297	$57,884	$2,681	$12,726
1996	2,293	$55,032	$2,740	$14,756
1997	2,293	$54,344	$3,056	$17,143
CAGR	0.2%	16.7%	21.1%	26.1%

another way of looking at the relationship between management's performance and the market's assessment of that performance. Figure 9.4 presents Wal-Mart's P/E ratios and M/B ratios between 1987 and 1997.

Price/Earnings Ratio. The P/E ratio links the firm's common stock share price to the income statement. The ratio equals the market value of Wal-

Mart's common stock divided by net income. In other words, the market price of the firm's common stock can be expressed as a multiple of the firm's net income. Wal-Mart's average P/E ratio of 24.6 between 1987 and 1997 means that the market value of its common stock has traded at 24.6 times its reported earnings.

▶───────────────────────────────────────

Between 1987 and 1997, Wal-Mart's common stock traded, on average, at 24.6 times its earnings.

───────────────────────────────────────◀

However, as we can see from Figure 9.4, Wal-Mart's common stock has traded well above and well below the 24.6 average P/E ratio. In 1993, Wal-Mart's common stock was trading at 33.4 times its earnings; in 1997, Wal-Mart's common stock was trading at 17.8 times its earnings.

Market/Book Ratio. The M/B ratio expresses the relationship between the market value of a firm's common stock and the shareholders' equity section of the balance sheet. The M/B ratio equals the market value of the firm's common stock divided by the shareholders' equity reported in the balance sheet (the firm's book value). Since shareholders' equity equals the cumulative amount of common stock, retained earnings, and translation adjustments, the M/B ratio is typically much lower than the P/E ratio. The M/B ratio is another way of looking at the relationship between management's performance and the market's assessment of that performance.

Wal-Mart's average M/B ratio of 5.8 for the ten-year period between 1987 and 1997 means that the market value of its common stock has traded at 5.8 times its reported shareholders' equity.

▶───────────────────────────────────────

Between 1987 and 1997, Wal-Mart's common stock traded, on average, at 5.8 times its reported shareholders' equity.

───────────────────────────────────────◀

As we can see from Figure 9.4, Wal-Mart's common stock has traded well above and well below the 5.8 average M/B ratio. In 1988, Wal-Mart's

Figure 9.4   Wal-Mart Price/Earnings and Market/Book Ratios (for the Years Ended January 31)

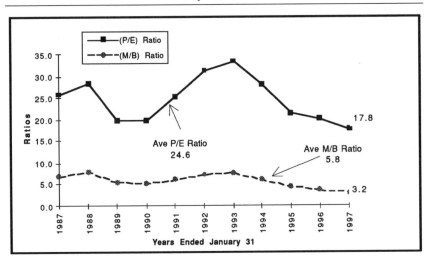

Year Ended January 31	Price/Earnings (P/E) Ratio	Market/Book (M/B) Ratio
1987	25.8	6.9
1988	28.3	7.9
1989	19.7	5.5
1990	19.7	5.3
1991	25.2	6.1
1992	31.4	7.2
1993	33.4	7.6
1994	28.1	6.1
1995	21.6	4.5
1996	20.1	3.7
1997	17.8	3.2
Average	24.6	5.8

common stock was trading at 7.9 times its book value; in 1997, Wal-Mart's common stock was trading at 3.2 times its book value.

As we can see from Figures 9.3 and 9.4, the market valuation process is not static. The market value for the common stock for all publicly traded firms, including Wal-Mart, ebbs and flows with the changes in expectations of what investors think the stock of a firm like Wal-Mart is worth in the capital marketplace. From a business strategy perspective, managers need to focus on running the business with one eye toward the market. However, managers also have to realize that the market price of their firm's common stock is also affected by investor expectations about the financial performance of other firms.

To develop a better understanding of the broader capital marketplace, we are going to take a closer look at Wal-Mart as one part of a greater whole, as represented by the S&P 500. Within the context of the S&P 500, we will be able to see how well Wal-Mart has performed compared to a market basket of 500 U.S. companies.

WAL-MART AND THE S&P 500

In addition to providing a full set of financial statements to shareholders on a quarterly and annual basis, the Securities and Exchange Commission (SEC) requires firms to make additional disclosures to shareholders in the notice of the annual meeting of shareholders (typically referred to as the firm's proxy statement).

For our present purposes, we are most interested in the stock performance graph that presents the cumulative total shareholder return for each firm as compared to the overall S&P 500 index and typically a more specific index consisting of firms in the same industry.

Figure 9.5 presents Wal-Mart's cumulative total return[1] compared to the S&P 500 index and the S&P retail stores composite index. The amounts reported in Figure 9.5 are based on the assumption that a shareholder invested $100 in Wal-Mart's common stock, $100 in a market basket of firms representing the entire S&P 500 index, and $100 in a more specific market basket consisting of all firms included in the S&P retail stores index.

As we can see from Figure 9.5, from 1992 through 1997, Wal-Mart underperformed both the S&P 500 index and the S&P retail stores index. Between these dates the total return on an investment in the S&P 500 would have equaled 17.1%; the S&P retail stores index, 6.5%; and Wal-Mart, −1.9%. In retrospect, it looks as if it would have been a good idea to sell our Wal-Mart stock at the end of 1993 and reinvested that money in a market basket of S&P 500 stocks. However, as mentioned above, the market price of Wal-Mart's common stock is now (July 1997) trading around $36.00 per share. If the stock price holds at $36.00 or increases even fur-

Figure 9.5 **Comparison of Five-Year Cumulative Total Return* among Wal-Mart Stores, the S&P 500 Index, and the S&P Retail Stores Composite Index**

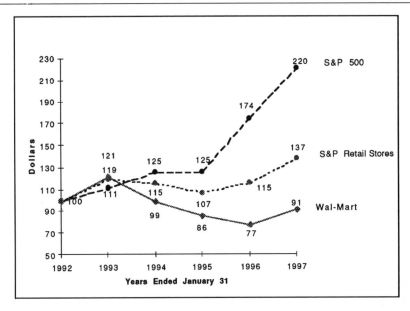

Year Ended January 31	S&P 500	S&P Retail Stores	Wal-Mart Stock
1992	100	100	100
1993	111	119	121
1994	125	115	99
1995	125	107	86
1996	174	115	77
1997	220	137	91
CAGR	17.1%	6.5%	−1.9%

*Assumes dividends are reinvested at the prevailing market price.

Source: Wal-Mart Stores, Inc., Notice of Annual Meeting of Shareholders, June 6, 1997.

ther, the performance graph included in the 1998 notice of annual meeting to shareholders will look substantially better.

From the standpoint of trying to understand the business through financial information, Figure 9.5 is interesting for several reasons.

- As investors, we are provided with information to help us assess how well we have done or might have done by investing or not investing in Wal-Mart's common stock. If we do not think that management is doing what it takes to turn things around, we just might want to invest our money elsewhere.

- As managers, we do not have the luxury of just selling our Wal-Mart stock and moving on. If some managers decided to leave Wal-Mart based on this information, the new managers would be faced with the problem of figuring out how to come up with a strategy to get Wal-Mart back on track in terms of creating value for its shareholders.

- As individuals trying to understand Wal-Mart's business, we might want to expand the horizon of our backward glance to see if a longer time horizon might provide a different perspective for speculating about how Wal-Mart's stock might perform in the future.

In Figure 9.6, we have extended the time horizon to ten years versus the five years included in Figure 9.5. However, instead of including the effects of a $100 investment in the S&P 500 retail stores index, we have included an index based on $100 of book value of Wal-Mart's shareholders' equity.

As we can see from Figure 9.6, the total return of a $100 investment in Wal-Mart's common stock would have grown to $487 by January 31, 1997, versus $383 for a similar investment in a market basket of S&P 500 common stocks. The 17.2% CAGR for Wal-Mart exceeded the growth rate for the S&P 500 by 2.8 percentage points.

When we look at the increase in Wal-Mart's book value, we see that $100 of book value increased to $997 over the same time period, a 25.9% CAGR. If the market was correcting for an overvaluation during the mid-1990s, it would appear that the market is in the process of correcting for a current undervaluation compared to the increase in book value.

In closing out this introduction to the market valuation process, we would just like to draw the reader's attention to the fact that the time horizons for looking at actual past performance and expected future performance affect the way we "see" a company. In looking to the future, which past performance record is more representative of Wal-Mart's future performance—the ten-year performance record, or the five-year performance record? Do you think Wal-Mart's common stock is overvalued or undervalued?

Figure 9.6 Wal-Mart S&P 500, Total Return, and Book Value Cumulative Total Return, $100 Investment, January 31, 1987–1997

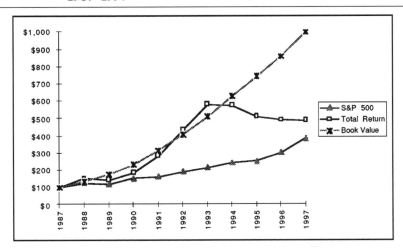

Year	S&P 500	Total Return	Book Value
1987	$100	$100	$100
1988	$125	$153	$133
1989	$120	$143	$177
1990	$151	$184	$233
1991	$162	$282	$313
1992	$188	$437	$405
1993	$214	$579	$508
1994	$239	$572	$624
1995	$251	$509	$739
1996	$302	$489	$859
1997	$383	$487	$997
CAGR	14.4%	17.2%	25.9%

Source: Value Line Investment Survey and Economic Report of the President of the United States.

Our goal in this chapter has been to start the process of linking market information to the firm's overall business strategy. In the first part of this chapter, we added some information about the market value of Wal-Mart's common stock to the summary version of the SPM. In keeping with the management philosophy underlying the DuPont executive charting system discussed in Chapter 1, we tried to develop a basic understanding about the market's perception of Wal-Mart's financial performance.

In the second part of the chapter, we looked at Wal-Mart within the context of the broader capital marketplace. After defining the P/E ratio and the M/B ratio, we discussed how the market evaluated Wal-Mart's performance in terms of these two ratios. Given a basic understanding of this market terminology, we compared Wal-Mart's common stock performance to a market basket of other firms as represented by the S&P 500.

As we saw in Chapters 7 and 8 on the SFM, management relied on a combination of internal equity financing and external debt financing to grow the business between 1987 and 1997.

In Chapter 10, we begin the process of seeing how the market establishes a price for a firm's long-term debt. The discussion in Chapter 10 will then serve as the foundation for the discussion in Chapter 11, where we look at how the market values establish a price for a firm's common stock. In Chapter 12, we will then add what we have learned about the market valuation process to create a version of the SPM that integrates market- and management-based measures of financial performance into a single management system.

NOTES

1. A firm's total return or the total return related to a stock index is based on the appreciation in the market value of the firm's common stock and dividend declarations. For the purpose of the total return calculation, any dividends declared are assumed to be reinvested in the firm's common stock.

CHAPTER 10

Market Valuation: Long-Term Debt

The markets for debt and equity securities are like the markets for producer and consumer products. It all boils down to prices and quantities. How much would we be willing to pay for a new computer, a new software package, or an exclusive contract with Michael Jordan to advertise our firm's consumer products? How much would we be willing to pay lenders for the right to borrow $100 million for the next 15 years? How much would we be willing to pay for 100 shares of Wal-Mart's common stock? How much money would we be willing to invest in U.S. treasury bonds or in a mutual fund specializing in growth firms in Southeast Asia?

The old adage "buy low and sell high" reflects everyone's dream of making a good return on their investment. Customers want to pay the lowest price for the products they buy. At the same time, suppliers want to receive the highest price possible for the products they sell. A market transaction takes place when buyers and sellers agree on the price to be paid for the quantity of product to be exchanged. In the case of debt and equity securities of publicly traded companies, all we have to do is look in the business section of most daily newspapers and we can see the price investors actually paid for these securities the previous day.

In this chapter and Chapter 11, we are going to take a closer look at how the market establishes the price that investors pay for the privilege of owning the debt and equity securities of a particular firm—in our case, Wal-Mart. We will be looking at Wal-Mart from the perspective of a long-term creditor. As we shall see, the dynamics of the capital marketplace are based, in general terms, on two factors: (1) the logic of *risk and return* and (2) *growth*.

The greater the perceived risk associated with a particular investment, the greater the expected return. Firms that grow the business (through sales), grow earnings (net income), and grow cash flow to shareholders (through dividends) typically trade at higher prices than firms in the same industry that are not growing as fast.

We will begin our discussion of the market valuation process by looking at the issues associated with risk and return and then take a closer look at the issues associated with growth.

DEBT AND EQUITY SECURITIES

Firms like Wal-Mart "buy" money on the capital markets to finance the growth of the business that cannot be financed from internal sources (internal equity financing). Management can buy money to finance the future of the firm by issuing long-term debt or common stock.[1] In the case of long-term debt, creditors lend money to the firm in exchange for the borrower's promise to pay interest and repay principal in the future. In the case of common stock, shareholders invest money in the firm in exchange for management's promise to be held accountable for the future success of the firm.

Debt Financing: Management borrows money from lenders in exchange for its promise to pay interest and repay principal at some time in the future.

Equity Financing: Management raises money from shareholders in exchange for its promise to be held accountable for the future success of the firm.

As we shall see in the remainder of this chapter, lenders "sell" money today in exchange for the right to receive money (a stream of cash flows) in the future. In Chapter 11, we will see that shareholders also sell money today in exchange for the right to receive money (a stream of cash flows) in the future. In the case of long-term debt, the stream of cash flows is more certain (and therefore less risky) than the stream of cash flows associated with common stock (which is therefore more risky).

Question: When we think about lending our money to someone, which potential borrower do you think is most likely to make the interest payments and repay the principal on that loan?

Answer: The U.S. government.

Before taking a closer look at how the market values the long-term debt of firms like Wal-Mart, it is helpful to see how the market values the long-term debt of the U.S. government. As we shall see, a very strong relationship exists between the interest rates associated with U.S. government debt (treasury bonds) and the market price of a firm's debt and equity securities. The interest on U.S. government securities represent the "risk-free" return on investment that investors use to determine what they would be willing to pay for more risky investments like corporate debt and equity securities.

In general, as interest rates on risk-free government bonds go up, investors demand higher returns on corporate debt and equity securities. And like any other products that are bought and sold at the market, prices vary with conditions and circumstances. When it comes to government securities, the price of U.S. treasury bonds varies with the general rate of inflation. As the rate of inflation goes up, the interest rate investors expect to receive on U.S. treasury bonds goes up. As the rate of inflation goes down, the interest rate investors expect to receive on U.S. treasury bonds goes down.

Figure 10.1 presents the general relationship between annual inflation rates in the U.S. economy and the interest rates on ten-year U.S. treasury bonds between 1987 and 1997. As we can see, the interest rates on U.S. treasury bonds were higher than the rate of inflation for each of these ten years.

Economists typically refer to the difference between interest rates and inflation rates as the *real* interest rate. For the year ended December 31, 1987, the real interest rate was 4.74% (8.39% interest rate minus the 3.65% inflation rate). For the year ended December 31, 1996, the real interest rate was 3.49% (6.44% interest rate minus the 2.95% inflation rate). Over the entire ten-year period, the average annual real interest rate was 3.77% (7.43% average interest rate minus the 3.66% average inflation rate).

Figure 10.1 U.S. Economy Inflation Rates and Interest Rates[1] (for the Calendar Years Ended December 31, 1987–1996)

Year Ended	Inflation Rates	Interest Rates
1987	3.65%	8.39%
1988	4.14%	8.85%
1989	4.82%	8.49%
1990	5.40%	8.55%
1991	4.21%	7.86%
1992	3.01%	7.01%
1993	2.99%	5.87%
1994	2.56%	6.27%
1995	2.83%	6.57%
1996	2.95%	6.44%
Average	3.66%	7.43%

[1]Interest rates on ten-year U.S. treasury bonds. Inflation rates based on changes in the consumer price index.

Source: Economic Report of the President of the United States.

Given this relationship between inflation rates and interest rates, it is not difficult to see why analysts and investors anxiously anticipate the quarterly announcements of changes in the consumer price index (CPI). An increase in the CPI is likely to trigger a demand for higher interest rates on U.S. treasury bonds in order to maintain the same real interest rate. Since U.S. treasury bonds are supposed to be risk-free investments, with the effective interest rate tied to inflation, it should not be too hard to imagine the ripple effect on the interest rates of the more risky corporate debt.

Figure 10.2 presents the relationships among ten-year U.S. treasury bonds and Moody's Aaa- and Baa-rated corporate bonds. Corporate bonds receiving Moody's Aaa rating represent the highest quality long-term corporate bonds or notes payable on the market. They are only slightly more risky than investing in U.S. treasury bonds. Bonds rated Baa are considered investment-grade bonds and are slightly more risky than Aaa-rated bonds or notes and therefore carry a higher interest rate.

As we might expect, lower-rated bonds or notes carry higher interest rates to offset the higher perceived risk. As we can see from Figures 10.1 and 10.2, the average interest rate on U.S. treasury bonds was 7.43% between 1986 and 1996. The average interest rate on Aaa-rated corporate bonds was 8.47% and the average interest rate on Baa-rated bonds was 9.35%. In terms of the language of risk and return, investors earned, on average, a risk premium of 1.04% on Aaa-rated corporate bonds over the U.S. treasury bonds. Investors earned, on average, another risk premium of 0.88% by investing in Baa-rated corporate bonds versus Aaa-rated corporate bonds.

In addition to the market information about the interest rates associated with corporate debt carrying different risk assessments, Moody's and Standard and Poor's rate the individual debt issues of publicly traded companies. For example, Moody's gives Wal-Mart's long-term debt an Aa rating and Standard and Poor's gives Wal-Mart's long-term debt an AA rating. Both rating agencies consider Wal-Mart's debt to be high quality. According to the Moody's and Standard and Poor's rating definitions, firms with Aa- and AA-rated debt have a very strong capacity to pay interest and repay principal. Aa- and AA-rated debt differ only slightly from Aaa- and AAA-rated debt, the highest ratings assigned by both rating agencies.

Figure 10.3 presents selected information about Wal-Mart's long-term debt as of January 31, 1997.[2] The principal or face amount of the debt is preceded by the fiscal year when the debt was issued and the year in which the principal is to be repaid. The stated interest rate represents the percentage of the principal that will be paid out in interest on an annual basis. Using the 9.10% long-term debt issued in 1991 as an example, Wal-Mart would make annual payments to lenders of $45,500,000.

Figure 10.2   Interest Rates on U.S. Treasury Bonds and Corporate Bonds[1] (for the Years Ended December 31, 1987–1996)

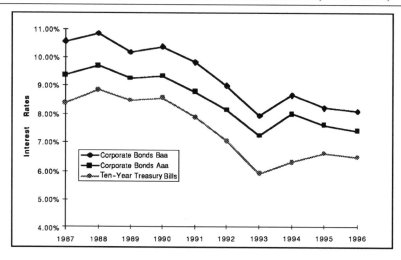

Year	Ten-Year Treasury Bills	Corporate Bonds Aaa	Corporate Bonds Baa
1987	8.39%	9.38%	10.58%
1988	8.85%	9.71%	10.83%
1989	8.49%	9.26%	10.18%
1990	8.55%	9.32%	10.36%
1991	7.86%	8.77%	9.80%
1992	7.01%	8.14%	8.98%
1993	5.87%	7.22%	7.93%
1994	6.27%	7.97%	8.63%
1995	6.57%	7.59%	8.20%
1996	6.44%	7.37%	8.05%
Average	7.43%	8.47%	9.35%

[1]Ten-year treasury bonds and Moody's Aaa and Baa rated bonds.
Source: Economic Report of the President of the United States.

Interest Payment = Principal × Stated Interest Rate

$45,500,000 = $500,000,000 × 9.10%

Figure 10.3 Wal-Mart Long-Term Debt as of January 31, 1997

Year Issued	Year Due	Principal Amount (in Millions)	Stated Interest Rate		Market Interest Rates					
				1990	1991	1992	1993	1994	1995	1996
1986	2000	$100	10.88%	9.28%	9.17%	7.55%	8.11%	8.44%	9.81%	Retired
1991	2000	$500	9.10%		8.69%	7.25%	7.31%	6.03%	8.30%	6.42%
1992	2001	$750	8.63%			7.29%	7.33%	5.98%	8.23%	6.50%
1992	1996	$250	8.00%			6.39%	5.94%	4.84%	7.39%	Retired
1993	1997	$500	5.50%				6.37%	5.42%	8.00%	Retired
1993	1999	$500	6.13%				6.97%	5.68%	8.19%	6.37%
1994	2023	$250	6.75%					7.14%	8.49%	7.33%
1994	1998	$500	5.50%					5.57%	8.09%	5.94%
1994	2003	$500	6.50%					6.18%	8.23%	6.64%
1994	2013	$500	7.25%					6.97%	8.47%	7.17%
1994	2005	$750	5.88%						8.32%	6.85%
1994	2003	$250	6.38%						8.27%	6.65%
1995	2004	$500	7.50%						8.27%	6.76%
1995	2006	$250	8.00%						8.32%	6.87%
1995	2024	$250	8.50%						8.67%	7.71%
1996	2002	$300	6.75%							6.61%
1994	1998	$250	EB* 5.13%							
1995	1999	$250	EB 8.75%							
1996	1998	$250	EB 7.00%							
1996	2000	$250	EB 6.13%							
1996	2002	$200	EB 6.75%							

*EB = Eurobonds.

The interest payments associated with the other long-term debt would be computed in a similar fashion. The principal amount of the debt and the stated rate of interest determine the annual (or monthly or quarterly) payments to be made to lenders.

Knowing the principal amount and the stated rate of interest, we can compute the contractual interest payment to be made. However, we cannot determine how much lenders are willing to pay in order to receive a 9.10% stated rate of interest and a principal payment of $500 million in the year 2000. In order to take this next step, we need to know the market rate of interest associated with the firm's long-term debt.

The market rates of interest associated with each of Wal-Mart's long-term debt issues are shown in the columns to the right of the stated rate of interest as of January 31, 1990 through 1996. For the $500 million of 9.10% long-term debt issued in 1991, the market rate of interest has fluctuated between a high of 8.69% in 1991 and a low of 6.42% in 1996.

Given the relationship between inflation and interest rates on U.S. treasury bonds (Figure 10.1) and the relationship between U.S. treasury bonds and corporate bonds (Figure 10.2), the fluctuations in the market rates of interest for Wal-Mart's long-term debt make perfect sense. Even though the stated rate of interest and principal amounts remain the same, the market rate of interest varies with changes in the overall economy.

If we think of borrowing money in exchange terms, firms like Wal-Mart "sell" a stream of cash flows to lenders who pay a lump sum of money today to "buy" the right to receive this stream of cash flows in the future. The market interest rate on the day the bonds or notes payable are issued determines the amount of money the lender and borrower will give and receive in exchange.

MARKET VALUATION OF LONG-TERM DEBT

We will illustrate how the market valuation process works with respect to external debt financing using the $500 million of 9.10% long-term debt issued by Wal-Mart in 1991. For the initial example, we will assume that the market rate of interest equaled the stated rate of interest when Wal-Mart borrowed the money.[3]

Figure 10.4 presents the stream of cash flows that Wal-Mart sold to lenders at the beginning of 1991 (shown as of the fiscal year ended January 31, 1990). As we can see, Wal-Mart agreed to pay lenders $955 million over a ten-year period in exchange for the $500 million needed to finance that part of the long-term investment plan not financed from internal sources in 1991 (see Chapter 8 for the discussion of internal equity and external debt financing).

Determining the specific amount of money to be received by Wal-Mart and paid by the lenders is the responsibility of financial professionals working at Wal-Mart and the lending institutions. However, from a management perspective, all we need to understand is the logic of the time value of money underlying the market valuation process.

TIME VALUE OF MONEY

The essence of the market valuation process involves reducing a stream of future cash flows down to a single dollar equivalence amount that

Figure 10.4 **Wal-Mart Schedule of Cash Flows, $500 Million, 9.10%**
Long-Term Debt (Amounts in Millions)

Year Ended January 31	Principal Payment	Interest Payments	Total Cash Flow
1990		$0.0	$0.0
1991		$45.5	$45.5
1992		$45.5	$45.5
1993		$45.5	$45.5
1994		$45.5	$45.5
1995		$45.5	$45.5
1996		$45.5	$45.5
1997		$45.5	$45.5
1998		$45.5	$45.5
1999		$45.5	$45.5
2000	$500.0	$45.5	$545.5
Totals	$500.0	$455.0	$955.0

equates what borrowers will receive to what lenders will pay to make the deal happen. Both borrowers and lenders factor the time value of money into any decision to buy and sell money.

When we are concerned with the present value of a stream of future cash flows, we use present value analysis techniques. When we are concerned with the future value of a stream of future cash flows, we use future value analysis techniques.

The present value of $1 to be received in the future will be less than $1 today.

The future value of $1 received today will be more than $1 in the future.

We use the market rate of interest to determine both present values and future values. In a sense, present values and future values are two sides of the same time value of money coin. If the market rate of interest is 9.10%, the present value and future value of $1 for one year are calculated as follows:

Present Value of $1 = $1 ÷ (1 + Interest Rate)

$.9166 = $1 ÷ (1 + 9.10%)

Future Value of $1 = $1 × (1 + Interest Rate)

$1.091 = $1 × (1 + 9.10%)

One dollar to be received one year from now is worth $.9166 today at 9.10% interest. Today's one dollar will be worth $1.0910 at the end of the year at 9.10% interest. All that the present value and future value analysis techniques do is apply the logic of the time value of money over a longer time horizon—ten years in this example.

Since Wal-Mart is committed to paying out the stream of cash flows shown in Figure 10.4, we need to identify a present value factor and a future value factor to associate with the cash flowing from Wal-Mart to lenders each year. Figure 10.5 presents the present value and future value factors needed to determine how much Wal-Mart will receive and lenders will pay for the $955 million stream of cash that will be flowing from 1991 through the year 2000.

Under the market interest rates column, we have shown the 9.10% interest rate for each of the ten years associated with this long-term debt issue. Once we go beyond a simple example of the market valuation process, the market interest rate can be allowed to vary on a yearly (or monthly or daily) basis.

The single-period present value factors are shown to the left of the market interest rates. The future value factors are shown to the right. At 9.10% interest, the present value of $1 equals $.917 and the future value $1.091 (rounded to the nearest three decimal places). The factors do not change from year to year because the interest rate does not change.

To the left of present value factors, we find the cumulative present value factors. To the right of the future value factors, we find the cumulative future value factors. As we can see, the cumulative present value factor associated with $1 to be received at the end of the year 2000 is 41.9¢. The cumulative future value of $1 is $2.389.

Figure 10.5 Time Value of Money: Present Value and Future Value Factors, 9.10% Market Interest Rates

Year Ended January 31	Cumulative Present Value Factors	Present Value Factor 1 + (1 + i)	Market Interest Rates (i)	Future Value Factor 1* (1 + i)	Cumulative Future Value Factors
1990	1.000	1.000	0.000%	1.000	1.000
1991	0.917	0.917	9.100%	1.091	1.091
1992	0.840	0.917	9.100%	1.091	1.190
1993	0.770	0.917	9.100%	1.091	1.299
1994	0.706	0.917	9.100%	1.091	1.417
1995	0.647	0.917	9.100%	1.091	1.546
1996	0.593	0.917	9.100%	1.091	1.686
1997	0.544	0.917	9.100%	1.091	1.840
1998	0.498	0.917	9.100%	1.091	2.007
1999	0.457	0.917	9.100%	1.091	2.190
2000	0.419	0.917	9.100%	1.091	2.389

Heads: The present value of $1 to be received at the fiscal year ended January 31, 2000, is 41.9¢.

Tails: The future value for $1 to be received at the fiscal year ended January 31, 2000, is $2.389.

The arrows connecting the present value factor column to the cumulative present values factor column show how each year's cumulative present value is determined.

The present value of $1 to be received at the fiscal year ended January 31, 1995, is 64.7¢.

64.7¢ = 1.000 × $.917 × $.917 × $.917 × $.917 × $.917

The arrows connecting the future value factor column to the cumulative future value factors column show how each year's cumulative future value is determined.

The future value of $1 to be received at the fiscal year ended January 31, 1995, is $1.546.

$1.546 = 1.000 × $1.091 × $1.091 × $1.091 × $1.091 × $1.091

Based on our experiences working in executive development programs, we know that managers appreciate a step-by-step buildup of the market valuation process. Even before we make any changes to this long-term debt example, managers can see that the cumulative present value and future value factors depend on the interest rates inserted into the market interest rates column of Figure 10.5.

LONG-TERM DEBT: MIND YOUR Ps AND Qs

The old adage "mind your Ps and Qs" refers to the advice tavern owners gave to the barmaids (and barmen?) in merry old England. Ps and Qs referred to pints and quarts of beer. If we do not know how many pints and quarts were sold, we will not know how much to charge the customers. In today's global markets, we would give managers the same type of advice. Mind your Ps (interest rates) and Qs (interest and principal payments).

When we combine the Ps from Figure 10.5 with the Qs from Figure 10.4, we can determine the present values and the future values of the entire stream of cash flows, as shown in Figure 10.6. The total stream of cash flows that Wal-Mart has agreed to pay in interest and principal is shown in the middle column of Figure 10.6. The amounts shown in the cumulative present value column equal the cash flow for the year times the cumulative present value factor for that year. For example, for 1995:

$29.4M = 0.647 × $45.5M

Figure 10.6 **Wal-Mart Present Values and Future Values, $500**
Million, 9.10% Long-Term Debt (Amounts in Millions)

Year Ended January 31	Cumulative Present Value	Cumulative Present Value Factors	Total Cash Flow	Cumulative Future Value Factors	Cumulative Future Value
1990	$0.0	1.000	$0	2.389	$0.0
1991	$41.7	0.917	$45.5	2.190	$99.6
1992	$38.2	0.840	$45.5	2.007	$91.3
1993	$35.0	0.770	$45.5	1.840	$83.7
1994	$32.1	0.706	$45.5	1.686	$76.7
1995	$29.4	0.647	$45.5	1.546	$70.3
1996	$27.0	0.593	$45.5	1.417	$64.5
1997	$24.7	0.544	$45.5	1.299	$59.1
1998	$22.7	0.498	$45.5	1.190	$54.2
1999	$20.8	0.457	$45.5	1.091	$49.6
2000	$228.3	0.419	$545.5	1.000	$545.5
Totals	$500.0		$955.0		$1,194.6

The total cumulative present value equals $500,000.

The amounts shown in the cumulative future value column equal the cash flow for the year times the cumulative future value factor for that year. For example, for 1995:

$$\$70.3M = 1.546 \times \$45.5M$$

As we can see, the total present value of the $955.5 million in total cash flow equals $500 million that Wal-Mart borrowed on January 31, 1990. The total future value equals $1.1946 billion. In other words, lenders would be willing to pay $500 million to Wal-Mart for the right to receive the $955 million stream of actual cash flows shown above. Over the course of the full ten-year period, the $955 million stream of cash flows would have accumulated to a total future value of $1.1946 billion by the year 2000 at 9.10% interest.

Figure 10.7 presents the same information with one small difference. The initial $500 million that Wal-Mart received from lenders is shown as a negative amount. By adding the $500 million to the total cash flow column, we see that the totals for the cumulative present value column (the net present value) and cumulative future value column (net future value) equal $0.

Question: What does it mean when the net present value and net future values equal $0?

Answer: You got what you paid for.

In today's highly sophisticated capital markets, we do not typically see how the logic of the time value affects what creditors will lend and borrowers will receive on any given day. However, even though managers cannot see the logic of the time value of money at work, it is always there.

Figure 10.7 Wal-Mart Net Present Values and Net Future Values, $500 Million, 9.10% Long-Term Debt (Amounts in Millions)

Year Ended January 31	Cumulative Present Value	Cumulative Present Value Factors	Total Cash Flow	Cumulative Future Value Factors	Cumulative Future Value
1990	($500.0)	$1.0	($500.0)	$2.4	($1,194.6)
1991	$41.7	0.917	$45.5	2.190	$99.6
1992	$38.2	9.840	$45.5	2.007	$91.3
1993	$35.0	0.770	$45.5	1.840	$83.7
1994	$32.1	0.706	$45.5	1.686	$76.7
1995	$29.4	0.647	$45.5	1.546	$70.3
1996	$27.0	0.593	$45.5	1.417	$64.5
1997	$24.7	0.544	$45.5	1.299	$59.1
1998	$22.7	0.498	$45.5	1.190	$54.2
1999	$20.8	0.457	$45.5	1.091	$49.6
2000	$228.3	0.419	$545.5	1.000	$545.5
Totals	$0.0		$455.0		$0.0

FAST FORWARD SIX YEARS

Assume that it is January 31, 1996, and all of Wal-Mart's original lenders need cash. Furthermore, Wal-Mart has no desire to retire the debt until the year 2000.

> **Question: What are these lenders to do?**
>
> **Answer: Sell the rights to receive the remaining cash flows to someone interested in earning the current market rate of interest.**

Refer to Figure 10.3, and you can see that Wal-Mart's $500 million of 9.10% long-term debt had a market interest rate of 6.42% as of January 31, 1996. If the original lenders want to sell their rights to receive the remaining cash flows from Wal-Mart, they must use the 6.42% market interest rate to determine how much cash they will receive from the new holders of Wal-Mart's debt.

Figure 10.8 presents the schedule of cash flows remaining to be paid by Wal-Mart to January 31, 2000. Figure 10.9 presents the present and future value factors associated with a 6.42% interest rate. As we can see from these figures, the logic of the time value of money establishes what the current group of lenders will receive from the new group of lenders who want to hold Wal-Mart's long-term debt.

As we can see, the cumulative present value of $1 to be received at the end of four years is 78.4¢ at a 6.42% market rate of interest. The cumu-

Figure 10.8   Wal-Mart Schedule of Remaining Cash Flows, $500 Million, 9.1% Long-Term Debt (Amounts in Millions)

Year Ended January 31	Principal Payment	Interest Payments	Total Cash Flow
1997		$45.5	$46
1998		$45.5	$46
1999		$45.5	$46
2000	$500.0	$45.5	$546
Totals	$500.0	$182.0	$682.0

Figure 10.9 **Time Value of Money—Present Value and Future Value Factors, 6.42% Market Interest Rates**

Year Ended January 31	Cumulative Present Value Factors	Present Value Factor 1 ÷ (1 + i)	Market Interest Rates (i)	Future Value Factor 1* (1 + i)	Cumulative Future Value Factors
1996	1.000	1.000	0.00%	1.000	1.000
1997	0.940	0.940	6.42%	1.064	1.064
1998	0.883	0.940	6.42%	1.064	1.133
1999	0.830	0.940	6.42%	1.064	1.205
2000	0.780	0.940	6.42%	1.064	1.283

lative future value of $1 is $1.283. At a lower rate of interest (6.42% versus 9.10%), the present value of $1 decreases at a slower rate and the future value of $1 increases at slower rate.

Figure 10.10 presents the net present values and net future values associated with the rights to receive the remaining cash flows. At a 6.42%

Figure 10.10 **Wal-Mart Net Present Values and Net Future Values, $500 Million, 9.10% Long-Term Debt, 6.42% Market Interest Rate (Amounts in Millions)**

Year Ended January 31	Cumulative Present Value	Cumulative Present Value Factors	Total Cash Flow	Cumulative Future Value Factors	Cumulative Future Value
1996	$0.0	1.000	$0.0	1.000	$0.0
1997	$42.8	0.940	$45.5	1.064	$48.4
1998	$40.2	0.883	$45.5	1.133	$51.5
1999	$37.8	0.830	$45.5	1.190	$54.2
2000	$425.3	0.780	$545.5	1.091	$595.1
Totals	$546.0		$682.0		$749.2

Question: What does not change in this analysis?

Answer: The logic of the time value of money analysis.

Figure 10.11 Wal-Mart Market Valuation Process, $100 Million, 10.875% Long-Term Debt, 9.100% Market Interest Rate (Amounts in Millions)

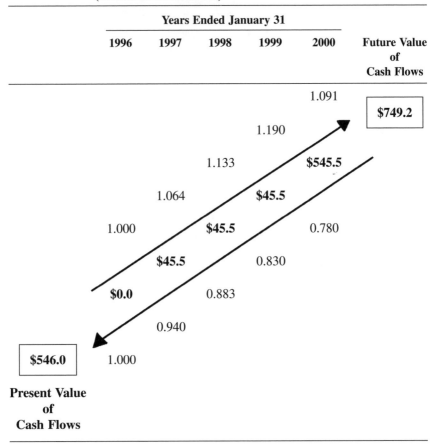

	Years Ended January 31					Future Value of Cash Flows
	1996	1997	1998	1999	2000	
					1.091	$749.2
				1.190		
			1.133		$545.5	
		1.064		$45.5		
	1.000		$45.5		0.780	
		$45.5		0.830		
$0.0			0.883			
		0.940				
$546.0	1.000					

Present Value of Cash Flows

market interest rate, lenders should expect to receive $749.2 million in exchange for their interests in Wal-Mart's long-term debt.

When we use examples of Wal-Mart's long-term debt to introduce the time value of money concepts into the market valuation process, we have to be careful not to get caught up in the finer points of debt financing. We want managers to develop a feel for the role that the time value of money plays in valuing debt securities so that we can move on to valuing equity securities — that is, common stock. All of the concepts introduced in this chapter are a means to that end.

Figure 10.11 presents a more visual representation of the market valuation process that we use to help managers see the time value of money at work.

When we look at how the market valuation process is applied to common stock in Chapter 11, the logic of the time value of money will not change. We will still use the same concepts to determine present values and future values. The main difference will revolve around how we incorporate risk into the calculation of present values and future values.

A second difference will involve the determination of the stream of future cash flows to be included in the valuation process. Cash flows associated with equity securities (common stock) involve more than the multiplication of a stated rate of interest by a known principal amount.

NOTES

1. For this introduction to the market valuation process, we will not deal with preferred stock issues, convertible debt, or more complex debt and equity securities. In today's global financial markets, the number of ways of packaging deals to buy and sell money is virtually unlimited. The term *financial instruments* is used to focus attention on the similarities and differences among the various financial products on the market today. A detailed discussion of the different types of financial instruments is beyond the scope of this book.

2. Market rates of interest obtained from the monthly S&P Bond Guide. No current market rates are reported for Eurobonds.

3. Since the market rate of interest on Aaa bonds was 11.37% for 1986, Wal-Mart's market rate of interest was probably around 12.00%.

CHAPTER 11

Market Valuation: Common Stock

In concluding our discussion of how the market values a firm's long-term debt, we indicated that the logic of the time value of money remains the same when the market values the firm's common stock. In the case of long-term debt, when we know the timing of the principal and interest payments over the life of the loan, we can create a stream of future cash flows and discount those cash flows back to the present to determine the net present value. That net present value then represents the amount of money the lender would be willing to pay to the borrower.

When the market values a firm's common stock, several aspects of the valuation process become more problematic. The three most significant differences between debt and equity valuation are:

1. There is no market rate of interest associated with common stock like there is with long-term debt. For common stock, financial analysts and investors use the term *cost of equity capital* to refer to the shareholders' expectations for a return on their investment in common stock.

2. Dividend payments are not the same as interest payments. Management is not obligated to pay a fixed dividend on a regular basis. Firms frequently change the amount and timing of their dividend payments. Some high-growth firms pay no dividends at all and reinvest all of their earnings into the business. Sometimes when a firm is facing financial difficulties, management suspends the dividend payments until the firm returns to profitability.

3. When a firm issues common stock, the stock remains outstanding forever. There is no date when the principal comes due and management is required to repurchase the outstanding shares of common stock. Aside from any dividends the firm may pay to its shareholders, the only other way shareholders can get additional cash from their investment is to sell their shares of stock to another investor or back to the company.

Given these differences between long-term debt and common stock, it is not surprising that investors consider common stock to be a riskier investment than long-term debt, and in exchange for assuming a greater risk, shareholders require a greater return on their investment.

Even though there is more uncertainty surrounding the returns associated with common stock, investors have reaped their rewards in the form of dividends and stock price appreciation over the years. Investments in common stock have consistently outperformed investments in corporate debt and U.S. treasury bonds.

In this chapter, we will see how financial analysts and investors go about the business of placing a value on a firm's common stock. We begin by describing the cost of equity capital and relating the cost of equity capital to the risk-free return on U.S. treasury bonds.

COST OF EQUITY CAPITAL

As discussed in Chapter 10, the cost of corporate debt is higher than the cost of U.S. treasury bonds. Since the U.S. government is less likely to go out of business than U.S. corporations, the government incurs a lower cost of debt (lower market interest rate) than corporations when it borrows money. In a similar fashion, the cost of equity capital is higher than the cost of corporate debt. In exchange for a promise of contractual interest and principal payments, investors expect a lower return on corporate debt than the return they expect when they buy the firm's common stock. When firms are successful, the higher risk associated with common stock is offset by the higher rewards (dividends and stock price appreciation).

Most managers understand the concept of the cost of equity capital at an intuitive level. If investing in common stock is more risky than investing in a firm's long-term debt, why shouldn't investors demand a higher return? An intuitive understanding of the cost of equity capital is typically sufficient until two specific events occur:

Managers, especially senior managers, are held accountable for increasing shareholder value (dividends plus stock price appreciation).

and

A significant portion of the managers' total compensation is tied to achieving the shareholder value target.

Suddenly, managers need to know the facts. Managers need to go beyond intuition and deal with concrete reality. The cost of debt is concrete. The cost of equity capital is somewhat less concrete.

Although individuals may differ in their personal risk preferences, a generally accepted procedure for calculating a firm's cost of equity capital does exist. The cost of equity capital is made up of three components:

1. The risk-free return associated with U.S. treasury bonds
2. A general market risk premium associated with any common stock investment
3. A risk premium associated with a specific common stock relative to the overall stock market

In working with managers to help them understand the business, we have found that it is much easier to understand the cost of equity capital concept if we can see how all of the components fit together for a particular firm.

Figure 11.1 presents the cost of equity capital for the overall economy and Wal-Mart for the ten-year period January 31, 1988, through January 31, 1997. As mentioned above, we build the cost of equity capital for the economy and a particular firm on a foundation of the risk-free return associated with ten-year U.S. treasury bonds (T bonds).

Figure 11.1   Overall Economy, Cost of Equity Capital Calculations (1988–1997)

Year Ended December 31	Ten-Year T Bonds[1]	Market Risk Premium	Cost of Equity Capital (CofC)
1988	8.39%	2.70%	11.09%
1989	8.85%	2.70%	11.55%
1990	8.49%	2.70%	11.19%
1991	8.55%	2.70%	11.25%
1992	7.86%	2.70%	10.56%
1993	7.01%	2.70%	9.71%
1994	5.87%	2.70%	8.57%
1995	6.27%	2.70%	8.97%
1996	6.57%	2.70%	9.27%
1997	6.44%	2.70%	9.14%
Average	7.43%	2.70%	10.13%

Source: Economic Report of the President for 1997.

OVERALL ECONOMY

The cost of equity capital for the overall economy equals the risk-free interest rate on U.S. treasury bonds plus a market risk premium for investing in common stock.

Ten-Year Treasury Bonds.   The risk-free interest rate on ten-year treasury bonds provides the foundation for estimating a firm's cost of equity capital. We have followed the common practice of using the ten-year treasury bond rate. However, the same type of cost of equity calculations can be made using rates associated with 3-, 5-, and 30-year treasury bonds. As discussed more fully in Chapter 10, the market interest rate on U.S. treasury bonds rises and falls with changes in the inflation rate.

Market Risk Premium.   The column for the market risk premium represents the historical returns earned by equity investors over and above the rate of return on ten-year treasury bonds. The estimate of 2.70% represents the additional return investors in the S&P 500 earned over treasury bonds for the period 1962 through 1988.[1]

For example, in 1988, investors in a market basket of S&P 500 common stocks were probably expecting a return of 11.09% on their investment. In 1997, those expectations had decreased to a 9.14% on their investment.

Expected Return: U.S. T Bond Rate + the Market Risk Premium

1988: 11.09% = 8.39% + 2.70%

1997: 9.14% = 6.44% + 2.70%

Like the market rate of interest on U.S. treasury bonds and long-term corporate debt, the cost of equity capital for the overall economy fluctuates from year to year in response to changes in the inflation rate.

While the overall cost of equity capital for the economy gives us a better feel for the relationship between U.S. treasury bonds and the risks associated with the stock market, we are still one step removed from understanding the cost of equity capital for a specific firm like Wal-Mart. To determine a firm's cost of equity capital, we must consider how risky the market considers a particular firm to be relative to the overall economy. In the next section, we will see how Wal-Mart's cost of equity capital differed from the overall economy.

WAL-MART'S COST OF EQUITY CAPITAL

Wal-Mart's cost of equity capital equals the cost of equity capital for the overall economy plus a risk premium (expressed as a relationship to the overall economy) for investing in this specific firm.

Beta (β). Beta (β) is a statistical measure of the volatility of the market rates of return on a particular common stock relative to the average rate of return of the market taken as a whole. Stocks with high Betas (greater than 1.00) are more volatile than the market taken as a whole. Stocks with low Betas (less than 1.00) are less volatile than the market taken as a whole. If the overall market is moving upward (a bull market), a firm with a high Beta is likely to provide higher returns to investors than a firm with a low Beta. However, if the overall market is moving downward (a bear market), a firm with a high Beta is more likely to experience a greater decline in value than a firm with a low Beta.

For Wal-Mart or any other publicly traded firm, the firm-specific cost of equity capital is calculated in the following manner:

$$\text{Firm-Specific Cost of Equity Capital} = \text{Risk-Free Interest Rate} + \left(\text{Beta} \times \text{Market Risk Premium} \right)$$

Figure 11.2 presents all of the information needed to make the cost of equity capital calculations for Wal-Mart. The overall market cost of equity capital is presented on the right-hand side of the figure for comparison purposes. As we can see from this figure, Wal-Mart's Beta has not remained constant over time. Between 1988 and 1996, Wal-Mart's common stock was more volatile than the market taken as a whole. However, in 1997, Wal-Mart's Beta fell to 1.00, indicating that Wal-Mart's common

Figure 11.2 Wal-Mart Cost of Equity Capital Calculations (1988–1997)

Year Ended December 31	Ten-Year T Bonds[1]	Beta (β)[2]	Market Risk Premium	Wal-Mart Cost of Equity Capital	Market Cost of Equity Capital
1988	8.39%	1.25	2.70%	11.77%	11.09%
1989	8.85%	1.25	2.70%	12.23%	11.55%
1990	8.49%	1.25	2.70%	11.87%	11.19%
1991	8.55%	1.25	2.70%	11.93%	11.25%
1992	7.86%	1.25	2.70%	11.24%	10.56%
1993	7.01%	1.30	2.70%	10.52%	9.71%
1994	5.87%	1.30	2.70%	9.38%	8.57%
1995	6.27%	1.25	2.70%	9.65%	8.97%
1996	6.57%	1.10	2.70%	9.54%	9.27%
1997	6.44%	1.00	2.70%	9.14%	9.14%
Average	7.43%	1.22	2.70%	10.72%	10.13%

[1]*Source:* Economic Report of the President for 1997.
[2]*Source:* Annual Value Line Investment Surveys.

stock was increasing and decreasing along with the overall market. Between 1988 and 1995, investors expected the return on their investment in Wal-Mart's common stock to increase at a faster rate than the market as a whole.

The calculation of any firm's specific risk premium equals Beta multiplied by the overall market risk premium. Wal-Mart's risk premium for 1988 and 1997 are calculated as shown below:

Wal-Mart's Risk Premium = Beta (β) × Market Risk Premium

1988: 3.38% = 1.25 × 2.70%

1997: 2.70% = 1.00 × 2.70%

As we can see, Beta reflects the fact that the specific risk associated with a particular firm becomes less volatile as the market price of the stock increases and decreases with fluctuations in the overall market.[2]

Cost of Equity Capital. A firm's cost of equity capital represents the combination of the cost of equity capital for the overall economy plus a firm-specific risk premium. The formula for determining the cost of equity capital is:

$$\text{Cost of Equity Capital} = \text{Risk-Free Interest Rate on U.S. Treasury Bills} + \left(\text{Beta} \times \text{Market Risk Premium} \right)$$

Wal-Mart's cost of equity capital for 1988, 1997, and the average for the ten-year period is:

1988: 11.77% = 8.39% + (1.25 × 2.70%)

1997: 9.14% = 6.44% + (1.00 × 2.70%)

Average: 10.72% = 7.43% + (1.22 × 2.70%)

Based on our experiences working with management groups, working through the calculation of a firm's cost of equity capital appears to be a necessary evil. However, once managers know how the cost of equity capital is calculated, their intuitive understanding of risk and return is strengthened. All that remains to be done is to show how a firm's cost of equity capital relates to the broader economy.

Figure 11.3 presents the cost of equity capital for the overall economy and for Wal-Mart compared to the inflation rate and the interest rate on ten-year treasury bonds.

As we can see from Figure 11.2, the cost of equity capital for the economy taken as a whole and a particular firm rises and falls with changes in the inflation rate and interest rates on U.S. treasury bonds. As we can also see, in 1996 and 1987 Wal-Mart's firm-specific risk premium disappeared. As the world's largest retailer, Wal-Mart represents a significant part of the U.S. economy. Wal-Mart is not the same high-risk company that went public back in 1970.

STREAM OF EQUITY CASH FLOWS

Once we calculate the cost of equity capital for any firm, we have jumped over our first hurdle. The cost of equity capital for common stock will be used to determine the present value factors and future value factors we will need to compute the net present value and net future value of a stream of equity cash flows.

As discussed in Chapter 10, the stream of cash flows associated with a firm's long-term debt equals the interest and principal payments specified in the debt agreement. Given the amount and timing of the interest and principal payments, the stream of cash flows can be discounted back to the present or accumulated into the future at the market rate of interest.

The equivalent stream of cash flows associated with a firm's common stock equals the periodic dividend payments plus an estimate of the terminal or residual value of the stock that investors might receive if they sold their shares in the future. The terminal value plays the same role in the valuation of a firm's common stock as the final principal payment played in the valuation of a firm's long-term debt.

Figure 11.3   Wal-Mart Inflation Rates, Interest Rates, and the Cost of Equity Capital (1988–1997)

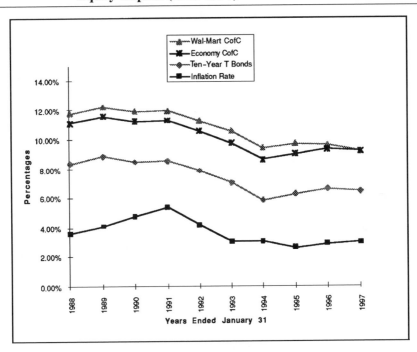

Year Ended December 31	Inflation Rate	Ten-Year T Bonds	Economy CofC	Wal-Mart CofC
1988	3.65%	8.39%	11.09%	11.77%
1989	4.14%	8.85%	11.55%	12.23%
1990	4.82%	8.49%	11.19%	11.87%
1991	5.40%	8.55%	11.25%	11.93%
1992	4.21%	7.86%	10.56%	11.24%
1993	3.01%	7.01%	9.71%	10.52%
1994	2.99%	5.87%	8.57%	9.38%
1995	2.56%	6.27%	8.97%	9.65%
1996	2.83%	6.57%	9.27%	9.54%
1997	2.95%	6.44%	9.14%	9.14%
Average	3.66%	7.43%	10.13%	10.72%

Figure 11.4 presents the information about Wal-Mart's common stock (on a per-100-share basis) that we will use to illustrate the mechanics of

the market valuation process.[3] For this illustration, we will be using 20/20 hindsight. We will go back to January 31, 1987, to see what investors might have been willing to pay for 100 shares of Wal-Mart's common stock. Of course, our perfect knowledge of all of the economic events that occurred between 1987 and 1997 was pure speculation at the beginning of this ten-year period.

At the end of fiscal 1988, Wal-Mart was earning 28¢ per share, paying 3¢ in dividends, and retaining the other 25¢ to grow the business. When we multiply the per-share data by 100 shares, we get the information presented in Figure 11.4.

Over this ten-year period, Wal-Mart earned a total of $798 on 100 shares of common stock, paid $110 in dividends, and retained $688 to grow the business. Given these facts (which would have been predictions back at the beginning of 1988), the question becomes one of using this information to put a value on Wal-Mart's common stock. How do we incorporate this earnings and dividends information into our time value of money calculations to estimate the present and future values of 100 shares of Wal-Mart's common stock?

Figure 11.4   Wal-Mart Earnings, Dividends, and Retained Earnings, 1988–1997 (per 100 Shares)

Year Ended January 31	Earnings	Dividends	Retained Earnings
1988	$28	$3	$25
1989	$37	$4	$33
1990	$48	$6	$42
1991	$57	$7	$50
1992	$70	$9	$61
1993	$87	$10	$77
1994	$102	$13	$89
1995	$117	$17	$100
1996	$119	$20	$99
1997	$133	$21	$112
Totals	$798	$110	$688

Source: Annual Value Line Investment Surveys.

As discussed in Chapter 1, net income equals net earned assets. The net assets *earned* by management on behalf of the shareholders can either be paid to shareholders in the form of dividends or reinvested in the business. When management declares and pays dividends, the shareholders must decide what to do with the money they receive. When management *retains* all or part of those earnings, they decide what to do with the money they retain.

From the investors' perspective, the only good reason for retaining or reinvesting all or part of the earnings is for management to grow the business and earn even more money on the shareholders' behalf. If management had no idea of how to grow the business and make more money on the shareholders' behalf, they might consider paying 100% of the earnings out in dividends. Theoretically, the firm that decided to pay out 100% of earnings in dividends would remain at its current size forever into the future.

If at the end of 1997, Wal-Mart decided to pay 100% of earnings to shareholders in the form of dividends, the holder of 100 shares of common stock would receive $133 in cash each year forever. Since charges like depreciation are included in the determination of net income, we can assume that management would use the money equal to the depreciation charges to replace productive assets as they wore out and to carry on other basic maintenance activities. Theoretically speaking and based on this set of assumptions, Wal-Mart would continue to generate $133 in earnings to be paid out in dividends every year from now until eternity.

As strange as paying out 100% of earnings in dividends may sound, this type of thinking is actually used to construct a stream of equity cash flows to be used in valuing a firm's common stock. As we shall see, financial analysts and investors typically make an assumption about when a firm will stop growing or start growing at a slower rate in the future. In the year the assumption of no growth is put into play, 100% of all future earnings are assumed to be paid out in dividends.

In Figure 11.5, we have converted information contained in Figure 11.4 into a stream of dividend payments to shareholders for 1988 through 1997 and a single terminal or residual value for the end of 1997. This is the information we will use to see how much we might have been willing to pay for 100 shares of Wal-Mart's common stock back at the beginning of 1988. We will also look to see how much that initial investment was expected to grow over the next ten years, assuming that investors were using Wal-mart's 10.72% average cost of equity capital in the valuation process (see Figures 11.1, 11.2, and 11.3).

Figure 11.5   Wal-Mart Earnings, Dividends, and Retained Earnings, 1988–1997 (per 100 Shares)

Year Ended January 31	Dividends	Terminal Value	Total Cash Flow
1988	$3		$3
1989	$4		$4
1990	$6		$6
1991	$7		$7
1992	$9		$9
1993	$10		$10
1994	$13		$13
1995	$17		$17
1996	$20		$20
1997	$21	$1,240	$1,261
Totals	$110	$1,240	$1,350

Dividends.   If we had owned 100 shares of Wal-Mart's common stock since the beginning of 1988, we would have received a total of $110 in dividends over ten years. As we can see from Figure 11.5, Wal-Mart increased the amount of dividends paid to shareholders each year, but dividend payments still only represented 13.8% of earnings over the entire ten-year period—82.2% of those earnings were retained to grow the business.

Terminal Value.   The terminal value shown for 1997 is calculated by dividing the earnings for 1997 by the cost of equity capital investors expected to earn on their investment over the ten-year period. As shown in Figure 11.2, Wal-Mart's average cost of equity capital equaled 10.72%.

▶

Terminal Value = Net Income ÷ Cost of Equity Capital

$1,240 = $133 ÷ 10.72%

◀

Now that we know how the terminal value was calculated, we can begin to talk about what it means and how it fits into the market valuation process.

As mentioned at the beginning of the chapter, the terminal value or residual value is equivalent to the principal payment that the lender receives at the end of the loan period. In exchange for the final payment, the loan is canceled and the borrower's obligation to the lender terminated.

In this case, the terminal value represents the amount of money the shareholders would expect to receive in exchange for their 100 shares of common stock at the end of 1997. Since they wanted to earned a 10.72% return on their investment, they would have had to receive $1,240.

The terminal value represents an estimate of what 100 shares of Wal-Mart's stock would be worth if the company earned $133 in net income every year and paid 100% of those earnings out in dividends.

Terminal Value × Cost of Equity Capital = Net Income
$1,240 × 10.72% = $133

The $1,240 represents the amount an investor would be willing to pay to receive $133 per year from now until eternity. Whether financial analysts and investors follow this particular approach or some similar approach, the objective of the market valuation process is the same: to seek out stocks that will allow investors to earn their cost of equity capital and exceed their cost of equity capital when management performs at a higher level of performance than originally expected.

With a cost of equity capital in hand and a schedule of equity cash flows prepared, the time value of money analysis can now be applied to the valuation of common stock following the same procedures we used to calculate the price of long-term debt in Chapter 10.

PRESENT VALUES AND FUTURE VALUES

Figure 11.6 presents the present value and future value factors we need to determine how much investors might have been willing to pay for 100 shares of Wal-Mart's common stock at the beginning of 1988 at a 10.72% cost of equity capital. As we can see from the figure, the present value of

$1 to be received in 1997 was 36.1¢ as of January 31, 1987. The future value of $1 invested on January 31, 1987, would have accumulated to $2.77 as of January 31, 1997. If management earned the investors' expected cost of equity capital, the $1 would have yielded a total return over the full ten-year period of 10.72¢.

When we combine the present value and future value factors from Figure 11.6 with the schedule of total cash flows from Figure 11.5, we can determine the present values and the future values of the entire stream of cash flows, as shown in Figure 11.7.

Figure 11.8 presents the same information with one important difference: The total cumulative present value of $503 shown at the bottom of the cumulative present value column in Figure 11.7 is shown as a negative amount (−$503) for 1987 in Figure 11.8.

As we can see from Figure 11.8, the total cumulative present value and total cumulative future value amounts equal $0 when we insert the $503

Figure 11.6 Time Value of Money, Present Value and Future Value Factors, 10.72% Cost of Equity Capital

Year Ended January 31	Cumulative Present Value Factors	Present Value Factor $1 \div (1 + i)$	Market Interest Rates (i)	Future Value Factor $1 * (1 + i)$	Cumulative Future Value Factors
1987	1.000	1.000	0.000%	1.000	1.000
1988	0.903	0.903	10.72%	1.107	1.107
1989	0.816	0.903	10.72%	1.107	1.226
1990	0.737	0.903	10.72%	1.107	1.357
1991	0.665	0.903	10.72%	1.107	1.503
1992	0.601	0.903	10.72%	1.107	1.664
1993	0.543	0.903	10.72%	1.107	1.842
1994	0.490	0.903	10.72%	1.107	2.040
1995	0.443	0.903	10.72%	1.107	2.258
1996	0.400	0.903	10.72%	1.107	2.501
1997	0.361	0.903	10.72%	1.107	2.769

Figure 11.7 Wal-Mart Net Present Values and Net Future Values, 10.72% Cost of Equity Capital (per 100 Shares)

Year Ended January 31	Cumulative Present Value	Cumulative Present Value Factors	Total Cash Flow	Cumulative Future Value Factors	Cumulative Future Value
1987	$0	1.000		▲ 2.769	$0
1988	$3	0.903	$3	2.501	$8
1989	$3	0.816	$4	2.258	$9
1990	$4	0.737	$6	2.040	$12
1991	$5	0.665	$7	1.842	$13
1992	$5	0.601	$9	1.664	$15
1993	$5	0.543	$10	1.503	$15
1994	$6	0.490	$13	1.357	$18
1995	$8	0.443	$17	1.226	$21
1996	$8	0.400	$20	1.107	$22
1997	$456	▼ 0.361	$1,261	1.000	$1,261
Totals	$503		$1,350		$1,394

as a negative amount for 1987. We can see that an investment of $503 in 100 shares of common stock might have generated future cash flows of $1,350 for a net cash flow of $847. This total stream of equity cash flows would have earned an investor the 10.72% cost of equity capital.

In order to make the discussion of the market valuation process relevant to managers, we expressed all of the calculations in terms of 100 shares of common stock. For most managers, buying or selling 100 shares of common stock is easy to visualize.

REALITY CHECK

A quick reality check on whether our valuation process makes any sense is to compare our results to the actual market price of Wal-Mart's common stock for fiscal 1987, the year before the cash flows associated with 100 shares of common stock would have started flowing to us.

Figure 11.8   Wal-Mart Present Values and Future Values, 100 shares of Common Stock at a 10.72% Cost of Equity Capital (per 100 Shares)

Year Ended January 31	Cumulative Present Value	Cumulative Present Value Factors	Total Cash Flow	Cumulative Future Value Factors	Cumulative Future Value
1987	($503)	1.000	($503)	▲ 2.769	($1,394)
1988	$3	0.903	$3	2.501	$8
1989	$3	0.816	$4	2.258	$9
1990	$4	0.737	$6	2.040	$12
1991	$5	0.665	$7	1.842	$13
1992	$5	0.601	$9	1.664	$15
1993	$5	0.543	$10	1.503	$15
1994	$6	0.490	$13	1.357	$18
1995	$8	0.443	$17	1.226	$21
1996	$8	0.400	$20	1.107	$22
1997	$456	▼ 0.361	$1,261	1.000	$1,261
Totals	($0)		$847		$0

▶━━━━━━━━━━━━━━━━━━━━━━━━━━━━━━━━━

Question: If we bought our hypothetical 100 shares of Wal-Mart's common stock on January 31, 1987, for $5.03 per share ($503 ÷ 100 shares), would the $5.03 have been even close to the actual market price for Wal-Mart's common stock?

Answer: Yes, it would have been in the ballpark.

For the fiscal year ended January 31, 1987, Wal-Mart's common stock traded between a low of $3.60 per share and a high of $6.70 per share. The average share price of $5.15 is within 12¢ of our $5.03 estimate.

━━━━━━━━━━━━━━━━━━━━━━━━━━━━━━━━━◀

Given the range of values that any firm's common stock trades at during any given year, it is not hard to see that investors differ to some degree in their assessments of a firm's expected future performance, their personal time horizons, and their estimation of cost of equity capital.

The market valuation process, as we have just described it, may not be perfect, but it does give managers a good understanding of what investors value: earnings and dividends.

In Chapter 12, we are going to revisit the Strategic Profit Model to integrate what we have just learned about the market valuation process with our understanding of the firm's financial performance, as reported in the financial statements.

NOTES

1. Ibbotson Associates, 1989.
2. Investment advisory services typically report a firm's Beta along with all of the other financial information they provide to their subscribers. The *Value Line Investment Survey* reports Beta for over 1,700 companies. These Betas are recalculated each time a new investment report is prepared for a company.
3. In order to make the discussion of the market valuation process relevant to managers, we will express all of the calculations in terms of 100 shares of common stock. For most managers, buying or selling 100 shares of common stock is easy to visualize.

CHAPTER 12

Market Valuation: The Strategic Profit Model Revisited

In Part One of this book, we discussed how managers can use the information found in the financial statements to better understand the business. In the first three chapters of Part Two (Chapters 9–11), we outlined the fundamentals of how the market values debt and equity securities. Given the market interest rates on long-term debt and estimating the shareholders' cost of equity capital, the basic logic and mechanics of the market valuation process were relatively straightforward.

The only trouble with looking at the firm from a market perspective is that managers find it difficult to translate the results of the market valuation process into their day-to-day responsibilities. That is where the Strategic Profit Model (SPM) comes back into the picture.

If we add information about the total market value of the firm's common stock and the cost of equity capital to the SPM, we can go a long way toward integrating market and management measures of performance into a single, integrated management communications framework.

In Chapter 1, we used the concept of return on equity (ROE) to integrate margin management, asset management, and financial management concepts into an overall management communications framework. In the initial development of the SPM, we did not include any market measures of financial performance.

In this chapter, we will show how the SPM may be extended to integrate market measures of performance with the financial measures of management performance. In Chapter 1, we saw that the market price of a firm's common stock is based, in part, on expectations of future earnings and cash flows. In this chapter, we shall see that the market price is also related, in part, to past performance of the firm as captured by the ROE. Although achieving a high (and sustainable) ROE while growing the business does not guarantee a high market valuation for the firm, the common stock of firms with consistently high ROEs typically trade at higher prices than firms with consistently lower ROEs.

We will begin the process of linking the market valuation process to management performance through the concept of "equity spread." We will examine Wal-Mart's performance from 1987 through 1997 through the concept of equity spread and see how the firm's equity spread can be integrated into the SPM. Once this is completed, managers can see how their performance and the performance of the entire firm fits into a broader market framework.

MANAGEMENT PERFORMANCE AND MARKET PERFORMANCE

By linking management's performance to the market's assessment of that performance, we will see the tension that almost always exists between managers, financial analysts, and investors. On the one hand, management must pay attention to the needs of customers, employees or associates, suppliers, and other creditors. On the other hand, management must be concerned about meeting the shareholders' expectations for a return on investment. Sam Walton highlights the tension that every CEO of a publicly traded company confronts:

> What really worried me over the years is not our stock price, but that we might someday fail to take care of our customers, or that our managers might fail to motivate and take care of our associates.

As business leaders, we absolutely cannot afford to get all caught up in trying to meet the goals that some retail analyst or financial institution in New York sets for us on a ten-year plan spit out of a computer that somebody set to compound at such-and-such a rate. If we do that, we take our eye off the ball. But if we demonstrate in our sales and our earnings every day, every week, every quarter, that we are doing our job in a sound way, we will get the growth we are entitled, and the market will respect us in a way we deserve.

If we fail to live up to somebody's hypothetical projection for what we should be doing, I don't care. It may knock our stock back a little, but we're in it for the long run. We couldn't care less about what is forecast or what the market says we ought to do. If we listened very seriously to that sort of stuff, we never would have gone into small-town discounting in the first place.[1]

Rather than taking sides (with CEOs like Sam Walton or some group of financial analysts or investors), we are going to use the concept of equity spread to illustrate this tension between management and the market.

CONCEPT OF EQUITY SPREAD

As discussed in Chapter 11, the firm's cost of equity capital is used to discount a stream of equity cash flows to estimate the market value of a firm's common stock. Based on this assessment of value, investors have two basic choices:

1. Buy: If they think that the current value of the firm is greater than the current market price.
2. Sell: If they think that the current value of the firm is less than the current market price.

In Chapter 11, we used the wisdom that comes from having 20/20 hindsight to value Wal-Mart's common stock. After creating a stream of equity cash flows and using Wal-Mart's average cost of equity capital (CofC) between 1987 and 1997, we estimated the value of 100 shares of common stock. As we saw, the value of $5.03 per share was very close to the average share price of $5.15 for the fiscal year ended January 31, 1987. In helping managers understand the business through financial information, we saw that a firm's cost of equity capital is a key measure of market performance.

When we link the market to management through the SPM, the cost of equity capital comes into play through the concept of equity spread. If a firm's ROE is greater than its CofC, management is said to be generating a positive equity spread. If the CofC is below the firm's ROE, management is generating a negative equity spread. As discussed in Chapter 11, the firm's CofC captures investor expectations by incorporating the effects of inflation, risk-free interest rates on U.S. treasury bonds, and market risk premiums into a single performance measure.

Since CofC is a measure of the market's expectations about a particular firm and since ROE is a measure of the firm's actual performance, there must be some way of combining these two measures into a single, more comprehensive performance measure. That is where the concept of equity spread demonstrates its value.

A firm's equity spread is defined in the following manner:

$$\text{Equity Spread} = \text{ROE} - \text{CofC}$$

Figure 12.1 presents Wal-Mart's equity spread for the years 1987 through 1997. As we can see from this figure, Wal-Mart generated a positive equity spread in each of these eleven years.

For every $1 of shareholders' equity, Wal-Mart generated 23.5¢ in profit in the years 1987 through 1997. 10.8¢ of that profit equaled Wal-Mart's cost of equity capital while the remaining 12.7¢ represented the equity spread over and above the cost of equity capital.

The equity spread concept is a useful addition to the ROE concept for two reasons. First, the equity spread calculation starts with ROE. As discussed in Part One of this book, the concept of ROE allows managers to see how profit margins, asset turnovers, returns on assets, and financial

Figure 12.1   Wal-Mart Equity Spreads (for the Years Ended January 31, 1987–1997)

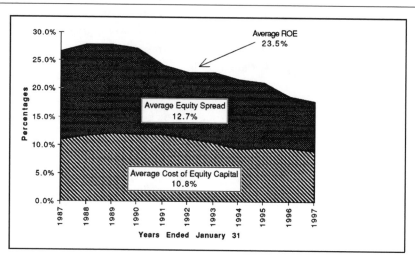

Year Ended January 31	Return on Equity	Cost of Capital	Equity Spread
1987	26.6%	11.1%	15.5%
1988	27.8%	11.8%	16.0%
1989	27.8%	12.2%	15.6%
1990	27.1%	11.9%	15.2%
1991	24.1%	11.9%	12.2%
1992	23.0%	11.2%	11.8%
1993	22.8%	10.5%	12.3%
1994	21.7%	9.4%	12.3%
1995	21.1%	9.6%	11.5%
1996	18.6%	9.5%	9.1%
1997	17.8%	9.1%	8.7%
Average	23.5%	10.8%	12.7%

leverage all come together through the SPM. Second, within an equity spread framework, management can see how well it is doing compared to the shareholders' cost of equity capital.

In developing a comprehensive business strategy, management has to balance the tension between the shareholders' expectations for a return on their investment and the firm's ability to meet those expectations. Although Wal-Mart exceeded the cost of equity capital in each of the ten years in our sample, the size of the spread declined over that period. Wal-Mart generated a 15.5% equity spread in 1987 but yielded only an 8.7% equity spread in 1997.

If the cost of equity capital had remained the same over the years 1987 through 1997 (11.1% in 1987), Wal-Mart's equity spread would have only been 6.7% in 1997. If management had been able to maintain the 26.6% ROE it was generating in 1987 while the cost of equity capital was falling, management would have generated a 17.5% equity spread in 1997. Over these years, Wal-Mart, like all other publicly traded firms, benefited from the effects of lower inflation rates and lower interest rates. As the data in Figure 12.1 suggest, if management had been able to stop or slow the decline in ROE that started to occur in 1991, Wal-Mart would have been able to reap the benefits of the substantial decline in the cost of equity capital that began in 1992.

From a management perspective, the firm's equity spread is made of one component that management can influence directly through its own actions (ROE) and a second component (the firm's CofC) that it can only influence indirectly. Management has no direct control over the inflation rate, the interest rate on U.S. treasury bonds, or how the market price of the firm's common stock fluctuates compared to the overall economy. However, management does have direct control over the firm's business, as measured by ROE. As mentioned above, that is where the SPM becomes useful.

EXPANDED SUMMARY VERSION OF THE SPM

Figure 12.2 presents an expanded summary version of Wal-Mart's SPM that allows us to look at the business all the way from a customer perspective (net sales) to an investor's perspective (equity spread). In terms of this figure, management's job is to ensure that all of the bases are covered. Every component of the model is being managed or influenced to benefit the major stakeholders in the business—customers, employees, suppliers, creditors, and shareholders.

Within the context provided by Figure 12.2, we can see that the addition of Wal-Mart's cost of equity capital and equity spread represents a convenient and systematic way of bringing the market and investors into a comprehensive strategy framework.

195

Figure 12.2   Wal-Mart Strategic Profit Model, Expanded Summary Version (for the Fiscal Years Ended January 31, 1987 and 1997 — Amounts in Millions)

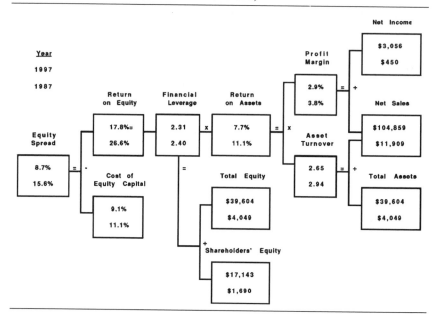

As we can see from Figure 12.2, management grew the business from $11.9 billion in net sales in 1987 to $104.9 billion in 1997. However, this growth has come at a cost to the shareholders.

In 1987, Wal-Mart earned 26.6¢ for every $1 of shareholders' equity and generated an equity spread of 15.6¢ on behalf of the shareholders.

In 1997, Wal-Mart earned 17.8¢ for every $1 of shareholders' equity and generated an equity spread of 8.7¢.

Given that throughout this book we have used the Wal-Mart example to demonstrate how to understand the business through financial informa tion, what aspects of the business would you focus on to reverse the decline in Wal-Mart's financial performance?

By adding market information to the SPM, managers can see how investors look at their firm relative to the stock of other publicly traded firms. Adding this market information accomplishes two objectives:

- Managers can see that they do not have to become financial analysts in order to understand what they have to do to create value for their shareholders. If management can increase the firm's ROE, they will have done everything under their control to increase the equity spread. The cost of equity capital is beyond their control.
- Once everyone on the management team sees the importance of growing the business and maintaining or improving the firm's ROE, managers can get back to the basics—improving margins and increasing asset turnover.

After using the financial information about Wal-Mart to help managers understand the business through financial information, we have come full circle. At this point, readers must decide where to go from here. One choice is to decide to learn more about the technical aspects of financial statement analysis and the market valuation process. The other choice is to go back to Chapter 1 and start the process all over again, only this time with your own company, a competitor, a supplier, or a potential investment opportunity.

Wal-Mart represents an example of how the models we have presented throughout this book may be used to understand any business through the use of financial information. The models presented in this book can be used to analyze any company. For publicly held companies, the information needed to complete the models is readily available to the general public.

Based on our experiences working with management groups, we know that the concepts underlying the SPM truly come to life when all of the members of a management team learn to speak the same language and use the SPM to help improve the financial performance of their firm.

NOTES

1. Sam Walton and John Huey, *Sam Walton, Made in America, My Story* (New York: Doubleday, 1992), 107–108.

Case Studies

Appendices/Introduction

As mentioned in the introduction, this book is about helping managers tell a story about the financial performance of their firm. In order to tell a convincing story, managers need to have some idea of what users of financial information consider to be important performance indicators. Managers also need to know how their decisions and actions can affect the financial performance of the firm as captured by these performance indicators.

In Chapters 1 through 12, we used Wal-Mart's financial statements to introduce two business strategy models that managers can use to help them make sense of the financial information found in those financial statements. The purpose of the case studies is to provide readers with additional examples of how the principles of financial statement analysis presented in this book may be applied to other high-profile companies.

The *Strategic Profit Model* (SPM) shows how all of the elements found in a firm's balance sheets and income statements are integrated together through the concept of return on shareholders' equity (ROE). We begin the analysis of any firm by starting with ROE and then breaking it down into its components parts:

- Profit Margin
- Asset Turnover
- Return on Assets
- Financial Leverage

The *Strategic Financing Model* (SFM) shows how all of the elements found in a firm's restructured balance sheets and financial flow statements allow us to understand the firm from a long-term investment and financing perspective. Given a basic understanding of this long-term perspective, we can then use the model to show how the firm's long-term financing and investment strategy is driven, in part, by the amount of internal equity financing generated by management. Generally speaking, a firm has access to three sources of long-term financing:

- External Debt Financing (Creditors)
- External Equity Financing (Shareholders)
- Internal Equity Financing (Management)

As we saw in the discussion of Wal-Mart's financial performance, these two business strategy models, along with market information about a firm's stock price, provide a powerful framework for understanding the business through financial information. Once managers have a basic understanding of how to look at financial statements and market information from a business strategy perspective, practice makes perfect: By applying the principles of financial statement analysis to a few other well-known firms, managers develop their ability to analyze other companies, particularly their own firms.

In recent years, we have used the financial statements of Microsoft, Coca-Cola, and Caterpillar, among other U.S. companies, to help managers begin the process of understanding the business through financial information. Since virtually every manager has some working knowledge of the products and services provided by these high-profile companies, we can usually jump right into the financial statement analysis without having to provide much background information about these firms. In telling a story about Microsoft, Coca-Cola, and Caterpillar, we will focus on what we believe to be the most significant aspects of each firm's business strategy, as revealed through the two business strategy models.

Microsoft.   Microsoft is the world's leading independent maker of computer software. Based on the market value of its common stock, Microsoft was ranked number five on the *Business Week* global 1,000 in 1997.

For a company that has only been in existence for 21 years, Microsoft is a premier exemplar of a well-managed, high-technology company that has created tremendous wealth for its shareholders. Between 1995 and 1996 alone, revenues increased from $5.94 billion to $8.67 billion, a 46% increase. By looking at Microsoft's financial performance from 1986 through 1996, we can see how CEO Bill Gates balanced risk taking on the technology side of the business with conservative risk management on the financial side of the business.

Coca-Cola. Coca-Cola is the world's largest soft drink company and holds one of the most widely known brand names in the world. Based on the market value of its common stock, Coca-Cola was ranked number two on the *Business Week* global 1,000 in 1997. Throughout its corporate history, Coca-Cola's success has revolved around its ability to convert raw materials into soft drink concentrates that it sells to bottlers.

Coca-Cola's publicly stated mission is to create economic value (dividends plus stock price appreciation) for its shareholders. Under the leadership of its late CEO Roberto Goizueta, Coca-Cola increased profit margins, returns on equity, and the per-share market value of its common stock.

Caterpillar. Caterpillar is the world's largest producer of earth-moving equipment. Based on the market value of its common stock, Caterpillar was ranked number 181 on the *Business Week* global 1,000 in 1997.

In the early 1980s, like many other industrial firms in the United States, Caterpillar was losing market share to its Japanese competitors and incurring financial losses for the first time in its history. Between 1982 and 1984, Caterpillar incurred net losses of $953 million. According to senior executives at Caterpillar, the company was operating at a 30% production cost disadvantage relative to its major Japanese competitor, Komatsu. Everyone at Caterpillar knew that something had to change.

Under the leadership of CEO Don Fites, the company was reorganized into decentralized profit center divisions based on product groups and customer markets. Between 1987 and 1997, Caterpillar solved its cost problem and began once again creating value (dividends plus stock price appreciation) for its shareholders.

With Wal-Mart and the cases of these three high-profile, high-performance companies, we will have applied the business strategy models to firms in four major U.S. industries: retail, computer software, consumer products, and heavy manufacturing. We believe that these examples provide a solid foundation for applying these principles of financial statement analysis to firms in any industry.

CASE STUDY DEVELOPMENT

For each of the case study companies, we will analyze the financial statements and market information about the company in three steps.

1. We will use the quick overview of the SPM to make sense out of financial information found in the firm's balance sheets and income statements. Based on what we find in this quick overview, we will indicate how readers can take a closer look at the most important component or components of the SPM for that firm: the margin-management, asset-management, or financial-management components of the model.

2. We will use the SFM to focus on the long-term investment and financing aspects of each firm's business strategy. As we shall see, the long-term financing and investment strategies differ across our three case study firms.

3. Using market value information about the S&P 500 and each firm's common stock, we will compare each firm's financial performance to the returns generated by the S&P 500.

The financial statement analyses of each case study firm closely parallel the thorough analysis of Wal-Mart that we used throughout the book. In order to keep each case study to a reasonable length, we have concentrated on the insights that can be gained from the summary versions of the SPM and SFM. We have also limited the discussion of the market valuation process to each firm's common stock.

We encourage readers to conduct their own more in-depth analysis of each firm by referring to specific chapters in the text for additional guidance.

Microsoft

Microsoft is the world's leading independent maker of computer software. Even though the company has only been in existence for 21 years, Microsoft is the premier exemplar of a well-managed, high-technology company that has created tremendous wealth for its shareholders. By looking at Microsoft's financial performance from 1986 to 1996, we can see how CEO Bill Gates balanced risk taking on the technology side of the business with conservative risk management on the financial side of the business.

In telling a story about the company, we will draw on the financial information reported in Microsoft's balance sheets and income statements and on market information about the company's common stock. We will focus on the most significant aspects of Microsoft's financial performance, as captured by our business strategy models. As we shall see, all of the parts of Microsoft's financial performance fit together to form a unified whole. It is just that one part, namely margin management, plays a greater role in Microsoft's overall business strategy than the other parts.

INCOME STATEMENTS AND BALANCE SHEETS

As mentioned in Chapter 1, a firm's balance sheets and income statements provide all of the information we will need to prepare a Strategic Profit Model (SPM) and a Strategic Financing Model (SFM) for any firm. In the case of the SFM, we restructure the balance sheets and create financial flow statements before we do the analysis. However, all of the key financial performance indicators that we will use to begin understanding the business are included in the balance sheets and income statements in one form or another.

Balance Sheets

Figure A.1 presents Microsoft's balance sheets for the fiscal years ended June 30, 1986 and 1996. Even before we start the financial statement analysis, we can see from the figure that several aspects of Microsoft's balance sheets are notable because they differ significantly from what we saw on Wal-Mart's balance sheets.

1. The most significant asset on the 1996 balance sheet is cash and equivalents of $6.9 billion. Microsoft has over five times as much money invested in cash and equivalents as it does in net productive assets.

2. Microsoft reports no inventory on its 1996 balance sheet. In fact, the unearned revenues of $560 million reported under current liabilities represent advance payments from customers for Microsoft's products.

3. Microsoft has no long-term debt. Aside from current liabilities, Microsoft reports a minority interest in the company of $125 million and $635 million of other liabilities.

As we shall see, these three observations will affect the way we interpret Microsoft's asset-management and financial-management strategies. For the moment, we can return to the overall comparison of 1986 with 1996 provided by Microsoft's balance sheet equations.

Assets = Liabilities + Shareholders' Equity
1986: $171M = $32M + $139M
1996: $10.093B = $3.185B + $6.098B

In terms of total assets, the Microsoft of 1996 was 59 times larger than it was in 1986.

Figure A.1 Microsoft Balance Sheets (for the Fiscal Years Ended June 30, 1986 and 1996 — Amounts in Millions)

	1986	1996
Assets		
Current Assets		
Cash and Equivalents	$103	$6,940
Receivables	$34	$639
Inventory	$8	$0
Other	$3	$260
Total Current Assets	$148	$7,839
Productive Assets		
Property, Plant, and Equipment	$31	$2,346
Accumulated Depreciation	($11)	($1,020)
Net Productive Assets	$20	$1,326
Other Assets	$3	$928
Total Assets	$171	$10,093
Liabilities and Shareholders' Equity		
Liabilities		
Current Liabilities		
Accounts Payable	$7	$808
Unearned Revenues	$0	$560
Other Current Liabilities	$23	$1,057
Total Current Liabilities	$30	$2,425
Minority Interest and Other Liabilities		
Minority Interest	$0	$125
Other Liabilities	$2	$635
Total MI & Other Liabilities	$2	$760
Total Liabilities & MI	$32	$3,185
Shareholders' Equity		
Common Stock	$51	$2,924
Retained Earnings	$88	$3,984
Total Shareholders' Equity	$139	$6,908
Total Equity	$171	$10,093

Income Statements

Figure A.2 presents Microsoft's statements of income and retained earnings for the fiscal years ended June 30, 1986 and 1996.[1] Microsoft's income statement differs from Wal-Mart's income statements in two ways.

Figure A.2 **Microsoft Statements of Income and Retained Earnings (for the Fiscal Years Ended June 30, 1986 and 1996 — Amounts in Millions)**

	1986	1996
Net Revenues	$198	$8,671
Total Revenue	$198	$8,671
Costs and Expenses		
Cost of Revenues	$41	$1,188
R&D	$21	$1,432
Operating Expenses	$75	$2,973
Other Expenses (Income)	($5)	($301)
Total Costs and Expenses	$132	$5,292
Income before Income Taxes	$66	$3,379
Provision for Income Taxes	$27	$1,184
Net Income	$39	$2,195
Dividends	$0	$0
Adjustments to Retained Earnings		($1,539)
Retained Earnings, Beginning Balance	$49	$3,328
Retained Earnings, Ending Balance	$88	$3,984

1. Since R&D (research and development) represents a significant aspect of Microsoft's business strategy, the income statements disclose the amount of money the company spends on R&D ($21 million in 1986 and $1.432 billion in 1996).

2. In 1996, Microsoft reported an adjustment to retained earnings of $1.539 billion. The great majority of that adjustment ($1.344 billion) was related to the repurchase of common stock.

The expenses associated with R&D will be reflected in the margin-management component of the SPM. The fact that Microsoft charges part of the cost of repurchasing common stock to retained earnings will affect how we interpret senior management's long-term financing and investment strategy.

If Microsoft's balance sheets provide us with snapshots of the company at different points in time, income statements provide us with information about Microsoft's financial performance on behalf of the shareholders in specific years. Microsoft's income statement equations for 1986 and 1996 provide us with basic information on how well management has performed on behalf of the shareholders.

Net Income = Revenue − Expenses (net)

1986: $39M = $198M − $159M

1996: $2.195B = $8.671B − $6.476B

In 1986, Microsoft generated $198 million in revenue and incurred $159 million in expenses. The net income of $39 million represents the increase in net assets (assets − liabilities) *earned* by management on behalf of the shareholders during the year. In 1996, Microsoft generated $8.7 billion in revenue while incurring $6.5 billion in expenses. In 1996, management *earned* $2.2 billion in net assets on behalf of the shareholders. The net income reported for 1996 was 56 times the net income reported in 1986.

Like our comparison of the two balance sheet equations, the comparison of the two income statement equations provides some initial insights into the business. When we add the return on equity (ROE) calculation to the analysis, we can begin to gain additional insights into the business by seeing how the balance sheets and income statements are interrelated. ROE provides the bridge between the firm's balance sheets and income statements.

Return on Equity

Return on shareholders' equity (ROE) links Microsoft's income statements to its balance sheets.

For the fiscal years ended June 30, 1986 and 1996:

$$ROE = Net\ Income \div Shareholders'\ Equity$$

1986:   28.1% = $39M ÷ $139M

1996:   31.8% = $2.195B ÷ $6.098B

Stated in dollars ($) and cents (¢) terms,

In 1986, Microsoft generated 28.1¢ in profit for every $1 of shareholder's equity.

In 1996, Microsoft generated 31.8¢ in profit for every $1 of shareholders' equity.

By increasing ROE from 28.1¢ to 31.8¢, management was able to generate an additional $256 million in net income on shareholders' equity of $6.908 billion.

ROE represents a convenient way of linking the balance sheet to the income statement. It provides the anchor for taking a closer look at Microsoft through the SPM. No matter how deep we delve into the details of Microsoft's financial performance, when we resurface, the ROEs for 1986 and 1996 will have remained the same: 28.1% in 1986 and 31.8% in 1996.

The quick overview of the SPM shows how all of the financial aspects of Microsoft's business strategy fit together in an integrated management framework.

STRATEGIC PROFIT MODEL: QUICK OVERVIEW

Figure A.3 presents the quick overview of Microsoft's SPM for 1986 and 1996 using just four elements taken from Microsoft's income statements and balance sheets: net revenues, net income, total assets, and shareholders' equity. Stated in dollars and cents terms:

> In 1986, Microsoft generated 28.1¢ in profit on every $1 of shareholders' equity; in 1996, Microsoft generated 31.8¢.

In the process of growing the business between 1986 and 1996, Microsoft experienced a 3.7¢ increase in ROE. With the quick overview provided by the SPM, we can now take a more in-depth look at the individual components contributing to Microsoft's ROE in 1986 and 1996 and the 3.7¢ increase over the ten-year period.

As with Wal-Mart, we begin the discussion of the financial aspects of Microsoft's business strategy with the margin-management component of the SPM.

Margin Management

As we can see from Figure A.3, Microsoft's profit margin increased from 19.7% to 25.3%. From a management perspective:

> Microsoft earned 19.7¢ in profit for every $1 of net revenues in 1986; in 1996, Microsoft earned 25.3¢ in profit.

Between 1986 and 1996, Microsoft was able to increase its margins by 5.6¢ on every $1 of net revenues.

> The 5.6¢ increase in profit margin translates into $486 million of net income on net revenues of $8.7 billion.

Figure A.3   Microsoft Strategic Profit Model: Quick Overview (for the Fiscal Years Ended June 30, 1986 and 1996 — Amounts in Millions)

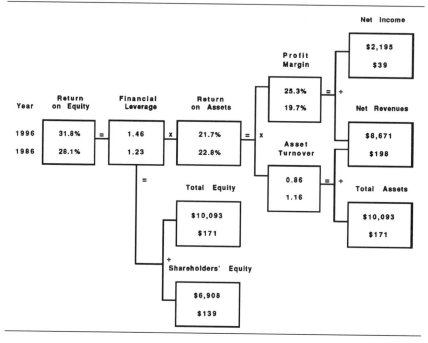

Between 1986 and 1996, net revenues increased at a 45.9% compound annual growth rate (CAGR), net expenses increased by 44.9% per year, and net income increased by 49.6%.

From a financial perspective, the key to Microsoft's success is reflected in the margin-management component of the SPM. Although we need to see how asset management and financial management fit into Microsoft's overall business strategy, the heart of that strategy is reflected in the profit margins.

Asset Management

As we can see from Figure A.3, Microsoft's asset turnover decreased from $1.16 in 1986 to 86¢ in 1996.

In 1986, Microsoft generated $1.16 in net revenue for every $1 of total assets; in 1996, Microsoft generated 86¢ in net revenue.

All things considered, management (and shareholders) would prefer to generate more dollars in net revenues per $1 of assets than less. The greater the asset turnover, the greater the amount of customer financing management has generated with a given amount of assets.

Between 1986 and 1996, total assets increased at a 50.3% CAGR compared to the 45.9% growth rate for net revenues. Any time total assets are increasing at a faster rate that net revenues, asset turnover is going to decrease. However, we must remember that any increase or decrease must be evaluated within the context of the firm's overall business strategy.

In Microsoft's case, the decrease in asset turnover of 30¢ per $1 of assets is somewhat misleading. Included in the $10.1 billion in total assets for 1996 is $6.9 billion in cash and equivalents (see Figure A.1). If cash and equivalents are excluded from the compound growth calculations, total assets increased at a more modest 46.8% CAGR.

With the $6.9 billion in cash and equivalents, Microsoft has enough cash on hand to invest in other high-technology companies or acquire these companies outright without having to borrow money or issue additional common stock. Microsoft could also use some of that cash to reacquire shares of its common stock on the open market.

If Microsoft used $5 billion of its cash on hand to buy back common stock, asset turnover would increase to $1.70, a 54¢ increase over the $1.16 in asset turnover for 1986.

In our work in executive programs, we caution managers to look at concepts like asset turnover on a relative basis within the context of the firm's overall business strategy. Most of the senior executives we know would love to be in Microsoft's position of having a lower asset turnover and more cash.

Return on Assets

As we can see from Figure A.3, Microsoft's return on assets (ROA) decreased from 22.8% in 1986 to 21.7% in 1996.

In 1986, Microsoft earned 22.8¢ in profit for every $1 of total assets; in 1996, Microsoft earned 21.7¢.

However, if Microsoft had used $5 billion of cash to reacquire its outstanding common stock, the company would have been generating 43.1¢ in profit for every $1 of total assets.

By keeping $6.9 billion in its war chest, Microsoft has an extremely strong balance sheet. In terms if financial strength, *Value Line* gives Microsoft an "A++," its strongest rating for financial strength.

As we can see from Figure A.3, Microsoft's key to operating success lies not in asset management, but in its ability to generate increasing profit margins while growing the business. Given Microsoft's overall return on equity of 31.8%, most investors seem to be quite happy in having Bill Gates add to the war chest.

Integrating Margin and Asset Management through ROA

In order to help managers consolidate what they are learning about Microsoft, it helps to return to the SPM song we learned for Wal-Mart.

In 1996:

For every $1 of assets, Microsoft generated 86¢ in net revenues.

For every $1 of net revenues, Microsoft earned 25.3¢ in profit.

Multiplying the profit margin by the asset turnover, for every $1 of assets, Microsoft generated 21.7¢ in profit in 1996.

Compared to 1986, Microsoft grew the business by 1996 while increasing profit margins. At the same time, Microsoft accumulated a war chest of $6.9 billion in cash assets. In 1986, Microsoft maintained 190 days' net revenues in cash and equivalents. By 1996, the number of day's net revenues in cash and equivalents had grown to 292 days. It would appear that Microsoft's biggest asset-management challenge is to find the right investment opportunities that will allow the company to stay on the cutting edge of technology.

Financial Leverage

As we can see from Figure A.3, financial leverage increased from 1.23 in 1986 to 1.43 in 1996.

▶

In 1986, Microsoft utilized $1.23 in total equity for every $1 of shareholders' equity; in 1996, Microsoft utilized $1.46.

◀

Managers in firms in rapidly changing, high-technology industries such as the computer industry, must focus on the business risks associated with the competitive marketplace. They do not want to make their job more difficult by taking on what they believe to be the unnecessary financial risks associated with borrowing money.

As we can see from Figure A.1, Microsoft has no long-term debt. In 1996, aside from its current liabilities, Microsoft had a $125 million responsibility to minority shareholders in joint ventures projects and other liabilities of $635 million. We also noted that $560 million of current liabilities represented advance payments from customers for Microsoft's products.

▶

In 1986, of the 23¢ of financial leverage, 22¢ represented current liabilities; in 1996, 35¢ of the 46¢ represented liabilities.

◀

In telling a financial story about Microsoft from a management perspective, there is no need to dwell on financial leverage. The low level of financial leverage just reinforces Microsoft's "A++" financial strength rating.

Although not a significant part of Microsoft's overall business strategy, the 23¢ increase in financial leverage also has a positive effect on ROE.

Return on Equity: Closing the Loop

As mentioned at the beginning of this case study, the concept of ROE provides us with the opportunity to interrelate all of the financial information included in the balance sheets and income statements into a comprehensive management framework. The SPM is then used to see how all of the parts fit together to form a greater whole. After managers see how all of the parts fit together, they can focus on developing their communication skills. For that part of the learning experience, we return to the SPM song. The 1996 version of Microsoft's SPM song goes something like this:

For every $1 of assets, Microsoft generated 86¢ in net revenues.

For every $1 of net revenues, Microsoft earned 25.3¢ in profit.

Multiplying the profit margin by the asset turnover, we know that for every $1 of assets, Microsoft generated 21.7¢ in profit.

When we multiply ROA by the $1.46 in total assets management controlled for every $1 of shareholders' equity, we see that Microsoft generated 31.8¢ in profit for every $1 of shareholders' equity invested in the business.

In a more in-depth analysis of the financial aspects of Microsoft's business strategy, we would focus our attention on the margin-management component of the SPM. Between 1986 and 1996, Microsoft was able to grow net revenues at a 45.9% CAGR while growing net income at a 49.6% compound annual rate. We would encourage readers to look at the margin-management component of the SPM to see how Microsoft accomplished that feat.

STRATEGIC FINANCING MODEL

As discussed in Chapters 7 and 8, we restructure a firm's balance sheets to focus on the long-term investment and financing aspects of the firm's business strategy. From the restructured balance sheets, we then create a financial flow statement that shows how the long-term investment and financing base has changed over the ten-year period.

Restructuring the Balance Sheets

Figure A.4 presents Microsoft's restructured balance sheets for 1986 and 1996. As we can see, Microsoft's long-term investment is made up of working capital, gross productive assets, and gross other assets. Microsoft's long-term financing base consists of minority interest financing, external equity financing, and internal equity financing.

Several aspects of Microsoft's restructured balance sheets are notable because they differ significantly from what we saw on Wal-Mart's restructured balance sheets.

1. Of the $7.8 billion of current assets in 1996, cash and equivalents accounted for $6.9 billion. Even with $2.4 billion in current liabilities, Microsoft had over $5.4 billion invested in working capital.
2. Microsoft's external equity financing included common stock and $3 billion of common stock that was repurchased and charged against retained earnings. The $3 billion of common stock repurchased and subtracted from the common stock outstanding was added back to retained earnings.
3. Accumulated depreciation and other liabilities were also added back to retained earnings in arriving at internal equity financing.

As we shall see, these three observations will affect the way we interpret how Microsoft financed the business from 1986 to 1996.

The financial-control equations underlying Microsoft's restructured balance sheets for 1986 and 1996 are presented on the next page:

Figure A.4 Microsoft Restructured Balance Sheets (for the Fiscal Years Ended June 30, 1986 and 1996 — Amounts in Millions)

	1986	*Change*	1996
Long-Term Investment			
Current Assets	$148	*$7,691*	$7,839
Current Liabilities	$30	*$2,395*	$2,425
Working Capital	$118	*$5,296*	$5,414
Gross Productive Assets	$31	*$2,315*	$2,346
Gross Other Assets	$3	*$925*	$928
Total Long-Term Investment	$152	*$8,536*	$8,688
Long-Term Financing			
Minority Interest Financing			
Minority Interest	$0	*$125*	$125
Total Minority Interest	$0	*$125*	$125
External Equity Financing			
Common Stock	$51	*$2,873*	$2,924
Common Stock Repurchased	$0	*($2,956)*	($2,956)
Total External Equity	$51	*($83)*	($32)
Internal Equity Financing			
Retained Earnings	$88	*$3,896*	$3,984
Common Stock Repurchased	$0	*$2,956*	$2,956
Accumulated Depreciation	$11	*$1,009*	$1,020
Other Liabilities	$2	*$633*	$635
Total Internal Equity	$101	*$8,494*	$8,595
Total Long-Term Financing	$152	*$8,536*	$8,688

▶

Long-Term Investment = Long-Term Financing

1986: $152M = $152M

1996: $8.688B = $8.688B

◀

The first observation we can make is that Microsoft's long-term financing and investment base in 1996 was 57 times larger than it was back in 1986. From a long-term investment and financing perspective, Microsoft's "A++" financial strength rating is reflected in the fact that it has $5.4 billion invested in working capital and no external debt financing. Whether we look at balance sheets or restructured balance sheets, Microsoft's financial conservatism shines through. The only question that remains to be answered is *how* Microsoft financed the business over this ten-year period. As we saw with Wal-Mart, in order to answer that question, it helps to look at the financial flow statement.

Financial Flow Statement

Figure A.5 presents Microsoft's financial flow statement for the ten-year period ended June 30, 1996. As we can see, the financial flow statement differs from the restructured balance sheets in two ways.

1. The details included in the restructured balance sheets have been omitted from the financial flow statement.
2. The long-term financing activity has been placed above the long-term investment activity. The financial flow statement includes a summary of the net revenues generated by Microsoft from 1986 to 1996.

By focusing on the "change" column of Figure A.5, we can construct the financing-the-business component of the SFM, as presented in Figure A.6.

In keeping with the theme of being financially conservative, the fact that Microsoft only required $42 million in external financing between 1986 and 1996 is somewhat astounding. For every $1 of net revenues, Microsoft has only one-tenth of a cent (0.1¢) of additional external financing.

As we can see from Figure A.6, Microsoft acquired 0.4¢ in minority interest financing from its joint venture partners and it actually reduced its external equity financing by 0.3¢ per $1 of net revenues. Between 1986 and 1996, Microsoft increased common stock by $2.9 billion. During that same period, it has also repurchased $3.0 billion of common stock. The net effect was a 0.3¢ decrease in external equity financing.

219

Figure A.5 Microsoft Financial Flow Statement (for the Ten Years Ended June 30, 1996 — Amounts in Millions)

Long-Term Financing	1986	*Change*	1996
Minority Interest Financing	$0	*$125*	$125
External Equity Financing	$51	*($83)*	($32)
Internal Equity Financing	$101	*$8,494*	$8,595
Total Long-Term Financing	$152	*$8,536*	$8,688

Long-Term Investment	1986	*Change*	1996
Working Capital	$118	*$5,296*	$5,414
Gross Productive Assets	$31	*$2,315*	$2,346
Gross Other Assets	$3	*$925*	$928
Total Long-Term Investment	$152	*$8,536*	$8,688

Year	Net Revenues
1987	$346
1988	$591
1989	$804
1990	$1,183
1991	$1,843
1992	$2,759
1993	$3,753
1994	$4,649
1995	$5,937
1996	$8,671
Ten-Year Total	$30,536

Heart of the Story

Since Microsoft did not go outside to finance the business, all of the financing had to come from internal sources.

Figure A.6   Microsoft Strategic Financing Model: Financing the Business (for the Fiscal Years Ended June 30, 1986 and 1996 — Amounts in Millions)

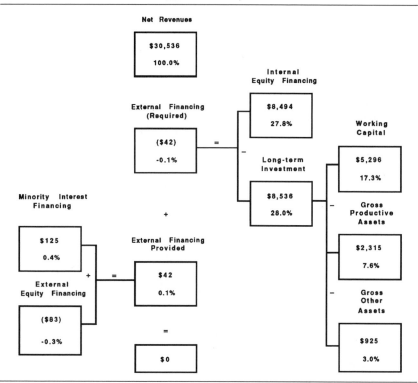

Between 1986 and 1996, management generated $30.536 billion of customer financing (net revenues). Of that amount, $8.494 billion of internal equity financing was made available to grow the business.

The $8.494 billion represented 27.8¢ of every $1 of net revenues.

As we can see from Figure A.6, Microsoft invested its internal equity financing in working capital (17.3¢), gross productive assets (7.6%), and gross other assets (3.0%). And as discussed above, Microsoft had $6.9 billion of cash and equivalents on hand at the end of 1996. That $6.9 billion translates into 22.4¢ of all of the net revenues generated by the company between 1986 and 1996.

Business Strategy Revisited

By using the quick overview from the SPM and the financing-the-business component of the SFM, we have been able to show how management increased Microsoft's ROE while growing the business. By looking at each component of the SPM, we were able to see that the heart of Microsoft's business strategy is captured by the margin-management component of the SPM.

Microsoft increased its profit margin from 19.7% in 1986 to 25.3% in 1996 while increasing net revenues at a 45.6% CAGR. The decrease in asset turnover is somewhat misleading in that Microsoft accumulated a $6.5 billion war chest of cash and equivalents. If Microsoft used $5 billion of that cash to buy back additional shares of common stock, its ROA would be over 40%.

A $5.0 billion repurchase of common stock would reduce shareholder's equity from $6.9 billion to $1.9 billion. The stock repurchase would have the effect of increasing financial leverage from 1.43 to 2.67. Combined with a 40% ROA, it would not be impossible for Microsoft to be generating an ROE of over 100% ($2.195 billion of net income ÷ $1.908 billion of shareholders' equity = 115%).

As it turns out, Microsoft's business strategy is not to generate the highest possible ROE. Microsoft uses the internal equity financing generated from the business to increase its investment in productive and other assets (10.6¢ of net revenues between 1986 and 1996). However, most of the 27.8¢ in internal equity financing went to increasing the investment in working capital. In fact, the $6.9 billion in cash and equivalents on hand in 1996 represents 22.4¢ of the 27.8¢ in internal equity financing between 1986 and 1996.

Given this phenomenal business and financial performance, we are well-positioned to understand how the market has valued Microsoft since 1986.

MARKET VALUATION

Back in 1986, we doubt if any investors could have imagined how a company with net income of $39 million would be generating $2.2 billion in net income by 1996.

Figure A.7 presents the relationship between the market value of Microsoft's common stock and the two management measures of financial performance we use to calculate Microsoft's ROE: net income and shareholders' equity. With the benefit of 20/20 hindsight, we can see that Microsoft's total market value (common shares outstanding times the market price per share) increased at a slightly faster rate than the increases in net income and shareholders' equity.[2]

As we can see from Figure A.7, Microsoft's common stock outstanding only increased at a 2.5% CAGR between 1986 and 1996. A close examination of Microsoft's annual reports shows us that the total increase of 28.0% ($1.176B ÷ $919M) is due primarily to employees exercising their stock options and buying additional shares through employee stock-purchase plans.

Over this ten-year period, the market value of the common stock outstanding increased at a 52.5% CAGR. During this same period, net income increased at a 49.6% compound annual rate and shareholders' equity increased at a 47.8% compound annual rate.

As mentioned in Chapters 9 through 12, financial analysts and shareholders determine the value of the firm's common stock. The price of a firm's common stock is influenced by the recommendations of financial analysts at the major investment firms and what each of us is willing to pay for the firm's common stock. Firms like Microsoft have no direct influence over the market price of their firm's common stock, but they do have an indirect influence through their actions.

From the quick overview of the SPM, we saw that the primary way Microsoft increased ROE was through its margin-management strategy. From the financing-the-business component of the SFM, we saw that Microsoft actually reduced the amount of external equity financing used to run the business between 1986 and 1996. The growth rates for net income (49.6%) and shareholders' equity (47.8%) reflect the combination of these two aspects of Microsoft's overall business strategy.

For the company taken as a whole, Microsoft has been a success in terms of both growth in market value and financial performance. The only question that remains to be answered is how well this performance has

Figure A.7 **Microsoft Market and Management Measures of Performance (for the Years Ended June 30 — Shares and Dollar Amounts in Millions)**

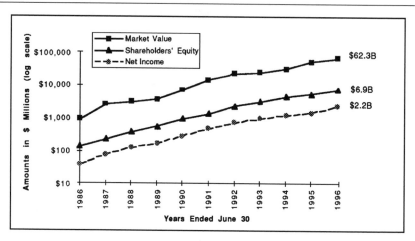

Year Ended June 30	Common Stock Outstanding	Market Value	Net Income	Shareholders' Equity
1986	919	$919	$39	$139
1987	949	$2,704	$78	$239
1988	966	$3,091	$124	$376
1989	983	$3,685	$171	$562
1990	1,023	$7,010	$279	$919
1991	1,045	$14,008	$463	$1,351
1992	1,089	$21,881	$708	$2,193
1993	1,128	$23,744	$953	$3,242
1994	1,162	$30,270	$1,210	$4,450
1995	1,176	$49,216	$1,453	$5,333
1996	1,176	$62,328	$2,195	$6,908
CAGR	2.5%	52.5%	49.6%	47.8%

benefited individual shareholders relative to other firms (possible investments) in the capital marketplace.

Figure A.8 presents Microsoft's relative market performance compared to the S&P 500 between 1986 and 1996. The comparison is based on a hypothetical investment of $100 in a market basket of S&P 500 common stocks and a $100 investment in Microsoft's common stock. Figure A.8

**Figure A.8 Microsoft S&P 500, Total Return, and Book Value
Cumulative Total Return, $100 Investment, June 30, 1986
(Amounts in Millions)**

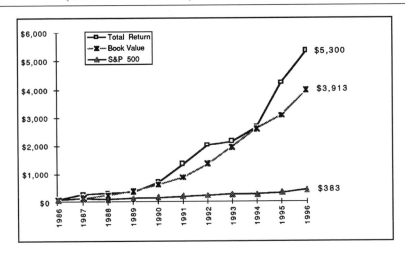

	S&P	Microsoft Total	Book
Year	500	Return	Value
1986	$100	$100	$100
1987	$125	$285	$167
1988	$120	$320	$260
1989	$151	$375	$380
1990	$162	$685	$600
1991	$188	$1,340	$860
1992	$214	$2,010	$1,340
1993	$239	$2,105	$1,913
1994	$251	$2,605	$2,553
1995	$302	$4,185	$3,020
1996	$383	$5,300	$3,913
CAGR	14.4%	48.7%	44.3%

Source: Value Line Investment Survey and Economic Report of the President of the United States.

also includes a comparison to $100 of book value for Microsoft's common stock.

For every $100 invested in a market basket of S&P 500 common stocks, that investment would have increased to $383 by 1996.[3] That in vestment would have generated an annual return of 14.4% compounded annually. If that $100 was invested in Microsoft's common stock, that investment would have increased to $5,300 by 1996. That investment would have generated an annual return of 48.7% compounded annually. As we can see from Figure A.8, the total return on Microsoft's common stock tracks quite closely with the increase in the book value (shareholders' equity) of Microsoft's common stock (44.3%).

Like the other cases included in this book, we have tried to show that the principles of financial statement analysis presented in this book can help managers develop a better understanding of any business. If we were to go into a more in-depth analysis, we would return to the SPM and take a closer look at each of its components. For Microsoft, this more in-depth look would focus on the margin-management component of the SPM.

In the case that follows, we will use the principles of financial statement analysis to see what we can learn about Coca-Cola, the world's largest soft drink company and holder of one of the most widely known brand names in the world.

NOTES

1. We refer to the statement of income and retained earnings as simply the income statement to simplify the discussion of key concepts. From a practical perspective, the statement of income and retained earnings provides us with two important pieces of financial information: (1) the amount of dividends that were declared during the year, and (2) the amounts of any charges or credits made to retained earnings that bypassed the income statement.

2. We have plotted the relationships between market value, net income, and shareholders' equity using a log scale in order to present the information in a meaningful manner. If we did not use a log scale, the amounts reported for net income and shareholders' equity would barely get above the X axis.

3. The total return for a $100 investment in a market basket of S&P 500 common stocks assumes that any dividends received were reinvested to buy additional shares of common stock at the prevailing market price. Over this ten-year period, firms in the S&P 500 paid annual dividends of slightly over 3% of the market value of the firms' common stock. Over this same period, Microsoft paid no dividends to shareholders.

Coca-Cola

Coca-Cola is the world's largest soft drink company and holds one of the most widely known brand names in the world. Throughout its corporate history, Coca-Cola's success has revolved around its ability to convert raw materials into soft drink concentrates that it sells to bottlers. Coca-Cola's publicly stated mission is to create economic value (dividends plus stock price appreciation) for its shareholders.

By looking at Coca-Cola's financial performance from 1986 to 1996, we can see how the company's late CEO, Roberto Goizueta, capitalized on Coca-Cola's brand names and worldwide distribution system to make the company a high-growth, international competitor.

In telling a story about the company, we will draw on the financial information reported in Coca-Cola's balance sheets and income statements and in market information about the company's common stock. We will focus on the most significant aspects of Coca-Cola's financial performance as captured by our business strategy models. As we shall see, Coca-Cola managed every component of the Strategic Profit Model (SPM) to increase the company's return on equity (ROE) over the years 1986 to 1996. As captured in the Strategic Financing Model (SFM), senior management increased the overall profitability of the company while growing the business and returning excess cash to its shareholders by repurchasing shares of common stock.

INCOME STATEMENTS AND BALANCE SHEETS

As mentioned in Chapter 1, a firm's balance sheets and income statements provide all of the information we will need to prepare an SPM and an SFM for any firm. We can begin to understand the business through the financial performance indicators calculated from any firm's balance sheets and income statements.

Balance Sheets

Figure B.1 presents Coca-Cola's balance sheets for the fiscal years ended December 31, 1986 and 1996. As we can see, Coca-Cola's balance sheets look very similar to Wal-Mart's balance sheet. Unlike Microsoft, Coca-Cola does not have a large cash war chest. The most notable difference between Coca-Cola and Wal-Mart is in the shareholders' equity section of the balance sheet.

As of December 31, 1996, Coca-Cola had repurchased $10.3 billion in common stock (treasury stock[1]). Between 1986 and 1996, Coca-Cola repurchased over $9.6 billion in common stock. As we shall see, the repurchase of outstanding common stock plays a significant role in management's overall business strategy.

Returning to the overall comparison of 1986 with 1996 provided by Coca-Cola's balance sheet equations, we see that Coca-Cola has roughly doubled in size between 1986 from 1996.

Assets = Liabilities + Shareholders' Equity
1986: $8.373B = $4.858B + $3.515B
1996: $16.161B = $10.005B + $6.156B

Compared to 1986, total assets for 1996 increased by 93%, total liabilities by 106%, and shareholders' equity by 75%. Coca-Cola grew, but nowhere near as fast as Microsoft. What is considered a growth business in the beverage industry is quite a bit different from a growth business in the computer software industry.

Figure B.1 Coca-Cola Balance Sheets (for the Fiscal Years Ended December 31, 1986 and 1996 — Amounts in Millions)

	1986	1996
Assets		
Current Assets		
Cash and Equivalents	$888	$1,658
Receivables	$1,081	$1,641
Inventory	$933	$952
Other	$837	$1,659
Total Current Assets	$3,739	$5,910
Productive Assets		
Property, Plant, and Equipment	$2,790	$5,581
Accumulated Depreciation	($1,026)	($2,031)
Net Productive Assets	$1,764	$3,550
Other Assets	$2,870	$6,701
Total Assets	$8,373	$16,161
Liabilities and Shareholders' Equity		
Liabilities		
Current Liabilities		
Accounts Payable	$1,333	$2,972
Current Debt Due	$725	$3,397
Other	$697	$1,037
Total Current Liabilities	$2,755	$7,406
Long-Term Liabilities		
LT Debt	$1,011	$1,116
Other LT Liabilities	$711	$1,182
Deferred Income Taxes	$381	$301
Total LT Liabilities	$2,103	$2,599
Total Liabilities	$4,858	$10,005
Shareholders' Equity		
Common Stock	$714	$1,916
Treasury Stock	($705)	($10,320)
Retained Earnings	$3,624	$15,127
Equity Adjustments	($118)	($567)
Total Shareholders' Equity	$3,515	$6,156
Total Equity	$8,373	$16,161

Income Statements

Figure B.2 presents Coca-Cola's statements of income and retained earnings for the fiscal years ended December 31, 1986 and 1996.[2] Coca-Cola's income statements look very similar to Wal-Mart's income statements. Unlike Microsoft, we do not see any research and development expenses or large adjustments to retained earnings related to the repurchase of common stock. Coca-Cola accounts for all of these repurchases through its treasury stock account.

While Coca-Cola's balance sheets provide us with snapshots of the company at different points in time, income statements provide us with information about Coca-Cola's financial performance on behalf of the shareholders in specific years. Coca-Cola's income statement equations for 1986 and 1996 provide us with basic information on how well management has performed on behalf of the shareholders.

Net Income = Revenue – Expenses (Net)

1986: $934M = $8.668B – $7.734B

1996: $3.492B = $18.546B – $15.054B

In 1986, Coca-Cola generated approximately $8.7 billion in revenue and incurred $7.7 billion in expenses. The net income of $934 million represents the increase in net assets (assets – liabilities) *earned* by management on behalf of the shareholders during the year. In 1996, Coca-Cola generated $18.5 billion in revenue while incurring $15.0 billion in expenses. In 1996, management *earned* $3.5 billion in net assets on behalf of the shareholders. The net income reported for 1996 is 274% greater than the net income reported in 1986.

Like our comparison of the two balance sheet equations, the comparison of the two income statement equations provides some initial insights into the business. When we add the ROE calculation to the analysis, we can begin to gain additional insights into the business by seeing how the balance sheets and income statements are interrelated. ROE provides the bridge between the firm's balance sheets and income statements.

Figure B.2 Coca-Cola Statements of Income and Retained Earnings (for the Fiscal Years Ended December 31, 1986 and 1996 — Amounts in Millions)

	1986	1996
Net Revenues	$8,668	$18,546
Total Revenue	$8,668	$15,546
Cost and Expenses		
Cost of Sales	$4,644	$6,738
S, G, and A	$2,699	$7,893
Interest Charges	$186	$286
Interest/Other Income (net)	($372)	($967)
Total Costs and Expenses	$7,157	$13,950
Income before Income Taxes	$1,511	$4,596
Provision for Income Taxes	$577	$1,104
Net Income	$934	$3,492
Dividends	($402)	($1,247)
Adjustments to Retained Earnings	$0	$0
Retained Earnings, Beginning Balance	$3,092	$12,882
Retained Earnings, Ending Balance	$3,624	$15,127

Return on Equity

Return on shareholders' equity (ROE) links Coca-Cola's income statements to its balance sheets.

For the fiscal years ended December 31, 1986 and 1996:

ROE = Net Income ÷ Shareholders' Equity

1986: 26.6% = $934M ÷ $8.668B

1996: 56.7% = $3.492B ÷ $18.547B

Stated in dollars (\$) and cents (¢) terms,

In 1986, Coca-Cola generated 26.6¢ in profit for every \$1 of shareholder's equity.

In 1996, Coca-Cola generated 56.7¢ in profit for every \$1 of shareholders' equity.

By increasing ROE from 26.6¢ to 56.7¢, management was able to generate an additional \$191 million in net income on shareholders' equity of \$6.156 billion.

As mentioned throughout the book, ROE represents a convenient way of linking the balance sheet to the income statement. ROE provides the anchor for taking a closer look at Coca-Cola through the SPM. No matter how deep we delve into the details of Coca- Cola's financial performance, when we resurface, the ROEs for 1986 and 1996 will have remained the same — 26.6% in 1986 and 56.7% in 1996.

The quick overview of the SPM shows how all of the financial aspects of Coca-Cola's business strategy fit together in an integrated management framework.

STRATEGIC PROFIT MODEL: QUICK OVERVIEW

Figure B.3 presents the quick overview of Coca-Cola's SPM for 1986 and 1996 using just four elements taken from Coca-Cola's income statements and balance sheets: net revenues, net income, total assets, and shareholders' equity.

Stated in dollars and cents terms,

In 1986, Coca-Cola generated 26.6¢ in profit on every \$1 of shareholders' equity; in 1996, Coca-Cola generated 56.7¢.

Figure B.3   Coca-Cola Strategic Profit Model: Quick Overview (for the Fiscal Years Ended December 31, 1986 and 1996 — Amounts in Millions)

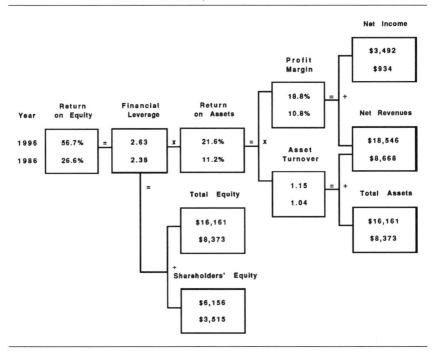

In the process of growing the business between 1986 and 1996, Coca-Cola experienced a 30.1¢ increase in ROE, an increase greater than the 1986 ROE. With the quick overview provided by the SPM, we can now take a more in-depth look at the individual components contributing to Coca-Cola's ROE in 1986 and 1996 and the 30.1¢ increase over this ten-year period.

As with Wal-Mart, we begin the discussion of the financial aspects of Coca-Cola's business strategy with the margin-management component of the SPM.

Margin Management

As we can see from Figure B.3, Coca-Cola's profit margin increased from 10.8% to 18.8%. From a management perspective,

233

Coca-Cola earned 10.8¢ in profit for every $1 of net revenues in 1986; in 1996, Coca-Cola earned 18.8¢ in profit.

Between 1986 and 1996, Coca-Cola was able to increase its margins by 8.0¢ on every $1 of net revenues.

The 8.0¢ increase in profit margin translates into $1.5 billion of net income on net revenues of $18.5 billion.

Between 1986 and 1996, net revenues increased at a 7.9% compound annual growth rate (CAGR), net expenses increased by 6.9% per year, and net income increased by 14.1%.

Like Microsoft, the key to Coca-Cola's success is reflected in the margin-management component of the SPM. Although we need to see how asset management and financial management fit into Coca-Cola's overall business strategy, the heart of that strategy is reflected in the profit margins.

Asset Management

As we can see from Figure B.3, Coca-Cola's asset turnover increased from 1.04 in 1986 to 1.15 in 1996. In terms of dollars and cents,

In 1986, Coca-Cola generated $1.04 in net revenue for every $1 of total assets; in 1996, Coca-Cola generated $1.15 in net revenue.

Coca-Cola achieved this increase in asset turnover by growing total assets at a slower rate than the growth in net revenues. Between 1986 and 1996, total assets increased at a 6.8% CAGR compared to the 7.9% growth rate for net revenues. However, we must remember that any increase or decrease must be evaluated within the context of the firm's overall business strategy.

In Coca-Cola's case, the increase in asset turnover of 11¢ per $1 of assets translates into $1.6 billion fewer assets needed to generate $18.5 billion in net revenues. If Coca-Cola had maintained the 1986 asset turnover of $1.04 in 1996, the company would have needed $17.8 billion in total asset to generate $18.5 billion in net revenues instead of $16.2 billion.

Return on Assets

As we can see from Figure B.3, Coca-Cola's return on assets (ROA) increased from 11.2% in 1986 to 21.6% in 1996.

▶───

In 1986, Coca-Cola earned 11.2¢ in profit for every $1 of total assets; in 1996, Coca-Cola earned 21.6¢.

The 10.4 percentage-point increase in ROA translates into $1.7 billion in profit on $16.2 billion in total assets. At a 11.2% ROA, Coca-Cola would have only generated $1.8 billion in net income versus the $3.5 billion earned in 1996.

───◀

As it did with Microsoft, *Value Line* gives Coca-Cola an "A++," the strongest possible financial strength rating.

As we can see from Figure B.3, Coca-Cola's key to operating success lies in its ability to generate increasing profit margins while growing the business and using fewer assets in the process. Between 1986 and 1996, net revenues increased at 7.9% per year, net income at 14.1% per year, and total assets at 6.8% per year. The net result of growing net income at a faster rate than net revenues and growing total assets at a slower rate is reflected in ROA. Between 1986 and 1996, Coca-Cola's ROA increased by over 90%.

Integrating Margin and Asset Management through ROA

In order to help managers consolidate what they are learning about Coca-Cola, it helps to return to the SPM song we learned for Wal-Mart.

In 1996,

For every $1 of assets, Coca-Cola generated $1.15 in net revenues.

For every $1 of net revenues, Coca-Cola earned 18.8¢ in profit.

Multiplying the profit margin by the asset turnover, for every $1 of assets, Coca-Cola generated 21.6¢ in profit in 1996.

Compared to 1986, Coca-Cola grew the business while increasing both profit margins and asset turnover.

Financial Leverage

As we can see from Figure B.3, financial leverage increased from 2.38 in 1986 to 2.63 in 1996.

In 1986, Coca-Cola utilized $2.38 in total equity for every $1 of shareholders' equity; in 1996, Coca-Cola utilized $2.63.

Between 1986 and 1996, total equity increased at a 6.8% CAGR while total liabilities increased at a 7.5% CAGR and shareholders' equity increased at a 5.8% CAGR.

Unlike Microsoft with no long-term debt, nothing in the total-equity section of Coca-Cola's balance sheet can be pointed to account for the 25¢ increase in financial leverage. As we shall see from our discussion of the SFM, Coca-Cola has slowly been restructuring the liabilities and shareholders' equity section of the balance sheet.

If Coca-Cola had maintained its 1986 financial leverage of $2.38, ROE management would have generated a 51.4% ROE given the 21.6% ROA in 1996.

Even at $2.63 in financial leverage, Coca-Cola still maintains its "A++" financial strength rating.

Return on Equity: Closing the Loop

As mentioned at the beginning of this case study, the concept of ROE provides us with the opportunity to interrelate all of the financial information included in the balance sheets and income statements into a comprehensive management framework. The SPM is then used to see how all of the parts fit together to form a greater whole. After managers see how all of the parts fit together, they can focus on developing their communication skills. For that part of the learning experience, we return to the SPM song.

The 1996 version of Coca-Cola's SPM song goes something like this:

▶─────────────────────────────────────

For every $1 of assets, Coca-Cola generated $1.15 in net revenues.

For every $1 of net revenues, Coca-Cola earned 18.8¢ in profit.

Multiplying the profit margin by the asset turnover, we know that for every $1 of assets, Coca-Cola generated 21.6¢ in profit.

When we multiply ROA by the $2.63 in total assets management controlled for every $1 of shareholders' equity, we see that Coca-Cola generated 56.7¢ in profit or every $1 of shareholders' equity invested in the business.

─────────────────────────────────────◀

In a more in-depth analysis of the financial aspects of Coca-Cola's business strategy, we would focus our attention on each of the financial elements making up the margin-management, asset-management, and financial-management components of the SPM.

Whereas Microsoft's primary focus is on margin management, Coca-Cola works all of the components of the SPM. Between 1986 and 1996, Coca-Cola was able to grow net revenues at a 7.9% CAGR while growing net income at a 14.1% compound annual rate. At the same time, total assets (and therefore total equity) increased at a 6.8% CAGR and shareholder's equity was held to a 5.8% growth rate. The net effect of managing all of the components of the SPM is that Coca-Cola's ROE increased by over 113% between 1986 and 1996.

STRATEGIC FINANCING MODEL

As discussed in Chapters 7 and 8, we restructure a firm's balance sheets to focus on the long-term investment and financing aspects of the firm's business strategy. From the restructured balance sheets, we then create a financial flow statement that shows how the long-term investment and financing base changed over the ten-year period.

Restructuring the Balance Sheets

Figure B.4 presents Coca-Cola's restructured balance sheets for 1986 and 1996. As we can see, Coca-Cola's long-term investment is made up of working capital, gross productive assets, and gross other assets. Coca-Cola's long-term financing base consists of external debt financing, external equity financing, and internal equity financing.

Two aspects of Coca-Cola's restructured balance sheets are notable because they differ significantly from what we saw on Wal-Mart's restructured balance sheets.

1. In 1986, Coca-Cola had $984 million invested in working capital. In 1996, Coca-Cola's working capital was a negative $1.5 billion.
2. Coca-Cola's external equity financing includes common stock and treasury stock. In 1986, Coca-Cola's net external equity financing was $9 million. In 1996, net external equity financing equaled a negative $8.4 billion.

As we shall see, these two observations will affect the way we interpret how Coca-Cola financed the business between 1986 and 1996.

The financial control equations underlying Coca-Cola's restructured balance sheets for 1986 and 1996 are presented below:

Long-Term Investment = Long-Term Financing
1986: $6.644B = $6.644B
1996: $10.786B = $10.786B

Figure B.4 **Coca-Cola Restructured Balance Sheets (for the Fiscal Years Ended December 31, 1986 and 1996 — Amounts in Millions)**

	1986	Change	1996
Long-Term Investment			
Current Assets	$3,739	$2,171	$5,910
Current Liabilities	$2,755	$4,651	$7,406
Working Capital	$984	($2,480)	($1,496)
Gross Productive Assets	$2,790	$2,791	$5,581
Gross Other Assets	$2,870	$3,831	$6,701
Total Long-Term Investment	$6,644	$4,142	$10,786
Long-Term Financing			
External Debt Financing			
LT Debt	$1,011	$105	$1,116
Other LT Liabilities	$711	$471	$1,182
Total External Debt	$1,722	$576	$2,298
External Equity Financing			
Common Stock	$714	$1,202	$1,916
Treasury Stock	($705)	($9,615)	($10,320)
Total External Equity	$9	($8,413)	($8,404)
Internal Equity Financing			
Retained Earnings	$3,624	$11,503	$15,127
Accumulated Depreciation	$1,026	$1,005	$2,031
Deferred Income Taxes	$381	($80)	$301
Equity Adjustments	($118)	($449)	($567)
Total Internal Equity	$4,913	$11,979	$16,892
Total Long-Term Financing	$6,644	$4,142	$10,786

Coca-Cola's long-term financing and investment base in 1996 had increased by over 62% since 1986. The financial flow statement helps us understand how senior management increased this long-term investment and financial base.

Financial Flow Statement

Figure B.5 presents Coca-Cola's financial flow statement for the ten-year period ended December 31, 1996. As we can see, the financial flow statement differs from the restructured balance sheets in two ways.

1. The details included in the restructured balance sheet have been omitted from the financial flow statement.
2. The long-term financing activity has been placed above the long-term investment activity. The financial flow statement includes a summary of the net revenues generated by Coca-Cola between 1986 and 1996.

By focusing on the "change" column of Figure B.5, we can construct the financing-the-business component of the SFM, as presented in Figure B.6. As we can see from this figure, Coca-Cola was actually able to reduce it external financing by $7.8 billion or 6.2¢ of every $1 of total revenue generated between 1986 and 1996.

Between 1986 and 1996, Coca-Cola borrowed $576 million to support the business over the long term (0.5¢ of every $1 of total revenue).

However, over that same ten-year period, Coca-Cola also reduced its total external equity financing by $8.4 billion. 6.6¢ of every $1 of total revenue generated over the ten-year period went to reduce the overall level of external equity financing.

Since Coca-Cola reduced its overall level of external financing, it still had to be generating more internal equity financing than it could use in the business and still generate values for the shareholders.

Figure B.5 Coca-Cola Financial Flow Statement (for the Ten Years Ended December 31, 1996 — Amounts in Millions)

Long-Term Financing	1986	*Change*	1996
External Debt Financing	$1,722	*$576*	$2,298
External Equity Financing	$9	*($8,413)*	($8,404)
Internal Equity Financing	$4,913	*$11,979*	$16,892
Total Long-Term Financing	$6,644	*$4,142*	$10,786

Long-Term Investment	1986	*Change*	1996
Working Capital	$984	*($2,480)*	($1,496)
Gross Productive Assets	$2,790	*$2,791*	$5,581
Gross Other Assets	$2,870	*$3,831*	$6,701
Total Long-Term Investment	$6,644	*$4,142*	$10,786

Year	Total Revenue
87	$7,658
88	$8,338
89	$8,966
90	$10,236
91	$11,572
92	$13,074
93	$13,957
94	$16,172
95	$18,018
96	$18,546
Ten Year Total	$126,537

Between 1986 and 1996, management generated $126.537 billion of customer financing (total revenue). Of that amount, $11.979 billion of internal equity financing was made available to grow the business or return to shareholders in the form of stock repurchases.

The $11.979 billion represented 9.5¢ of every of $1 of total revenue.

As we can see from Figure B.6, Coca-Cola did not have to invest any of its internal equity financing in the business. In fact, the $2.5 billion decrease in working capital freed up another 2¢ per $1 of total revenue to be used in other parts of the business.

The $11.979 billion of internal equity financing plus the $2.480 billion reduction in working capital provided management with $14.459 billion to invest in other parts of the business or return to shareholders.

The $14.459 billion represented 11.5¢ of every of $1 of total revenue.

As we can see from Figure B.6, Coca-Cola invested $2.8 billion in productive assets and $3.8 billion in other assets. A closer look at Coca-Cola's financial statements shows that the increase in other assets primarily represents investment in affiliated companies. After making those long-term investments, Coca-Cola had $7.8 billion that was not needed to run the business. If you recall from the Microsoft case, management decided to build a war chest of cash and equivalents from the internal equity financing generated by management. Coca-Cola decided to return that money to its shareholders and actually borrow a small amount of money to run the business over the long term.

Business Strategy Revisited

By using the quick overview from the SPM and the financing-the-business component of the SFM, we have been able to show how management increased Coca-Cola's ROE while growing the business. By looking at each component of the SPM, we were able to see that Coca-Cola worked on all aspects of the SPM as part of its overall business strategy.

**Figure B.6   Coca-Cola Strategic Financing Model: Financing the
Business (for the Fiscal Years Ended December 31, 1986
and 1996 — Amounts in Millions)**

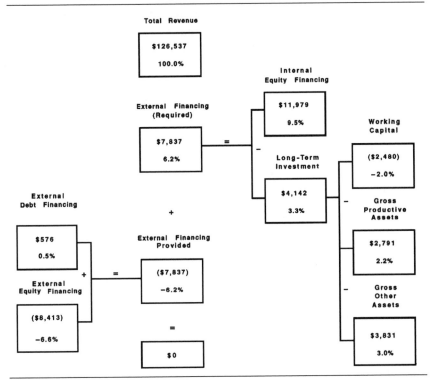

Coca-Cola increased its profit margin from 10.8% in 1986 to 18.8% in 1996. Asset turnover increased from 1.04 in 1986 to 1.15 in 1996, and financial leverage increased from 2.38 to 2.63. The combined effect of each of these increases was to increase ROE from 26.6% to 56.7%.

Coca-Cola increased net revenues by 7.9% per year and kept expenses to a 6.9% annual increase, resulting in a 14.1% increase in net income. As with expenses, total assets increased at a slower rate (6.8%) than net revenues (7.9%). The combined effects of expense control and increased asset utilization resulted in an the increase in ROA from 11.2% in 1986 to 21.6% in 1996.

The increase in financial leverage was caused in part by management's decision to repurchase shares of common stock. Both total liabilities

(7.5%) and shareholders' equity (5.8%) grew slower than net revenues (7.9%). However, the slower growth in shareholder's equity resulted from offsetting effects. While retained earnings were increasing from $3.6 billion in 1986 to $15.1 billion in 1996, treasury stock repurchased had increased from $705 million to $10.3 billion. The $8.4 billion reduction in external equity financing was helped in part by management's ability to free up $2.5 billion of working capital.

As we have seen, Coca-Cola's business strategy is captured quite nicely through our two business models. Management pursued growth and high ROEs, as captured by the SPM, and restructured its long-term investment and financing foundation, as captured by the SFM.

Given Coca-Cola's success as measured by the amounts reported in the financial statements, we need to see how the market has valued the company's performance.

MARKET VALUATION

Back in 1986, many investors viewed Coca-Cola as a low growth, conservative, "blue chip" company. At that time, Coca-Cola was not considered to be a growth company. We doubt that many investors would have predicted how the company would do under the leadership of its late CEO, Roberto Goizueta. With the 20/20 hindsight we have become accustomed to using, we can look to see how the market has valued a company that went from generating a net income of $934 million in 1986 to generating $3.5 billion in 1996.

Figure B.7 presents the relationship between the market value of Coca-Cola's common stock and the two management measures of financial performance we use to calculate Coca-Cola's ROE: net income and shareholders' equity. As we can see, Coca-Cola's total market value (common shares outstanding times the market price per share) increased at a substantially faster rate than the increases in net income and shareholders' equity.[3] As we can also see, Coca-Cola's common stock outstanding actually decreased at a 2.1% compound annual rate over the ten-year period. Coca-Cola's common stock outstanding decreased $599 million from $3,080 billion in 1986 to $2,481 billion in 1996. In relative terms, the total decrease of 19.4% ($599M ÷ $3,080B) can be attributed primarily to Coca-Cola's strategy of returning cash to shareholders by repurchasing common stock outstanding.

Figure B.7 Coca-Cola Market and Management Measures of Performance (for the Years Ended December 31—Shares and Dollar Amounts in Millions)

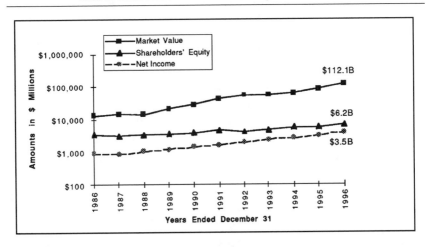

Year Ended December 31	Common Stock Outstanding	Market Value	Net Income	Shareholders' Equity
1986	3,080	$13,552	$934	$3,515
1987	2,979	$15,192	$916	$3,224
1988	2,838	$14,333	$1,045	$3,345
1989	2,696	$20,895	$1,193	$3,486
1990	2,673	$27,398	$1,382	$3,849
1991	2,658	$41,330	$1,618	$4,426
1992	2,614	$52,927	$1,884	$3,888
1993	2,595	$53,585	$2,188	$4,584
1994	2,552	$58,821	$2,554	$5,235
1995	2,505	$80,899	$2,986	$5,392
1996	2,481	$112,141	$3,492	$6,156
CAGR	−2.1%	23.5%	14.1%	5.8%

Over this ten-year period, the market value of the common stock out-standing increased at a 23.5% CAGR. During this same period, net income increased at a 14.1% compound annual rate and shareholders' equity increased at a 5.8% compound annual rate. As we can see, Coca-Cola's strategy of growing the business by increasing net income (and profit margins) while reducing shareholders' equity through stock repurchases has paid-off handsomely in terms of the increased market value of Coca-Cola's common stock.

As mentioned in Chapters 9 through 12, financial analysts and share-holders determine the value of the firm's common stock. The price of a firm's common stock is influenced by the recommendations of financial analysts at the major investment firms and what each of us is willing to pay for the firm's common stock. Firms like Coca-Cola have no direct in-fluence over the market price of their firm's common stock, but they do have an indirect influence through their actions.

From the quick overview of the SPM, we saw that the primary way Coca-Cola increased ROE was through its margin-management, asset-management, and financial-management strategies. From the financing-the-business component of the SFM, we saw that Coca-Cola actually reduced its investment in working capital and the amount of external equity financing used to run the business from 1986 to 1996. The growth rates for net income (14.1%) and shareholders' equity (5.8%) reflect the combination of these two aspects of Coca-Cola's overall business strategy.

For the company taken as a whole, Coca-Cola has been a success in terms of both growth in market value and financial performance. The only question that remains to be answered is how well this performance ben-efited individual shareholders relative to other firms (possible invest-ments) in the capital marketplace.

Figure B.8 presents Coca-Cola's relative market performance com-pared to the S&P 500 between 1986 and 1996. The comparison is based on a hypothetical investment of $100 in a market basket of S&P 500 com-mon stocks and a $100 investment in Coca-Cola's common stock. Figure B.8 also includes a comparison to $100 of book value for Coca-Cola's common stock. As we can see, for every $100 invested in a market basket of S&P 500 common stocks, that investment would have increased to $383 by 1996.[4] That investment would have generated an annual return of 14.4% compounded annually. If that $100 was invested in Coca-Cola's common stock, that investment would have increased to $1,228 by 1996. That investment would have generated an annual return of 28.5% com-pounded annually. As we can see, the total return on Coca-Cola's com-mon stock does not track very closely to the increase in the book value (shareholders' equity) of Coca-Cola's common stock (8.1%).

The total return to shareholders who held Coca-Cola's common stock increased substantially faster than the increase in book value (28.5% ver-sus 8.1%) and the market value of the S&P 500 (28.5% versus 14.4%). It

Figure B.8 **Coca-Cola S&P 500, Total Return, and Book Value Cumulative Total Return, $100 Investment, December 31, 1986 (Amounts in Millions)**

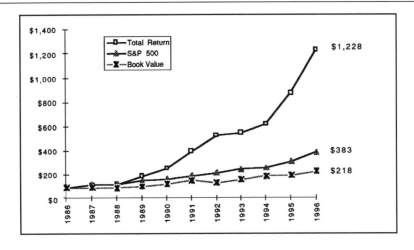

Year	S&P 500	Total Return	Book Value
1986	$100	$100	$100
1987	$125	$118	$95
1988	$120	$120	$94
1989	$151	$189	$104
1990	$162	$255	$124
1991	$188	$394	$146
1992	$214	$524	$131
1993	$239	$542	$155
1994	$251	$614	$180
1995	$302	$870	$189
1996	$383	$1,228	$218
CAGR	14.4%	28.5%	8.1%

Source: Value Line Investment Survey and Economic Report of the President of the United States.

would appear that investors like Coca-Cola's strategy of growing the business, increasing margins and returns (i.e., ROA, ROE), and returning cash to shareholders by repurchasing common stock.

Closing the Loop

As with the cases of Wal-Mart and Microsoft, we have tried to show that the principles of financial statement analysis presented in this book can help managers develop a better understand of any business. If we were to go into a more in-depth analysis, we would return to the SPM and take a closer look at each of its components. For Coca-Cola, this more in-depth look would begin by focusing on the margin-management component of the SPM and then taking a closer look at the asset-management and financial-management components of the model.

In the case that follows, we will use the principles of financial statement analysis to see what we can learn about Caterpillar, the world's largest producer of earthmoving equipment.

NOTES

1. Treasury stock includes shares of a firm's common stock that have been issued and then repurchased at a later date.

2. We refer to the statement of income and retained earnings as simply the income statement to simplify the discussion of key concepts. From a practical perspective, the statement of income and retained earnings provides us with two important pieces of financial information: (1) the amount of dividends that were declared during the year, and (2) the amounts of any charges or credits made to retained earnings that bypassed the income statement.

3. We have plotted the relationship between market value, net income, and shareholders' equity using a log scale in order to present the information in a meaningful manner. If we did not use a log scale, the amounts reported for net income and shareholders' equity would barely get above the X axis.

4. The total return for a $100 investment in a market basket of S&P 500 common stocks assumes that any dividends received were reinvested to buy additional shares of common stock at the prevailing market price. Over this ten-year period, firms in the S&P 500 paid annual dividends of slightly over 3% of the market value of the firms' common stock.

Caterpillar

Caterpillar is the world's largest producer of earthmoving equipment. In the early 1980s, like many other industrial firm in the United States, Caterpillar was losing market share to its Japanese competitors and incurring financial losses for the first time in its history. Between 1982 and 1984, Caterpillar incurred net losses of $953 million. According to senior executives at Caterpillar, the company was operating at a 30% production cost disadvantage relative to its major Japanese competitor, Komatsu. Everyone at Caterpillar knew that something had to change.[1]

Under the leadership of the CEO, Don Fites, the company was reorganized into decentralized profit center divisions based on product groups and customer markets. Between 1986 and 1996, Caterpillar solved its cost problem and began once again to create value (dividends plus stock price appreciation) for its shareholders.

In telling a story about the company, we will draw on the financial information reported in Caterpillar's balance sheets and income statements and market information about the company's common stock. For this illustration of how we use our business strategy models to focus on the financial performance of the business, we will focus on Caterpillar's machinery and engines business and set aside its financial products business and the company's investments in affiliated companies.[2]

Given the amount of detail provided by Caterpillar about its businesses in the annual reports, we were able to set up a hypothetical corporate holding company with investments in the machinery and engines (M&E) business, the financial products (FP) business, and affiliated companies. Viewed as a holding company, with three subsidiary businesses, a highly summarized version of Caterpillar's balance sheets and income statements for 1986 and 1996 would appear as in Figure C.1[3]

Figure C.1   Caterpillar Balance Sheets (for the Fiscal Years Ended December 31 — Amounts in Millions)

	1986	1996
Assets		
Investments in M&E Businesses	$2,847	$2,656
Investments in Affiliated Companies	$185	$701
Investments in FP Subsidiaries	$117	$759
Total Assets	$3,149	$4,116
Equity		
Equity in M&E Businesses	$2,847	$2,656
Equity in Affiliated Companies	$185	$701
Equity in FP Subsidiaries	$117	$759
Total Equity	$3,149	$4,116

Caterpillar Income Statements (for the Fiscal Years Ended December 31 — Amounts in Millions)

	1986	1996
Equity in Profit of M&E Business	$76	$1,225
Equity in Profit of Affiliated Companies	$6	$33
Equity in Profit of FS Subsidiaries	($6)	$103
Net Income	$76	$1,361

In the remainder of this case study, we will use complete balance sheet and income statement information for Caterpillar's machinery and engines business to run through our business strategy models. For the discussion of the market valuation process, we will revert back to the financial information reported for all of Caterpillar's operations.

As we can see from the highly summarized statements in Figure C.1, the investment in the M&E business accounted for 90.4% of total assets and 100% of net income in 1986 and 64.5% of total assets and 90.0% of net income in 1996.

INCOME STATEMENTS AND BALANCE SHEETS

As mentioned in Chapter 1, a firm's balance sheets and income statements provide all of the information we will need to prepare a Strategic Profit Model (SPM) and a Strategic Financing Model (SFM) for any firm. In the case of the SFM, we restructure the balance sheets and create financial flow statements before we do the analysis. However, all of the key financial performance indicators that we will use to begin understanding the business are included in the balance sheets and income statements in one form or another.

Balance Sheets

Figure C.2 presents Caterpillar's balance sheets for the M&E business (hereafter CAT M&E) for the fiscal years ended December 31, 1986 and 1996. Two aspects of CAT M&E's balance sheets are worth mentioning before we start the analysis.

1. The long-term liabilities for 1996 included an obligation of $1.887 billion for postemployment benefits. Like many other U.S. firms, Caterpillar began reporting is postemployment benefit obligations as a long-term liability in 1992.
2. The transfers to holding company for the M&E business are equivalent to the repurchase of common stock. As of December 31, 1986, the M&E business had transferred $302 million back to the holding company. By 1996, that amount had increased to $2.3 billion.

As we shall see, these two observations will affect the way we interpret the financial-management aspects of CAT M&E's overall business strategy. For the moment, we can return to the overall comparison of 1986 with 1996 provided by CAT M&E's balance sheet equations.

Assets = Liabilities + Shareholders' Equity

1986: $5.896B = $3.139B + $2.847B

1996: $10.474B = $7.818B + $2.658B

Figure C.2 Caterpillar Machinery and Engines Balance Sheets (for the Fiscal Years Ended December 31, 1986 and 1996 — Amounts in Millions)

	1986	1996
Assets		
Current Assets		
Cash and Equivalents	$124	$445
Receivables	$1,728	$2,960
Inventory	$1,211	$2,222
Other	$300	$876
Total Current Assets	$3,363	$6,503
Productive Assets	$2,433	$3,242
Net Productive Assets	$2,433	$3,242
Other Assets	$190	$729
Total Assets	$5,986	$10,474
Liabilities and Shareholders' Equity		
Liabilities		
Current Liabilities		
Accounts Payable	$1,089	$2,556
Current Debt Due	$619	$158
Other	$472	$1,151
Total Current Liabilities	$2,180	$3,865
Long-Term Liabilities		
LT Debt	$963	$2,018
Postemployment Benefit Obligation	$0	$1,887
Deferred Income Taxes	($4)	$48
Total LT Liabilities	$959	$3,953
Total Liabilities	$3,139	$7,818
Shareholders' Equity		
Common Stock	$714	$881
Transfers to Holding Company	($302)	($2,291)
Retained Earnings	$2,363	$3,904
Equity Adjustments	$72	$162
Total Shareholders' Equity	$2,847	$2,656
Total Equity	$5,986	$10,474

In terms of total assets, the CAT M&E of 1996 is 1.78 times larger than it was back in 1986. In terms of shareholders' equity. CAT M&E is actually 6.7% smaller than it was in 1986.

Income Statements

Figure C.3 presents CAT M&E's income statements for the fiscal years ended December 31, 1986 and 1996. CAT M&E's income statements look very similar to Wal-Mart's income statements and only differs in two significant ways.

Figure C.3 Caterpillar Machinery and Engines Income Statements (for the Fiscal Years Ended December 31, 1986 and 1996 — Amounts in Millions)

	1986	1996
Net Revenues	$7,321	$15,814
Total Revenue	$7,321	$15,814
Costs and Expenses		
Cost of Goods Sold	$5,952	$11,832
Operating Expenses	$942	$1,715
R&D	$178	$410
Interest/Other Expenses (net)	$150	$67
Total Costs and Expenses	$7,222	$14,024
Income before Income Taxes	$99	$1,790
Provision for Income Taxes	$23	$565
Net Income	$76	$1,225

1. Research and development (R&D) represents a significant aspect of CAT M&E's business strategy; therefore, the income statements disclose the amount of money the company spends on R&D ($178 million in 1986 and $410 million in 1996).
2. Since the M&E business is not a freestanding business, we did not prepare statements of income and retained earnings. However, the transfers to the holding company have been captured in the balance sheets.

The expenses associated with R&D will be reflected in the margin-management component of the SPM. The transfers to the holding company will affect how we interpret senior management's long-term financing and investment strategy for the M&E business.

If CAT M&E's balance sheets provide us with snapshots of the company at different points in time, income statements provide us with information about CAT M&E's financial performance on behalf of the shareholders in specific years. CAT M&E's income statement equations for 1986 and 1996 provide us with basic information on how well management has performed on behalf of the shareholders.

$$\text{Net Income} = \text{Revenue} - \text{Expenses (net)}$$
$$1986: \quad \$76M = \$7.321B - \$7.245B$$
$$1996: \quad \$1.225B = \$15.814B - \$14.589B$$

In 1986, CAT M&E generated \$7.3 billion in revenue and incurred \$7.2 billion in expenses. The net income of \$76 million represents the increase in net assets (assets − liabilities) *earned* by management on behalf of the shareholders during the year. In 1996, CAT M&E generated \$15.8 billion in revenue while incurring \$14.6 billion in expenses. In 1996, management *earned* \$1.2 billion in net assets on behalf of the shareholders. The net income reported for 1996 is 16.1 times the net income reported in 1986.

Like our comparison of the two balance sheet equations, the comparison of the two income statement equations provides some initial insights into the business. When we add the return on equity (ROE) calculation to the analysis, we can begin to gain additional insights into the business by seeing how the balance sheets and income statements are interrelated. ROE provides the bridge between the firm's balance sheets and income statements.

Return on Equity

Return on shareholders' equity links CAT M&E's income statements to its balance sheets.

For the fiscal years ended December 31, 1986 and 1996:

ROE = Net Income ÷ Shareholders' Equity

1986:   2.7% = $76M ÷ $2.847B

1996:   46.1% = $1.225B ÷ $2.656B

Stated in dollars and cents terms,

In 1986, CAT M&E generated 2.7¢ in profit for every $1 of share-holder's equity; in 1996, CAT M&E generated 46.1¢ in profit for every $1 of shareholders' equity.

By increasing ROE from 2.7¢ to 46.1¢, management was able to generate an additional $1.2 billion in net income on shareholders' equity of $2.7 billion.

ROE represents a convenient way of linking the balance sheet to the income statement. ROE provides the anchor for taking a closer look at CAT M&E through the SPM. No matter how deep we delve into the details of CAT M&E's financial performance, when we resurface, the ROEs for 1986 and 1996 will have remained the same — 2.7% in 1986 and 46.1% in 1996.

The quick overview of the SPM shows how all of the financial aspects of CAT M&E's business strategy fit together in an integrated management framework.

THE STRATEGIC PROFIT MODEL: QUICK OVERVIEW

Figure C.4 presents the quick overview of CAT M&E's SPM for 1986 and 1996 using just four elements taken from CAT M&E's income statements and balance sheets: net revenues, net income, total assets, and shareholders' equity. When material from this figure is stated in dollars and cents terms,

**Figure C.4   Caterpillar Machinery and Engines Strategic Profit
Model: Quick Overview (for the Fiscal Years Ended
December 31, 1986 and 1996—Amounts in Millions)**

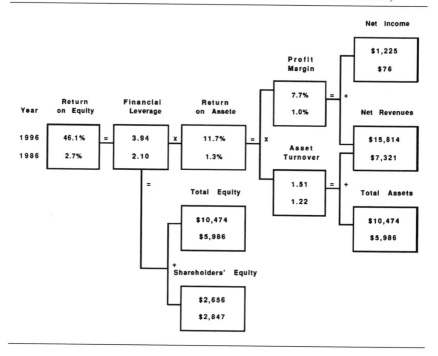

In 1986, CAT M&E generated 2.7¢ in profit on every $1 of share-
holders' equity; in 1996, CAT M&E generated 46.1¢.

In the process of growing the business between 1986 and 1996, CAT
M&E experienced a 43.4¢ increase in ROE. With the quick overview provided by the SPM, we can now take a more in-depth look at the individual components contributing to CAT M&E's ROE in 1986 and 1996
and the 43.4¢ increase over this ten-year period.

As with Wal-Mart, we begin the discussion of the financial aspects of
CAT M&E's business strategy with the margin-management component
of the SPM.

Margin Management

As we can see from Figure C.4, CAT M&E's profit margin increased from 1.0% to 7.7%. From a management perspective,

CAT M&E earned 1.0¢ in profit for every $1 of net revenues in 1986; in 1996, CAT M&E earned 7.7¢ in profit.

Over this ten-year period, CAT M&E was able to increase its margins by 6.7¢ on every $1 of net revenues.

The 6.7¢ increase in profit margin translates into $1.1 billion of net income on net revenues of $15.8 billion.

Between 1986 and 1996, net revenues increased at an 8.0% compound annual growth rate (CAGR), net expenses increased by 7.3% per year, and net income increased by 32.0%.

From a financial perspective, the key to growing net income at a 32.0% CAGR was slowing the rate of growth in expenses relative to the growth in net revenues. The difference in growth rates contributed to net income being 16.1 times larger in 1996 than it was in 1986.

If we took a closer look at the margin-management component of the SPM, we would see 6.5 percentage point increase in gross margin (from 18.7% to 25.2%) and a 2.0 percentage point decrease in operating expenses (from 12.8% to 10.8%).

Asset Management

As we can see from Figure C.4, CAT M&E's asset turnover increased from $1.22 in 1986 to $1.51 in 1996.

In 1986, CAT M&E generated $1.22 in net revenue for every $1 of total assets; in 1996, CAT M&E generated $1.51 in net revenue.

All things considered, management (and shareholders) would prefer to generate more dollars in net revenues per $1 of assets than less and that is exactly what Caterpillar did in its M&E business.

Between 1986 and 1996, total assets increased at a 5.8% CAGR compared to the 8.0% growth rate for net revenues. Any time net revenues are increasing at a faster rate than total assets, asset turnover is going to increase. However, we must remember that any increase or decrease must be evaluated within the context of the firm's overall business strategy.

In CAT M&E's case, the increase in asset turnover of 29¢ per $1 of assets resulted from better management of receivables, inventory, and productive assets. If we took a closer look at the asset-management component of the SPM, we would see that from 1986 to 1996, receivables decreased from 86.3 days' net revenues to 68.3 days', inventory decreased from 60.4 days' to 51.3 days', and productive assets decreased from 121.3 days' to 74.8 days'. In addition to margin management, asset management played a big part in Caterpillar's turnaround.

Return on Assets

As we can see from Figure C.4, CAT M&E's return on assets (ROA) decreased from 1.3% in 1986 to 11.7% in 1996.

In 1986, CAT M&E earned 1.3¢ in profit for every $1 of total assets; in 1996, CAT M&E earned 11.7¢.

The 10.4¢ increase in resulted in $1.1 billion in additional profits in 1996 on the $10.5 billion of total assets.

As mentioned at the beginning of the case, all managers and salaried employees are on an incentive compensation plan tied, in part, to ROA. From the looks of it, it appears that the incentive compensation program works.

Integrating Margin and Asset Management through ROA

In order to help managers consolidate what they are learning about CAT M&E, it helps to return to the SPM song we learned for Wal-Mart. In 1996,

▶

For every $1 of assets, CAT M&E generated $1.51 in net revenues.

For every $1 of net revenues, CAT M&E earned 7.7¢ in profit.

Multiplying the profit margin by the asset turnover, for every $1 of assets, CAT M&E generated 11.7¢ in profit in 1996.

◀

Compared to 1986, CAT M&E had by 1996 grown the business while increasing profit margins and asset turnover. During this period, profit margins increased 670%, and asset turnover increased by 24%. These increases together produced an 800% increase in ROA.

Financial Leverage

As we can see from Figure C.4, financial leverage increased from 2.10 in 1986 to 3.94 in 1996.

▶

In 1986, CAT M&E utilized $2.10 in total equity for every $1 of shareholders' equity; in 1996, CAT M&E utilized $3.94.

◀

However, 71¢ of that increase was due to the increase in postemployment benefits from $0 in 1986 to $1.9 billion in 1996. That increase accounted for 71¢ of the $1.84 increase in financial leverage.

Between 1986 and 1996, total equity increased at a 5.8% CAGR and total liabilities increased at 9.6%. Shareholders' equity declined by 0.7% per year.

Return on Equity: Closing the Loop

As mentioned at the beginning of this case study, the concept of ROE provides us with the opportunity to interrelate all of the financial information included in the balance sheets and income statements into a comprehensive management framework. The SPM is then used to see how all of the parts fit together to form a greater whole. After managers see how all of the parts fit together, they can focus on developing their communication skills. For that part of the learning experience, we return to the SPM song.

The 1996 version of CAT M&E's SPM song goes something like this:

For every $1 of assets, CAT M&E generated $1.51 in net revenues.

For every $1 of net revenues, CAT M&E earned 7.7¢ in profit.

Multiplying the profit margin by the asset turnover, we know that for every $1 of assets, CAT M&E generated 11.7¢ in profit.

When we multiply ROA by the $3.94 in total assets management controlled for every $1 of shareholders' equity, we see that CAT M&E generated 46.1¢ in profit for every $1 of shareholders' equity invested in the business.

Between 1986 and 1996, CAT M&E was able to grow net revenues at a 8.0% CAGR while growing net income at a 32.0% compound annual rate. Over that same period of time, total assets and total equity increased at a 5.8% CAGR and shareholders' equity decreased by 0.7% per year.

STRATEGIC FINANCING MODEL

As discussed in Chapters 7 and 8, we restructure a firm's balance sheets to focus on the long-term investment and financing aspects of the firm's business strategy. From the restructured balance sheets, we then create a financial flow statement that shows how the long-term investment and financing base has changed over the ten-year period.

Restructuring the Balance Sheets

Figure C.5 presents CAT M&E's restructured balance sheets for 1986 and 1996. As we can see, CAT M&E's long-term investment is made up of working capital, gross productive assets, and gross other assets. CAT M&E's long-term financing base consists of external debt financing, external equity financing, and internal equity financing.

Two aspects of CAT M&E's restructured balance sheets are notable because of the difference from what we saw on Wal-Mart's restructured balance sheets.

1. The amounts reported for productive assets on the balance sheets and the amounts reported for gross productive assets on the restructured balance sheets are the same. Caterpillar does not disclose the dollar amounts for accumulated depreciation in its balance sheets. Therefore, the accumulated depreciation cannot be added back to retained earnings.
2. CAT M&E's external debt financing includes the $1.9 billion in postemployment benefits. From a long-term financing perspective, this obligation is equivalent to borrowing money from employees.

As we shall see, these two observations will affect the way we interpret how CAT M&E financed the business over ten-year period between 1986 and 1996.

The financial control equations underlying CAT M&E's restructured balance sheets for 1986 and 1996 are presented below:

Long-Term Investment = Long-Term Financing

1986: $3.806B = $3.806B

1996: $6.609B = $6.609B

Figure C.5 Caterpillar Machinery and Engines Restructured Balance Sheets (for the Fiscal Years Ended December 31, 1986 and 1996 — Amounts in Millions)

	1986	*Change*	1996
Long-Term Investment			
Current Assets	$3,363	*$3,140*	$6,503
Current Liabilities	$2,180	*$1,685*	$3,865
Working Capital	$1,183	*$1,455*	$2,638
Gross Productive Assets	$2,433	*$809*	$3,242
Gross Other Assets	$190	*$539*	$729
Total Long-Term Investment	$3,806	*$2,803*	$6,609
Long-Term Financing			
External Debt Financing			
LT Debt	$963	*$1,055*	$2,018
Postemployment Benefit Obligation	$0	*$1,887*	$1,887
Total External Debt	$963	*$2,942*	$3,905
External Equity Financing			
Common Stock	$714	*$167*	$881
Transfers to Holding Company	($302)	*($1,989)*	($2,291)
Total External Equity	$412	*($1,822)*	($1,410)
Internal Equity Financing			
Retained Earnings	$2,363	*$1,541*	$3,904
Deferred Income Taxes	($4)	*$52*	$48
Equity Adjustments	$72	*$90*	$162
Total Internal Equity	$2,431	*$1,683*	$4,114
Total Long-Term Financing	$3,806	*$2,803*	$6,609

In 1996, CAT M&E's long-term investment and financing base was 1.74 times larger than it was back in 1986.

The only question that remains to be answered, is *how* CAT M&E actually financed the business over this period. As we saw with Wal-Mart, in order to answer that question, it helps to look at the at the financial flow statement.

Financial Flow Statement

Figure C.6 presents CAT M&E's financial flow statement for the ten-year period ended December 31, 1996. As we can see, the financial flow statement differs from the restructured balance sheets in three ways.

1. The details included in the restructured balance sheet have been omitted from the financial flow statement.
2. The long-term financing activity has been placed above the long-term investment activity.
3. The financial flow statement includes a summary of the net revenues generated by CAT M&E between 1986 and 1996.

By focusing on the "change" column of Figure C.6, we can construct the financing-the-business component of the SFM, as presented in Figure C.7.

As we can see from Figure C.7, CAT M&E only required $1.1 billion (1.0¢ of the total revenue for 1986–1996) of external financing to run the M&E business. However, in the process of raising that $1.1 billion, CAT M&E was changing the mix of debt and equity financing. The M&E business actually reduced its external equity financing by $1.8 billion (1.6¢). At the same time, it increased its external debt financing by $2.9 billion (2.5¢).

The Heart of the Story

Since CAT M&E only went outside to finance $1.1 billion of the M&E business (1.0¢), the majority of financing had to come from internal sources.

▶────────────────────────────

Between 1986 and 1996, total revenue equaled $116.5 billion. Of that amount, $1.7 billion of internal equity financing was made available to grow the business.

The $1.7 billion represented 1.4¢ of every $1 of total revenue generated over the ten-year period 1986–1996.

────────────────────────────◀

**Figure C.6   Caterpillar Machinery and Engines Financial Flow
Statement (for the Ten Years Ended December 31, 1996 —
Amounts in Millions)**

Long-Term Financing	1986	Change	1996
External Debt Financing	$963	*$2,942*	$3,905
External Equity Financing	$412	*($1,822)*	($1,410)
Internal Equity Financing	$2,431	*$1,683*	$4,114
Total Long-Term Financing	$3,806	*$2,803*	$6,609

Long-Term Investment	1986	Change	1996
Working Capital	$1,183	*$1,455*	$2,638
Gross Productive Assets	$2,433	*$809*	$3,242
Gross Other Assets	$190	*$539*	$729
Total Long-Term Investment	$3,806	*$2,803*	$6,609

Year	Total Revenue
87	$8,180
88	$10,255
89	$10,882
90	$11,103
91	$9,838
92	$9,840
93	$11,235
94	$13,863
95	$15,451
96	$15,814
Ten-Year Total	$116,461

As we can see from Figure C.7, CAT M&E invested its internal equity
financing in working capital (1.2¢), gross productive assets (0.7%), and
gross other assets (0.5%). Between 1986 and 1996, CAT M&E invested
2.4¢ of every $1 of total revenue generated.

Figure C.7 Caterpillar Machinery and Engines Strategic Financing Model: Financing the Business (for the Fiscal Years Ended December 31, 1986 and 1996 — Amounts in Millions)

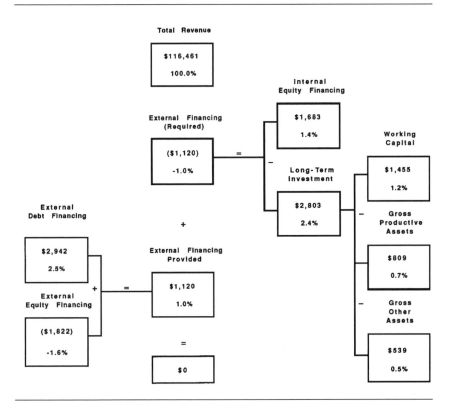

Business Strategy Revisited

By using the quick overview from the SPM and the financing-the-business component of the SFM, we have been able to show how management increased CAT M&E's ROE while growing the business. By looking at each component of the SPM, we were able to see that the heart of CAT M&E's business strategy is reflected in each component of the SPM: margin management, asset management, and financial management.

CAT M&E increased its profit margin from 1.0% in 1986 to 7.7% in 1996 while increasing net revenues at a 8.0% CAGR. Asset turnover increased from 1.22 to 1.54 by keeping the growth in total assets (5.8%) below the growth in net revenue (8.0%). Financial leverage increased from 2.10 to 3.94, due, in part, to having to include the postemployment benefits obligation on the balance sheet.

From a business strategy perspective, the most significant factor was management's decision to transfer $2.0 billion out of the business and back to the holding company. Over the ten-year period, this decision resulted in a 0.7% compound annual reduction in shareholders' equity.

The combined effects of managing all aspects of CAT M&E's SPM was to increase ROE from 2.7% to 46.1%.

This difference of 43.4 percentage points in ROE translated into $1.2 billion of net income on $2.7 billion of shareholders' equity.

To achieve a 2.7% ROE, CAT M&E's net income would only have equaled $72 million—quite a difference from $1.2 billion.

Given this phenomenal turnaround over ten years, we are well positioned to understand how the market has valued Caterpillar during this period. When we consider how the market values Caterpillar, we must remember that the company consists of all three subsidiaries.

MARKET VALUATION

Figure C.8 presents the relationship between the market value of Caterpillar's common stock and the two management measures of financial performance we use to calculate Caterpillar's ROE: net income and shareholders' equity. With the benefit of 20/20 hindsight, we can see that Caterpillar's total market value (common shares outstanding multiplied by the market price per share) increased at a slightly faster rate than the increase in shareholders' equity but quite a bit slower that the increase in net income.

As we can see from Figure C.8, Caterpillar's common stock outstanding actually decreased at a 0.4% compound annual rate between 1986 and 1996. It would appear that some of the cash transferred from the M&E business was used to repurchase common stock.

Figure C.8 **Caterpillar Market and Management Measures of Performance (for the Years Ended December 31—Shares and Dollar Amounts in Millions)**

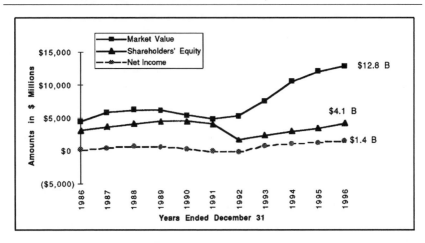

Year Ended December 31	Common Stock Outstanding	Market Value	Net Income	Shareholders' Equity
1986	395.3	$4,546	$76	$3,149
1987	405.7	$5,822	$348	$3,565
1988	405.7	$6,207	$616	$4,113
1989	405.7	$6,187	$497	$4,474
1990	403.6	$5,368	$210	$4,540
1991	403.7	$4,803	($135)	$4,040
1992	403.8	$5,209	($218)	$1,575
1993	407.5	$7,497	$681	$2,199
1994	400.9	$10,523	$955	$2,911
1995	388.0	$11,971	$1,136	$3,388
1996	380.7	$12,849	$1,361	$4,116
CAGR	−0.4%	10.9%	33.4%	2.7%

Over this ten-year period, the market value of the common stock outstanding increased at a 10.9% CAGR. During this same period, net income *for the entire company* increased at a 33.4% compound annual rate and shareholders' equity increased at a 2.7% compound annual rate.

As we can see from Figure C.8, the increase from $76 million in net income to $1.4 billion was not smooth. In 1991 and 1992, Caterpillar reported losses of $135 million and $218 million. Also, the decline in shareholders' equity from $4.0 billion in 1991 to $1.6 billion in 1992 reflects the cumulative charge against retained earnings for all of the postemployment benefit obligations that the company incurred in past years. However, since 1992, the market value of Caterpillar's common stock has increased at about the same rate as the increase in shareholders' equity.

As mentioned in Chapters 9 through 12, financial analysts and shareholders determine the value of the firm's common stock. The price of a firm's common stock is influenced by the recommendations of financial analysts at the major investment firms and what each of us is willing to pay for the firm's common stock. Firms like Caterpillar have no direct influence over the market price of their firm's common stock, but they do have an indirect influence through their actions.

From the quick overview of the SPM, we saw that the primary way that Caterpillar increased ROE in the M&E business was by working all three components of the SPM. From the financing-the-business component of the SFM, we saw that Caterpillar actually reduced the amount of external equity financing used to run that business from 1986 to 1996. For the company taken as a whole, the growth rates for net income (33.4%) and shareholders' equity (2.7%) reflect the combination of these two aspects of Caterpillar's overall business strategy.

The only question that remains to be answered is how well this performance benefited individual shareholders relative to other firms (possible investments) in the capital marketplace.

Figure C.9 presents Caterpillar's relative market performance compared the S&P 500 between 1986 and 1996. The comparison is based on a hypothetical investment of $100 in a market basket of S&P 500 common stocks and a $100 investment in Caterpillar's common stock. Figure C.9 also includes a comparison to $100 of book value for Caterpillar's common stock. As we can see, for every $100 invested in a market basket of S&P 500 common stocks, that investment would have increased to $383 by 1996.[4] That investment would have generated an annual return of 14.4% compounded annually. If that $100 was invested in Caterpillar common stock, that investment would have increased to $344 by 1996. That investment would have generated an annual return of 13.1% compounded annually.

As we can see from Figure C.9, Caterpillar's market performance was well below the S&P 500 between 1990 and 1992. However, in 1993, Caterpillar started to close the gap and eventually caught up to the S&P 500 in 1994. For those investors who bought Caterpillar's common stock in

**Figure C.9   Caterpillar S&P 500, Total Return, and Book Value
Cumulative Total Return, $100 Investment, December 31,
1986**

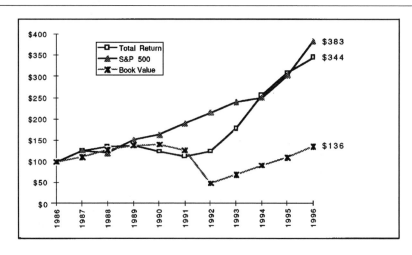

Year	S&P 500	Total Return	Book Value
1986	$100	$100	$100
1987	$125	$126	$110
1988	$120	$136	$127
1989	$151	$138	$138
1990	$162	$123	$141
1991	$188	$113	$126
1992	$214	$124	$49
1993	$239	$178	$68
1994	$251	$256	$91
1995	$302	$307	$110
1996	$383	$344	$136
CAGR	14.4%	13.1%	3.1%

Source: Value Line Investment Survey and Economic Report of the President of the United States.

1992, their total returns have far exceeded the returns of investors who bought the stock at the end of 1986.

Like the other cases included in this book, we have tried to show that the principles of financial statement analysis presented in this book can help managers develop a better understand of any business. If we were to go into a more in-depth analysis, we would return to the SPM and take a closer look at each of its components. For Caterpillar, this more in-depth look would focus on the margin-management component of the SPM.

NOTES

1. Stephen F. Jablonsky and Patrick J. Keating, *Changing Roles of Financial Management: Strategy, Control, Accountability, and Culture* (Financial Executives Research Foundation, 1998).
2. Although our approach to financial statement analysis is basically the same for industrial companies and financial service companies, profit margins, asset turnovers, return on assets, and financial leverage differ substantially between the two companies. The financial performance measures for Caterpillar are more meaningful when we focus on Caterpillar's core business, M&E.
3. While many large companies now own financing divisions and have other investments, their annual reports do not typically include the level of detail needed to make this type of analysis feasible. Since M&E represent Caterpillar's core business, our analysis will focus on that division. Later in the case, we will reintegrate the financial performance of the financial products business and the affiliated companies into the market valuation of the entire company.
4. The total return for a $100 investment in a market basket of S&P 500 common stocks assumes that any dividends received were reinvested to buy additional shares of common stock at the prevailing market price. Over this ten-year period, firms in the S&P 500 paid annual dividends of slightly over 3% of the market value of the firms' common stock.

Index